THE
Naked Manager

Selected Books by Robert Heller

ROBERT HELLER

THE
Naked Manager

Games Executives Play

T·T

Truman Talley Books

E. P. DUTTON
New York

Portions of this book appeared in slightly different form in *The Great Executive Dream*, by Robert Heller (1972).

Published in the United States by Truman Talley Books • E. P. Dutton,
a division of New American Library,
2 Park Avenue, New York, N.Y. 10016

Library of Congress Cataloging in Publication Data

Heller, Robert.
The naked manager.
"A Truman Talley book."
Bibliography; p.
Includes index.
1. Industrial management—Great Britain.
2. Industrial management—United States. I. Title.
HD70.G7H44 1985   658.4   85-10263
ISBN: 0-525-24314-3

Published simultaneously in Canada by
Fitzhenry & Whiteside Limited, Toronto

COBE

10 9 8 7 6 5 4 3 2
First Edition

to Matthew

Contents

CONTENTS

x

Introduction

The Age of
Cut and Thrust

This book is dedicated to all those executives who did the right thing for the wrong reason, and were acclaimed as geniuses and heroes; and to all those who did the wrong thing for the right, the wrong, or no reason at all and still hold their overpaid jobs.

Maybe there are less of the latter around than there used to be, though. Maybe there are more, many more, managements that actually do the right thing for the right reason. Deep recession and foreign competition have wonderfully concentrated the managerial mind—and wonderfully concentrated many a business on its real business, as described in these pages, which is to manage the affairs of the corporation so that everybody involved (employees, stockholders, customers, communities) has good cause to be profoundly thankful for management's work.

In the process of concentration, too, more and more managements have decried the nonsenses I describe; have thrown the rubbish out the window; and have set out, often with stunning and sudden success, not to do likewise—to make a break with the overmanaged, underproductive past. But nothing exceeds like excess. Just as the conglomerate cons and the merger mania of the 1960s were the product, the oil slick, if you will, of the Kennedy-Johnson boom, so the Reagan renaissance generated, and is still generating, a new collection of excrescences every bit as bothersome as any managerial nudity of the past.

Actually, the faults and the dangers are always the same. The dialogue and the actors may change, but every time the business cycle peaks, it's basically the same stupid plot. Only think back to that dedication to "those who still hold overpaid jobs" they don't deserve. Well, maybe more managers deserve their positions, but Americans are now, and rightly so, beginning to question whether these executives deserve their pay, or rather overpay.

Men who have never laid their own fortunes on the entrepreneurial line are making themselves multimillionaires, at the stockholders' expense, with no more trouble than it takes to arrange a bonus deal or stock-option scheme. If as much ingenuity had been spent on schemes for getting more productive collaboration from the rest of the work force, maybe the managerial elite would have presided over fewer losses of jobs and markets.

In many cases, the overpay will become still more excessive, because the corporation has been swollen by the megamergers that have passed with so little adverse comment, even at a time when the managements of earlier merged creations, still in sackcloth and ashes, are busy dismantling their failed agglomerations. Is there truly any economic point in du Pont buying Conoco, or U.S. Steel absorbing Marathon, or General Motors shelling out $2.5 billion for Electronic Data Systems? Weren't corporations such as these already supposed, long ago, to be too big for their own managerial good (setting aside the good of the community?). Or have the hardship and reshaping of the recession years so improved managerial competence and attitudes that these megadeals, and the host of lesser corporate combinations of unrelated businesses, will genuinely create new wealth elsewhere than in Wall Street?

There are no prizes for the right answers, which are very obvious. Indeed, the new conventional wisdom holds that agglomeration is the total contradiction of effective modern management, which aims for the minimum size of unit with the maximum amount of independence and informality. Set the people, or at least the business, free—and wonders will follow. That is part of the rationale for the leveraged buy out (LBO). But behind the facade of the LBO, other time-dishonored acts of managerial folly are being repeated on a still grander scale —a debt spree of unprecedented proportions.

It used to be thought imprudent to borrow more than half the worth of the company's equity. Some of the LBOs enter life as independents with 80 percent or more of their capital in the form of high-interest debt. The size of the deals, once confined to quite small spin-offs, usually from de-conglomerating mergers, has waxed greater and greater too—numbers in the billions now don't frighten the greedy bankers who finance the deals and who wax rich on the LBO proceeds.

So do quick-draw operators, the spiritual heirs of the conglomerators; in 1984 one executive used an LBO to create a $115 million fortune for himself out of thin air—while tripling his holding in the company. Once again, the economic justification of the phenomenon is hard to find. Once again, the gunslingers cloak their activities with the current language of fashionable management theory, in this case, merely the latest version of an old nostrum: managing a business as if it's your own.

The trouble is that too many managements have begun to treat the corporation as if it really were their own, another misdeed of the discredited past. The bad old days, though, threw up nothing more discreditable than today's golden parachutes and greenmail. God save the shareholder when executives can write themselves contracts that shower them with wealth should anyone, unwanted (or even wanted), acquire the company, devices so deplorable that the Reagan administration rightly tried to take action against them.

These golden parachutes had no justification of any kind, save in the minds and pockets of these who devised them. Greenmail, on the other hand, is not a situation of the executive's own choosing. The villians of these pieces are the predators, the corporate raiders who, using the aforementioned easy availability of bank money, or (still worse) junk bonds, for merger operations, launch a feasible bid for some constipated giant like Gulf Oil, Warner, or Walt Disney and place the victim's management in a terrible fix.

Either, one, they let the whole corporation pass (with themselves aboard) into the captivity of someone they dislike and perhaps despise; or, two, they find a white knight to buy the company instead, as Gulf found Socal, in which case their independence still goes; or, three, they buy back the predator's stock at a premium.

In cases two and three, the predator cleans up a lot of loot for a little trouble. But that money must come from somewhere, and in case three, that place is again the stockholders' pockets. As some of the afflicted have begun to argue—long, loudly, and legally—if the board of, say, Disney is prepared to pay Saul Steinberg of Reliance a fat premium on his stock to get rid of him, why shouldn't other holders get the same price? The answer, of course, is that the stock isn't worth it, and may be worth still less if, during the greenmail battle, the management has bought up companies (as Warner did Chris Craft) with the motive of making the attacker's task more difficult.

Small wonder that an affronted Congress has moved, though with scant effect, against greenmail as well as golden parachutes. But these are only the more conspicuous ways in which history is, unfortunately, repeating itself. The point shouldn't need stressing that the excesses of the 1960s were followed by, or led into, the period of American management's most abysmal postwar performance, as technology and market leadership, in industry after industry, passed to other companies, mostly Japanese ones, events that in 1960 or 1970 nobody would have thought remotely conceivable.

Could it happen again? Management in America, demonstrating anew the great national talent for regeneration, bloomed again in the early 1980s, as the new entrepreneurs in the Silicon Valley and elsewhere, in high technology and low, were joined by big corporation managers determined to right the wrongs of their predecessors.

I chronicled some of their feats in *The Supermanagers,* like Lee Iacocca's turnaround at Chrysler, the brilliant counterattack of John Opel's IBM in personal computers, Roger B. Smith's iconoclastic remaking of GM's basic automotive business. There were many other examples, large and small, of top-class well-dressed management, of executives not afraid either to recognize reality or to act on its imperatives.

It wasn't, of course, that the truth of the direct approach to management, as recommended in these pages and drawn from observed best practice over a quarter of a century, had suddenly been revealed to managers. The big corporations were reacting not so much to challenge as to threat—and the threat hasn't gone away.

That truth, the fact that American companies can no longer rely on the vast riches of a safe home market to maintain their world market share, is the biggest single reason for supposing that it won't happen again, that the merger, LBO, greenmail, executive pay, and other excesses of the mid-1980s aren't the preliminary to another lethal bout of managerial complacency and industrial underperformance.

These folderols and hot flushes of greed, too, have nothing

to do with the lives and concerns of the younger managers who are going to carry the ball for American management, whether their seniors like it or not. The sheer volume of new technology, the shortening time between innovation and imitation, the speed of change in the market and the workplace, all these demand by their nature that responsibility be pushed down the corporation into the hands of those who have to exercise it.

These coming generations of management are the people who have shown the most impatience with the dominant traditions of the big corporation. Maybe their impact on managerial life will, one day, turn this account of the follies and foibles of management into a historical document, like a record of the Great Plague. Maybe not, though, for management is an entirely human activity, and its failings are human ones.

Look at the overall statistics, in fact, and you see clear evidence that the all-too-human managers running American business as a whole are not emulating the thrusters mentioned above. The naked manager pays lip service to fashionable ideas —like the need for higher investment in modern plant and innovation. But what he actually does is a very different matter. American management has been spending billions upon billions in completely sterile operations that, just like those cons of the conglomerate era, have the sole purpose of elevating, not true performance, but untrue earnings per share.

In the first quarter of 1984, for a main instance, an enormous sum of $60 billion went, totally without economic justification, on buying back corporations' own stock. This far outweighed the amount, still vastly too large for comfort, lavished on LBOs—$6.3 billion in the first half of the same year. In the previous year, $68.6 billion went on other mergers and acquisitions, say Venture Economics, Inc., and W. T. Grimm & Co. As *Business Week* pointed out, in an anxiety-ridden article, that sum was nearly seventy times the money that the venture capitalists (supposedly the stars and leaders of the new American economy) invested in start-ups in 1983.

Worse still, spending on research and development (R & D), the fount of innovation, rose more slowly in 1983 than two years before (an 11 percent rise against 16 percent). Spending on innovation, as every manager must surely know by now, has to be backed up by capital investment. Yet in both 1982 and 1983 capital spending by manufacturers actually fell—it was the service industries that raised their investment. And that's not good enough. In fact, it's deadly dangerous.

In an era of unparalleled competitive cut and thrust, those who don't thrust stand a strong chance of being cut to pieces. That's why thrusters and nonthrusters alike need to ponder the myths of management and its realities more than ever before. It isn't a question of may the best man win. He will.

BOOK I

Power
Games

1

Why Successes Flop

The naked emperor in Hans Christian Andersen's story was magnificently dressed, not only in the public's mind but in his own. The business executive, ruler of economic empires richer than many nations, has gone one better. The public believes in him, he believes in himself, but his clothing is not simply that of personal prestige and power (though both can be great). The manager is wrapped in a rich and seamless garment, which, going by the name of management, has become a pervasive religion of our time. But management, like the emperor's clothes, does not exist. The prime myth of management is that it does.

Management's nonexistence explains why there are so many confused and conflicting attempts to define a pastime that all but monopolizes the waking hours of earnest men, many of them able, creative, and industrious; many of them none of these things. Any definition of management must be right, because almost any definition must fit something so amorphous and shifting. "Achieving results through other people" is one of the more popular definitions. It applies to the president of General Motors, but it also fits the madam of a brothel. And she is an executive facing real problems of personnel selection, marketing, and accountancy, not to mention her tax and legal arrangements.

The president of GM may not fancy the idea that a madam is in the same business, but she is—the business of business. All executives are in the same line of work, which is that of organizing something or somebody in such a way that somebody else, somehow or other, will pay for it. The job of a big business executive is basically the same as that of a small shopkeeper—turning a (more or less) honest penny. And the executive forgets this (as he often does) at his peril.

Efficient businesses and brilliant executives are those who turn the most pennies, make the most money. The public never bothers about the methods. It accepts the results as evidence of their excellence. And this seems perfectly right and proper. So the good executive is the effective one, and the effective executive is the good one—or is he?

Effectiveness means more than goodness, but not much more. This little difficulty explains how a professor of management can write "Effectiveness is best seen as something an executive produces from a situation by managing it appropriately." Substitute *effectively* for the last word in that mishmash and you have a sentence that means exactly the same, that is, nothing. There is no absolute criterion of managerial achievement. A manager is good and a company efficient only because others consider the results of their work good; their so-called goodness endures only as long as this good opinion holds.

Ivar Kreuger, the European match king, and Samuel Insull, the American utilities magnate, are early figures in a line that stretches to the crack of corporate doom. President after president, honest and less honest, has been turned into a hero figure, sometimes even without benefit of assiduous publicity. Behind the great collapses of companies and reputations—IOS, King Resources, National Student Marketing, Equity Financing, Penn Square, Continental Illinois, and so on—are collapsed heroes, feet of clay, now mostly forgotten names. Among fallen idol companies, some, like Litton, ITT, or Rolls-Royce, would be too conspicuous ever to forget even if they hadn't survived; others slid so far from grace that nobody remembers either their names or the exact astronomical height of their former price/earnings ratios.

In management, wonders nearly always cease. One day, events will surely expose any executive, in all his nakedness, for what he is: a fallible human being trying, with the help of others, who are equally fallible, to cope with circumstances that are constantly changing. In the kingdom of the uncertain, the one-eyed manager makes mistakes. And that is why corporate goodness, even measured on the standard scales, is infrequent. Any study of leading companies will show that few can claim to be good—if you define goodness as doubling profits in real terms in a decade, maintaining return on stockholders' equity over the ten years, and having only one off year.

The average performance of big companies is just that—average. In the United States, half of the five hundred largest companies had annual earnings per share growth of less than 7 percent in the period from 1973 to 1983; and any company that couldn't double its earnings in a grossly inflationary era, in which all manner of juggles for the painless boosting of earnings per share were still available, has no claims to any managerial skills, even low cunning.

Executives are not always to blame for mediocrity. Running large corporations, or middling, or small, is never easy. To run them effectively is always tough, and is sometimes impossi-

ble. This explains the management that is excellent in everything except its results—as in aluminum. You won't find a
harder-working, keener, better-developed bunch of men anywhere than in companies such as Alcoa and Alcan (heaven
knows why, because aluminum is the world's second most
boring industry, after cement). Yet the result of all their effort
and massed brainpower is an insignificant return on capital,
profitless growth, and a terrible proneness to accident. Alcan,
possibly the most expert of the groups erecting aluminum
smelters in Britain, naturally had the project that went most
grievously awry; and the whole industry has an uncontrollable
urge to plunge into excess capacity.

A former boss of Alcoa once made the immortal remark:
"There is no overcapacity, only underselling"—another of
those management sayings that read the same backward or
forward. Executives are bad judges of their own actions, their
own talents, their own stock prices. Every member of the board
thinks his company's shares are too cheap, although few are
foolish enough to buy them (they don't mind having them free).
Whenever a company boasts of its managerial excellence, sell
the shares; and if you own the firm, fire the boss.

Bids bring out the worst in executives. They can't judge
their own ability fairly, which is understandable. But they can
also be awful judges of other managers. When you hear a chief
executive say, "You should not forget that in buying a company we are buying management as a primary asset" (to quote
one merger fanatic), run for the hills. Management does not
exist, and here's this colossus paying good money for the invisible and evanescent. You can't buy management, but you can
very easily buy trouble. Better executives can, and often do,
walk out; and sometimes after the reality emerges from the
image, the worst ones have to be fired. An American group
bought a red-hot British growth company for a tycoon's ran-
som and discovered subsequently: "(a) it does not have good

reporting and control data; (b) the production output per person employed is very poor; (c) it has too many people for the job they are doing; (d) it has never really set good targets; (e) it is much too diversified." Otherwise, the buy was in pretty good shape.

The optical illusion of goodness arises from the one-idea phenomenon. Sigmund Freud called *The Interpretation of Dreams* his greatest work, noting that inspiration of this order came to a man only once in his lifetime. Companies and chief executives are subject to the same law. A company such as Apple has a large notion about small computers and a couple of brilliant men who can make it work. In the process the company's worth—and their fortunes with it—swells in half a dozen years from peanuts to $1.7 billion in 1982. All this proves, not that the Apple crew are supermanagers, but merely that their one super-idea was good, wonderfully good. The managers will look good as long as the big idea does, but so will all their other ideas, including the foolish ones, until—as happened to Apple when the small-computer market was invaded in overwhelming force by IBM—the profits are poleaxed and new men must be imported to remake the management and the success.

Skepticism in the face of success is an impudent posture. But corporate history must foster the skeptical approach. The eye-opener lies in the way that respectable, established, conservative corporations and their no less clean and decent executives start off in one direction and end up facing the other way, with equal ardor for both postures. Sad examples here are the copper companies, which once threw fortunes into the laps of other people in a doomed and silly effort to keep prices down —and then discovered the virtues of the free market they had sought to destroy.

In corporation land, you learn rapidly that there are some villains but no heroes. I once had to write the profile of an

7

oilman reputed to be the hero-genius behind one of the world's greatest companies. Research showed that, after an incomparable early career battling against the archenemy, he had long since sat on the sidelines. In despair, I asked the real boss to say what the hero did. "Well," he said, after deep thought, "he has the office next to mine." The profile, inevitably, perpetuated the legend. Nobody would have believed the reality, any more than most people would believe that a young family scion, famed (falsely) for internationalizing an introverted midwestern business, was once so claustrophobic that he held conferences in an open bus. Cured by his shrink, he then became so agoraphobic that he could work only in a windowless room.

Men like him, or the Cunard chairman who never took a ship to America, are the human factors, the real stuff of management—eccentric to the point of lunacy in a few cases, and generally odd enough in multitudinous smaller ways. Time and again, what happens in corporations cannot be explained by economics. It can only be understood by realizing that, naturally enough, men express in their work the same motive forces that drive them in their ordinary lives. Management is an arena for human behavior at its most naked—under stress, but freed from many restraints of civilization. You can yell and scream at a subordinate in a way that would not be tolerated even by a wife. You can force a man to lose all his assets, though you wouldn't trespass on his lawn. You can tell lies, but if the lies are good enough, they will be applauded as universal truth.

This is the background against which one Harry Figgie can be seen as a real management hero of our times. Figgie, a manager of brilliant reputation, had won high academic respect and an avid stock market following for his "nucleus theory of growth," which he applied to Automatic Sprinkler. The nucleus theory proved to be an empty sham. The reality was that in rapid succession Figgie bought a fire-hose nozzle company whose profits promptly fell from $939,000 to $76,636; a vacuum cleaner firm whose sales methods were outlawed just before acquisition; and a metal-bending defense contractor that managed to lose $8 million on a $6.3 million Pentagon contract. There are no theories of growth, nuclear or non-nuclear. There are only actions—intelligent, not so bright, and stupid. And the only thread binding the intelligent actions is that they work, as Figgie himself demonstrated after these dismal events. His company has not only changed its name since those days, first to ATO and then to Figgie International Holdings, but has also changed its theories and its spots and can consequently boast one of the better growth records among the *Fortune* 500.

The trouble is that in management, nothing succeeds like success—if you define the latter as winning a high, wide, and handsome management reputation. But pride goeth before a flop, as *Business Week* recently discovered, retreading the ground covered by *In Search of Excellence.* It found that "at least 14 of the 43 'excellent' companies" highlighted in that booming best-seller "have lost their lustre."

Worse still, several of them shouldn't have been in the book at all; notably Atari, a firm so appallingly mismanaged that it infringed all eight of the book's "attributes," or rules of management, and very nearly busted its miserable owners, Warner, in the process. But what did the *Business Week* analysis prove? First, that there are no universal rules of success (thus, Hewlett-Packard, which has "stumbled badly" in the critical microcomputer and superminicomputer markets, obeyed all eight commandments). Second, past success by no means equates with either future triumph or excellent management.

So what else is new? Speaking (or writing) personally, I've stressed both self-evident truths ad infinitum (if not ad nauseam) for the best part of two decades. But nothing will ever stop managers, especially at times of great uncertainty—like the 1980s—from seeking, and overvaluing, examples of appar-

9

ent certainty. All the same, the "Oops" analysis is valuable, maybe more so than the original study. For instance, eight of the fourteen flops didn't stay close to the customer—companies like Avon, Disney, Revlon, Tupperware, and Levi-Strauss, which are practically synonymous with consumer satisfaction.

Take the last-named. As long as the worldwide jeans market was booming, Levi's management could afford, paradoxically, to ignore it. "For so long we were [always] sold out. Our time was prioritized on getting more product, new factories, more raw materials. We were internationally oriented." As for the customers, "we let the relationship with our retailers fall into a sad state of disrepair, the company completely missed the powerful [and profitable] trend towards fashion jeans." Direct, in-the-home-sellers Avon and Tupperware similarly failed to spot or react to the blatant consequences of more women going out to work. Disney went on flogging clean and decent entertainment to an increasingly less wholesome marketplace.

Yet turn the clock back a decade and what proved to be crucial defects were being hailed as heroic virtues. Theories or methods of management can work wonders in individual companies at individual times, but only because they suit the way in which individual managers like to act in individual markets. The methods that Robert Townsend, of *Further Up the Organization,* used to run Avis were a marvelous way for Robert Townsend to run Avis. But they might paralyze a different company with different men—even Hertz. Yet executives, beset by corporate ailments, reach for a theory formed in a different context as if it were a broad-spectrum antibiotic, a wonder drug. They see their businesses as suffering patients requiring medical treatment, though there is seldom anything wrong with a company that better, or better-directed, executives won't cure. Executives, however, will undergo almost any treatment rather than amputation of themselves.

But self-amputation is far more effective for the stockholders. I know of two companies, one large, one gargantuan, that
found themselves with cuckoos in the nest—two tough, aggressive, ruthless entrepreneurs whose drive, hunger for profits,
and magical rapport with figures couldn't live with the passive,
profitless vagueness on the existing board. Laying their own
heads on the block, the older directors voluntarily handed the
ax to the new men. In the next few years, both companies grew
by such prodigious bounds that some of the superannuated
oldies became very wealthy—and they deserved every penny.
They followed the golden rule: if you can't do something yourself, find somebody who can—and then let him do it in his own
sweet way.

In contrast, many cures that less self-effacing boards may
purchase are subject to the same objection as psychoanalysis:
they are expensive; they take a lot of time; the patient does all
the work; and there's no way of telling that he wouldn't have
gotten better, anyway, with the mere passage of the years. If
it takes two years (to take one example from the past) to draw
up a new shop-floor management structure in a car company,
the problem won't be the same at the end as it was at the
beginning. That's why, in the discontinuous present, speed has
become of the essence. Today you not only have to fix it, you
must fix it fast.

Any improvement, however, can always be looked at two
ways. You can pat yourself on the back (as most executives do)
for your brilliant advance, or you can kick yourself for the
imbecility that made improvement necessary. If the executive
doesn't like one view through the telescope, he can turn it
around and look through the other end—precisely because
management is not a scientific and objective activity but a
subjective historical process, full of ifs and buts. Thus Roy Ash,
when president of Litton and forced to explain how the management wasn't to blame for errors that wiped out billions in

stock market value, had no trouble at all: "Operationally, we could have made sure of never facing the problem by never undertaking the venture." Nothing ventured, nothing lost, in fact. That's like the guilty party in a midair collision offering as excuse that if he had never learned to fly the accident would never have happened.

The literature and history of companies like Litton or ITT bear careful reading by anybody who believes that the emperor-manager is wearing clothes. In this book, although there are no heroes, there are Goodies and Baddies. The Baddies range from leading actors—the bankrupt or all-but-broke giant companies like International Harvester or Continental Illinois—to a strong supporting cast, many of them conglomerates like the two mentioned above, whose badness lies in the damage done by arrogant managers to innocent stockholders.

In the early 1970s, in addition to the Baddies, the Heavies —such as du Pont, General Electric, ICI, and General Motors —were conspicuous underperformers, companies that were neither very good nor at all poor but whose enormous potential for goodness was constantly frustrated by their own bad habits. Many such Heavies proved *in extremis* in the early 1980s, with GM leading the bunch, that the underperformance was indeed culpable; they changed their awful habits, and that enormous potential came bursting through onto the bottom line.

There are Goodies, too, in my books: men such as the gang at IBM, Lord Weinstock of General Electric, the bosses of Daimler-Benz, or Ryuzaburo Kaku of Canon; men (and there are many of them) who (unless and until I am proven wrong) can be trusted with the stockholders' money to the last line on the balance sheet.

Think before you act; the money isn't yours—the First Truth of Management—is a home truth. But management is a far more homely business than its would-be scientists suggest, more closely allied to cooking than any other human activity.

Like cooking, it rests on a degree of organization and on adequate resources. But just as no two chefs run their kitchens the same way, so no two managements are the same, even if they all went to the same business (or cooking) school. You can teach the rudiments of cooking, as of management, but you cannot make a great cook or a great manager.

In both activities, you ignore fundamentals at grave risk —but sometimes succeed. In both, science can be extremely useful but is no substitute for the art itself. In both, inspired amateurs can outdo professionals. In both, perfection is rarely achieved, and failure is more common than the customers realize. In both, practitioners don't need recipes that detail timing down to the last second, ingredients to the last fraction of an ounce, and procedures down to the last flick of the wrist; they need reliable maxims, instructive anecdotes, and no dogmatism. This is a cookbook for managers who want to get their clothes back.

2

The Stockholder
Finagle

To hear them tell it, big company directors on both sides of the Atlantic are quite dedicated to the stockholder. Strangely, devotion turns to irritation, almost a sense of betrayal, if the love object asks offensive questions about the company's performance at the annual general meeting. The stockholder whom the directors love is better than a good Victorian child or a chairman's yes-man, neither seen nor heard, one who merely collects his dividend (if any) and dutifully returns his proxy form if, by some mischance, one of the directors' projects needs a democratic rubber stamp.

Most top executives are sincere men. When they say they hold the stockholder dear, they really and truly mean it, because they truly can't imagine any conflict between the stockholder's interests, as seen by the directors, and the directors' own desires. What's good for the board of General Motors is good for the stockholders, and vice versa, more or less sums up the philosophy. Suppose that the stockholders would be better off with a whole new management. The existing managers won't share the horrible idea and they won't protect stockholders by lopping off their own heads. The stockholder is not expected to criticize. It's enough to know that managements, in deciding what they want, will have general objectives that directly promote the stockholder's everlasting comfort—or will they?

Rich targets for growth in earnings per share were once standard corporate objectives. (That was before a series of disasters, starting with the Nixon recession and proceeding through oil price shocks, hyperinflation, and the great deflation of the late 1970s, gave business hell—and brought it down to earth.) In happier days the hotter giants, the Honeywells and so on, dreamed of a 15 percent annual compound increase in earnings per share. The number was plucked out of the air: 10 percent looked too small, and 20 percent (doubling every three and one half years) absurdly large for a swollen corporation. A steady 15 percent clip, doubling monotonously every five years, would surely guarantee a high price/earnings ratio for all eternity.

But this corporate target has a secret advantage for the men in charge of companies. Earnings per share are engineered by dividing profits attributable to ordinary stockholders (that is, after tax and minority interest) by the number of shares in issue, which is a beautifully elastic sum on both sides. For instance, if Wonder Company A buys Wonder Company B with stocks, kindly valuing B at the same noble price/earnings ratio as its own, the earnings per share of A (now A plus B) stay exactly the same. But if A uses money borrowed at fixed interest, any margin between B's profits and the interest paid comes through as a straight, juicy increment in earnings per share.

As the conglomerates of the 1960s noted, many tricks can be worked around this basic dodge: simply buy earnings without diluting the equity, and by a stroke of the computer, management seems to achieve the results of years of honest toil. This cult of earnings per share has never been worshiped as widely in Britain as in the United States, where management has elaborated much the same concept into something (still widely used) called "return on invested capital" or "stockholders' equity."

The notion behind invested capital is that only the money that belongs to the stockholder counts. So you conveniently forget about loans, however overpowering, and take the often much tinier sum of stockholders' capital. This in turn relates to asset values that have been shrunk by so-called depreciation over the years. To this much skinnier residue, you apply the net profit figure—and the result is a much zestier index of performance than could be gotten in any other way. For example, Dr. Armand Hammer's Occidental Petroleum earned a worse-than-middling 7.8 percent on stockholders' equity in 1983 (with the advantage of an extraordinary credit, at that). As a percentage of assets, the miserable figure shrank to under 5 percent. At another of America's biggest corporations, Procter & Gamble, the return on the shareholders' loot was a much more handsome 18.8 percent. The return on assets figure? Only 10.6 percent. At Philip Morris, the tobacco champions, an awesome equity return of 22.4 percent shrinks to a mere 9.3 percent on assets. At Lockheed, the equity return was no less than 31.5 percent, but that on assets was less than a third of this exalted figure.

Few managements consciously fix their figures in the most flattering light—but that's what happens when they define their objectives by stockholders' finances alone. This is dangerous—it sustains the myth that high debt is good for the company, and it also misrepresents the motivation of the board. Though the director chatters about the stockholder as the owner of the company's assets, he doesn't really see the investor as a proprietor—and still less as a member of the company. The members, in the director's inner mind, are those sitting on the payroll, above all upper management itself.

The stockholders are remote licensers. They get a cut of any profits, and in return they license the managers to do as they please with the assets. More, they let managers do what they like (apart from outright theft) with the value of the shares. If the management longs to dilute those famous earnings per share by some overpriced acquisition, the stockholder can seldom kill the deal. And if the management wants to change the entire business of the company, the stockholder is expected to sit tight and watch, clapping loudly.

The tobacco companies, faced with evidence that they were merchants of death, could have taken their profits, remitted the maximum loot to stockholders for as long as the going was good, and then folded into graceful liquidation. No law ordains that American Brands (née Tobacco) or R. J. Reynolds must be preserved in perpetuity. Yet the company's executive officers (who would otherwise have liquidated themselves out of good jobs) proceeded to act as if in slavish obedience to such a law.

At all costs, the corporate entity must be perpetuated. So the stockholders, like it or not, are swiftly switched from owning a lucrative cigarette manufacturer, with minor diversified interests, to possessing heavily diversified companies with relatively minor interests in tobacco. True, R. J. Reynolds, Philip Morris, and American Brands, after their heavy plunge into strange waters (and liquors), came up swimming in 1984 with, on the *Fortune* 500 rankings, respectable figures: 157th, 42nd, and 131st in ten-year earnings-per-share growth

But while R. J. Reynolds, for example, heroically reduced the cigarette to under half its sales, the effort was full of appall-

17

ingly expensive mistakes (like a $1.6 billion shipping line eventually given away to shareholders) and costly pain; thus, at its canner, Del Monte (purchased at a price of $618 million), Reynolds had to close twelve businesses and thirty-eight plants. Its food and beverage buys included the equally troubled Kentucky Fried Chicken ("where just about everything that could go wrong had gone wrong," according to the man who took charge). Yet, thanks to radical surgery, this side did end up producing 38 percent of Reynolds' earnings on 29.4 percent of sales in 1983.

Like it or not, these stockholders who stuck with Reynolds had to go along with the board's creation, through years of such travail, of what management fondly sees as a consumer-products colossus, headed by non-tobacco men—including a chief executive (formerly of Procter & Gamble and Scott Paper) who had previously handled health and beauty products at Chesebrough-Pond's. The chief's top entourage, too, came mostly, not from tobacco, but from similar seminaries of branded goods. The big switch from cigarette men who wrongly thought themselves whizzes at consumer marketing to marketing men who reckoned they could also sell cigarettes may be marvelous for the management. But along the way the stockholders have been forced by corporate officers to pay prices for independent provision merchants—like those of Del Monte—that made the latter's stockholders positively drool.

Management's liberties are guaranteed by the weakness, apathy, and ignorance of stockholders, by the stockholders' lack of time to harass bad management, and by the stockholders' perpetual freedom, if disenchanted, to sell out. However, not all stockholders are weak, apathetic, and ignorant; at least, they shouldn't be. The directors' real masters are institutions: the investment concerns and foundations that control the dominating chunks of the equity; the banks that hand over short-term finance; the investment banks and merchant banks that are pipelines to the long-suffering investing public. These solid institutional citizens are not always stockholders—the banks in Britain and the United States do not, as on the Continent or in Japan, own industry. But in several respects the banks' interests are no different from the stockholders', individual or institutional: since they want their booty back, the banks—like the stockholders—need to ensure that inefficient management doesn't drain or dribble the money away.

Yet the institutions, on both sides of the Atlantic, are almost as supine as the little old lady in Toledo, Ohio, or Melton Mowbray, Leicestershire. When they do zero in on a lagging management, the move is ponderous and far too late. Take Lockheed (though you could just as well take Chrysler, Massey-Ferguson, or International Harvester, and there are plenty of others). In 1975, Robert Abboud, chairman of the First National Bank of Chicago, found himself all alone in demanding that Daniel Haughton, the aircraft manufacturer's chairman, be fired for the incompetence that had landed Lockheed with the Tristar jetliner and also, at that point, with a desperate need for $595 million just to stay alive. Bankers Trust led the other banks in total opposition to Abboud; he won, not because of the proven failure of the Haughton management but because of its proven propensity to bribe foreign potentates, including the Prime Minister of Japan, Kakuei Tanaka, and Prince Bernhard of the Netherlands.

Why did the dogs take so long to bark? The executives who lead financial institutions are, if anything, more conservative, more deeply dyed in tradition, happier to rest on seniority and security, and more thoroughly inbred than industrial directors. They have a vested interest in stability at the top, especially a top manned by personal friends or men of higher rank in the arcane lists of business snobbery. Those who run mammoth banks and insurance companies (let alone those who merely handle multimillion-pound investment portfolios) sel-

dom reach the exalted heights or salaries of captains of industry, and they feel the difference.

Most financial men are not especially knowing about business and business management, in their own trade or in other
people's. Financial institutions are better at burying their mil-
lion-dollar mistakes in multimillion aggregates than at display-
ing commercial drive, managerial acumen, and marketing enterprise. The expertise needed on Wall Street is not that of the
industrial executive suite—and the financier's judgment of directors is therefore fallible. That is why banks lend gigantic
sums to managements of bewildering incompetence and on
propositions of worse than dubious worth—like their dud loans
to real estate investment trusts, less developed countries, and
(very probably) overleveraged buyouts. The unsureness of investment managers and their bosses about how to judge management in industry partly explains their profound reluctance
to tackle nonperforming boards—and of those there is never
any shortage.

Even if you use their own soft criterion of growth in
earnings per share, the top fifty U.S. companies made a feeble
showing from 1973 to 1983: in four cases, earnings per share fell
over the decade; in seven further cases, they rose by less than
2 percent compounded annually; ten others grew by less than
10 percent; the magic 15 percent mark was hit in only four cases.
The next fifty largest were not much more inspiring. Four
showed declines; another fourteen grew by less than 7 percent;
and only seven managed 15 percent.

The recessions of the 1970s can't be blamed, either. In 1983,
a marvel for growth in sales, there were twenty companies in
the top fifty whose earnings per share were worse than in the
previous year; for the next fifty companies, the delinquents
were seventeen. As for return to investors, in which the stock
price is dominant, seventeen of the five hundred biggest companies produced a negative figure; stockholders had not obtained

a 7 percent annual return on their investment in sixty-two more cases. Yet few knives have leaped out; nothing has disturbed the slumber in the executive suite of such as U.S. Steel (with a negative 1973–83 growth rate of 12.7 percent for its earnings per share). Unless companies are on bankruptcy's brink (in which case the directors have other anxieties), dozing managements have little cause to fret about their mighty, weak stockholders. They need watch out for only a few uncommon enemies of their species. There's the corporate gadfly who seeks his or her own fortune by harassing managements on behalf of aggrieved stockholders; and the corporate raider, whose pounce may be sincere (he really wants the company) or cynical (he only wants the profits from greenmailing the victim). These two predators can overlap, as when a greenmailed board of directors (like Disney's in 1984) goes to such self-abasing lengths to escape one hunter, the raider, that the other scourge, the gadfly, gets handed a strong case for a stockholder suit.

But such animals are by definition rare, even in the corporate jungle and even though their numbers have lately multiplied. Both overlap, too, with a third foe of supine managements—the (equally rare) rich and determined individual investor. Some of these, like T. Boone Pickens, whose group picked up a billion from the corpse of Gulf Oil, bow out with the alacrity of any greenmailer; but others, the more interesting ones, insist on having their investment managed to success. Thus, coal tycoon George H. Love injected new management into Chrysler (he jacked it up high enough to plunge right back into disaster). Thus, Chicago financier Colonel Henry Crown twice intervened to arrest General Dynamics' slide into bankruptcy. Thus, to descend from the great to the middling, and from the public to the private, Victor Kiam turned a million of his own money into $12 million of pretax profits from Remington, the razor company whose previous owner, Sperry Rand, couldn't make a dime from the business.

Note, however, that both General Dynamics and Chrysler had recurrent bouts of financial nausea. Maybe even effective gingering up by rich shareholders has its limits: it often comes too late, when too much vitality and cash have already been sucked away by years of travail. The Kiam experience points the moral. It's when the rich shareholder also takes a stake in the management that you can more confidently expect miracles; when a Carlo de Benedetti puts in $12 million of his own cash as he takes managerial control of Olivetti, and turns his nest egg into a veritable cornucopia; or when Robert Maxwell, once the execrated scourge of New York whiz-kid Saul Steinberg, buys three quarters of a moribund printing company for $14.4 million—and a scant eighteen months later has managed and masterminded his family stake up to $200 million.

In such cases, though, the other stockholders are strictly along for the ride. The managing proprietor generally acts on the principle that God helps those who (literally) help themselves. Can anybody else save the stockholder? Investors could save themselves by trying to avoid companies that on past performance can't outdo the returns from a savings and loans. But most individual investment in stocks goes via the insurance companies and investment companies anyway, and the sheer weight of the money that they must invest presses them to buy into big companies, and with little discrimination. Only the heavyweights have enough shares on the market for heavy buying, and only large-scale purchases are any use to a large fund. Big companies and big investors are locked in to each other by nature, which is one good reason that the investment record of the great funds is generally so insipid: they are stuck with insipid investments.

The myth that men who run investment funds or manage companies can always do more with the stockholder's money than he could for himself still stands—despite its destruction by all manner of evidence. A theory of stock markets has, almost irrefutably, shown that stock prices follow a haphazard statistical pattern known to mathematicians as the "random walk." If so, all the painstaking "fundamental" analysis designed to prove that a company's stock price must soar is beside the point. In reality, security analysts, however closely they nuzzle up to an industry, judge the favored managements too kindly; being articulate men themselves, the analysts especially fall for executives who can actually talk.

It also follows that the expert is no more likely than the inexpert to pick a growth stock that grows. In 1970 top American investment professionals picked Viatron, an electronics outfit, and a company called National Student Marketing as the two hottest growth prospects of the year. Both slid down a slippery slope.

In the 1980s such examples of slithering have become too common to count, largely because of the high-tech phenomenon. Outsiders have no real means of judging the management (or for that matter the technology) of an Osborne or a Victor in a fast-moving business like computers—and because both companies went down with large quantities of supposedly expert venture capital clinging to the wrecks, it doesn't seem that insiders are necessarily any better placed. In fact, the greatest single start-up in history greatly proves the point. Trilogy Systems raised a towering $230 million to finance an IBM-crunching number-cruncher and a monstrously powerful monster chip. Its ambitions surfaced in 1980; in August 1984, in swift and disorderly succession, Trilogy, strapped for cash, abandoned both the giant computer and the gigantic chips. So much for the sharp insiders who financed, found, and finagled Trilogy's quarter of a billion precisely to pay for these two goodies.

The funniest tale in this genre is that of a data-processing company that had a rousing reception on Wall Street—until its sponsors saw the prospectus. Unlike other similar gee-whiz ventures, which were all losing money handsomely, this one was making profits. The sight of its price/earnings ratio, up over the 100 mark, so terrified the sponsors that they sold out of the stock; had it reported losses, they would happily have held on until some later deluge.

The fallback argument is that all equity investment, taking the lean years with the fat, will wax rich. First, the money purchases productive assets that (however inept their management) become worth more year after year through the simple magic of inflation; second, the company can do massively what the individual can seldom do—get "leverage" by borrowing at fixed interest, achieving double the financial horsepower from the same engine.

Both arguments rest on one unsafe assumption: that management will, year in, year out, boost earnings by a statistically significant amount. If, as in most companies, it doesn't, the market value of the stock, which is all that matters, may slump below the book value of the assets—let alone their supposed inflationproof real value. And all that leverage is mathematically bound to accelerate the profit declines nastily when, as happens more often than not, the company steps firmly on a banana skin.

Maybe there is a haphazard statistical pattern, a random walk, in profits. Since in most human affairs there is only a fifty-fifty chance of being right, half the actions of any company are likely to be wrong. Certainly the records of many corporations (after extracting the impact of acquisitions) look more random than planned, and in such circumstances the highly geared company is a menace to one and all.

Surveys by *Fortune* in the United States and *Management Today* in Britain show conclusively that the most profitable companies have the least debt and that the most indebted are the most likely to be unprofitable. *Fortune* found that the fifty highest-debt corporations among the five hundred biggest companies in the United States included fifteen in the lowest bunch for profitability and not one in the top fifty; the fifty lowest-debt companies included twenty-three, nearly half, in the top lot for profitability and not one in the bottom. In Britain, *Management Today* noted that the twenty lowest-debt companies had an average profitability that was 70 percent higher than that for the twenty highest-debt firms.

Like many earthshaking management finds, this one enshrines childish logic. If a company generates great profits, it rarely needs to borrow; if it needs to panhandle heavily, the overwhelming odds (as with an individual) are that it is earning too little. In most cases, it never will earn enough either—the borrowing becomes a permanent burden on the sore backs of management and unwitting or witting stockholders.

The combined impact of prolonged recession and mismanagement has demonstrated the hard truth about soft debt in two especially dramatic ways. First, management after management concentrated on "de-gearing"—cutting back the debt to equity ratio as fast as their finances would allow: Monsanto, for instance, reduced the size of its debt between 1980 and 1984 by a massive 31 percent to $1.1 billion, and that was a strictly run-of-the-mill case, one among thousands.

Second, the worst-hit (and worst-run) companies piled up such monstrous debts (Massey-Ferguson, International Harvester, Chrysler) that their all-too-numerous bankers couldn't afford to let the borrowers go bust and the loans go dead. In the now-classic case of Chrysler, of course, the two phenomena were combined. Lee Iacocca skillfully used the corporation's $2 billion debt overhang to pressure the bankers and the government to give him the time and space needed to de-gear on a heroic scale.

Financial institutions don't pause to wonder why they lend most generously to managements that show themselves least capable of making the money grow. Without its friendly neighborhood bankers, for instance, Lockheed would have gone to the wailing wall long ago. Yet the banks, on all external evidence, went on showing nothing but confidence in Lockheed's Daniel Haughton and his merry men as nine-figure sum after nine-figure sum was literally sunk into the company—as it was into the three other mighty miscreants listed above.

Lockheed's partner in calamity, Rolls-Royce, soaked the City of London for money time and again on the strength of a balance sheet that would have worried Mr. Micawber. And yet the big business executive, who finds it relatively easy to get around the allegedly sharp-eyed men with the big money, says that he is genuinely concerned about the little stockholder up-country. He can safely leave the stockholder to look after himself; nobody else will.

3

The American Daydream

Great ideas commonly turn false when they are most widely promulgated, applauded, and received. For a decade Europeans groaned under what J. J. Servan-Schreiber nicknamed "The American Challenge." Superefficient Americans were supposed to deploy the bottomless riches of magnificently organized corporations to trample, take over, and mesmerize European competition. But the thesis was untrue even then—and it got further from reality with every passing transatlantic flight.

In reality, American executives turned out to be no abler than Frenchmen, Japanese, Germans, or even Englishmen. U.S. corporations, including the most highly praised, suffer from all the same inefficiencies as their competitors. American technology, in most fields, is not some magical, insuperable advantage, and (so much for Servan-Schreiber) many European firms—even in Britain—outgrew the Americans by a

27

mighty margin over the 1970s. The beauty of the invader lies only in the eyes of the invaded.

For a start, the awesome figures of American invasion overstate the challenge. Take away oil and cars, and U.S. investment dwindles severely; and almost all the original investment in these capital-hungry industries dates back well before World War II. There are only a few exceptions, such as Continental Oil's unprofitable efforts to offload Libyan oil or Chrysler's stakes in Simca and Rootes, long since sold off to make the once highly profitable Peugeot's life a misery.

In computers, the most typical, most publicized, and most glamorous postwar industry, American dominance was based largely, not on the miracles of Pentagon-financed technology, but on IBM's prewar lead in punch-card machines; the Watson family business had 80 to 90 percent of this market back in 1935, more than it has ever managed in computers. In the new industries in which transatlantic hostilities have begun since the peace—chemicals, say, or convenience foods—Europeans have often had little trouble defending themselves, and Americans even less difficulty in losing glorious sums. Much of the superior quality of American management in Europe in fact consisted of this endearing ability to suffer losses that would have sent most Europeans to the poorhouse.

While admirable, in its way, the attribute is not on the curriculum of the Harvard Business School. But that seminary, and its like, were launching pads for the most truly challenging American invasion. More pervasive, and more profitable, than the computers of IBM were the acolytes of American management technology. They came from all sides—highly motivated professors of motivation, consultants commanding the world's highest fees, expatriate managers whose salaries (and tax positions) would embarrass an Italian boardroom, visiting lecturers of every posture, sellers of packaged management development aids—witch doctors whose spells, if they can't cure all corporate ailments, will definitely provide hours of harmless, profit-less diversion.

The arrival and acceptance of this flood seemed logical enough. When a powerful commission under Lord Franks, a former British ambassador to Washington, compared the de-fects of British management with American virtues, it saw one prime difference. The Americans had myriad business schools, Britain none. Ergo, build British business schools, native imita-tions of Harvard, and British management would improve. Nobody unkindly observed that the Germans, whose managers have also handily outstripped the British, had no business schools either; nor do the Japanese.

The Franks theory rested on two improbable or at least unprovable notions: that American business management actu-ally is more efficient and that the business schools have been critical in creating this lead. The grains of truth are only that management, as a body of theoretical knowledge, is almost entirely an American creation, and that business management, as a professional racket, attracts far more highly educated U.S. citizens than Britons or Frenchmen.

It is also true that American business, chasing the econo-mies of scale in the richest market in creation, and in a society that is indulgent toward high profits, has spawned corporations of immense success and, for all practical and some highly impractical purposes, unlimited resources. Some of these re-sources have been invested in some grave, sometimes despair-ing, attempts to combat the disadvantages of scale by con-structing new corporate systems. And these are truly built with a thoroughness and theoretical justification worthy of that great free enterpriser, Karl Marx.

But a system, or a management theory, or a posse of business-school graduates are only as good as their achieve-ments. Forget the long string of American disasters in Europe —the Betty Crocker cakes, the Dial soap, the Gerber baby foods, the Frigidaire refrigerators, the Campbell's soups (those lost $6.1 million in a single year as the obstinate British refused to change their tastes), and so on and so on. Consider instead events back home in corporations that, by common consent, are among America's finest.

Nobody can wander through the thickets of management lore for long without bumping into General Electric and American Telephone & Telegraph. GE is virtually a free business school: its investment in management theory, organization, and development is legendary. AT&T's fame spreads from the invention of the transistor in its Bell Labs via experiments in human relations and job organization to the courteous efficiency of the phone service. At least, that was the story until the New York telephone system had its coronary in 1969 and simply broke down.

Move on to 1984 and the communications colossus, with its arms, legs, fingers, and toes all missing after the amputation of its telephone network, rated the following encomium from *Business Week:* "Product shortages and customer defections have plagued the company's equipment manufacturing arm, while its long-distance unit has lost business to rivals and service snafus." Not surprisingly, the new, streamlined AT&T had missed its financial targets by several miles, earning only $1 billion in the first nine months of a year that was supposed to produce twice as much.

At GE matters have improved since the 1960s, when its record would have shamed any company. Between 1963 and 1969, while its sales doubled, its profits budged scarcely an inch —and over the decade from 1960, GE's rise in earnings per share was a pitiful 4.8 percent annually. That this was bad management, rather than possession of bad businesses, was amply demonstrated by GE's sharp improvement under sharper managers from 1973 to 1983, when earnings per share rose by an average 10.74 percent. All the same, that was only

127th among the *Fortune* 500, not much of a score for so supposedly expert a body of management.

The malfunctions of these two giants are in no way extraordinary, though: running a business with GE's 340,000 employees (the old unsplit AT&T had twice as many) is a crucifying task. Yet, oddly enough, no gleaming theory that the two have ever tried to implement has ever been soiled by the self-evident lack of success of these giant theorists.

The records had little to do with the damage inflicted on U.S. growth by Nixonian economics and the oil sheikhs. Right through the Kennedy-Johnson boom, the performance of GE was inferior. Its management of its computer business, stuck out on a limb in Arizona, was a dream of decentralized failure that ended only with a humiliating sellout. AT&T in New York was brought low, not by a shortfall in demand, but by inability to cope with the expansion that it stimulated through its own homey, costly advertising.

Neither GE nor AT&T lacked management talent at the time or lack it now. Very few American leviathans do. They all claim otherwise, but many consultants outside the United States agree that the American corporation, unchecked, multiplies executives like mice. Just as paperwork breeds paperwork (every memo demands at least one answer), so one executive breeds more executives (every executive vice-president needs at least two vice-presidents reporting to him).

This overbreeding and interbreeding of executives, mostly hot from the business schools, is the root of the fashion that reached its apotheosis at the end of the 1960s—the corporation decentralized on product lines, with management responsibility devolved to profit centers within profit centers, bound together by tight financial controls and meticulous forward planning, activated by regular reviews of plans and progress.

The system, imitated slavishly by one European corporation after another, seemed a sensible answer to diversity and to problems of maintaining individual responsibility and initiative inside the whale. With the rose-colored spectacles off, the system can be seen as a monumental bureaucracy, with veins made of paper, subject to blood clots at any point. To work at all, the system demands more layers of management, a great burgeoning of staff work, and heavy expenditure of line managers' time, simply to cover the control, planning, and review. Much of this managerial time is frittered away on meetings for "coordination," "consultation," and "approval"—in other words, in committees.

Take AT&T's macabre New York fiasco, as detailed by *The Wall Street Journal*. Under pressure for good figures, the New York profit center pushed up earnings by 16 percent in 1966 and 10 percent in 1967—and cut capital spending significantly in both years. Down the line, each subsidiary profit center was under strict budgetary control. This meant that in one area grossly overworked men were transferred from repairs to installations (a separate profit center on a separate budget) "to get them off the maintenance account." The installers, in turn, were the bottom of a line of command that ran through foremen, service superintendent, divisional superintendent, assistant vice-president, and operating vice-president to the president.

This was the long, long trail up which the bad news about New York's overload wound its way. AT&T executives, being human, were reluctant to face the facts—and the consequences for their budgets. A former sales manager from the main disaster area, Wall Street, told *The Wall Street Journal*, "We were well aware that these problems were coming, and we kept passing it up the line. But nothing much seemed to happen." The story has been repeated, and will go on being repeated, in many U.S. corporations with similar dire results. In this case, fifteen hundred expensive technicians were imported six months too late and an additional $200 million was pumped in as capital spending—also belated.

But Americans have a wondrous talent for regeneration. The big company has swung to other fashions, casting into outer darkness the kind of decentralization that isolated AT&T's top management so effectively from what it was supposed to be managing. The brightest business-school graduates are impatient with climbing the mountainsides of corporate bureaucracy. Recession and recovery have sharpened the reflexes of the American executive, shaken off some of his bonds, and flexed his managerial muscles. But the renewed might of management and money, coupled with America's wizard technology, financed by the taxpayer through defense contracts, has still not enabled U.S. business to win again as it always has done—or was supposed to.

That, though, was another American daydream. Some bitter U.S. disappointments of the recent past (GE, General Dynamics, Litton Industries, Lockheed, Ling-Temco-Vought, and so on) were all leading recipients of federal largesse. Although the United States spends so enormously on research and development, supplies defense plants and equipment free (with working capital thrown in), and gives most of its bounty to relatively few lucky companies, it gets a great deal of pain for its bounteous billions. Between the fiscal years of 1980 and 1982, one helicopter program studied by Booz Allen & Hamilton showed a doubled unit price, even though precious little had been changed. From 1977 to 1980 the Pentagon found the time it had to wait for A-10 and F-15 warplanes rising by ten months. With a similar stretch-out for the F-16, the delay bill was $4.7 billion. The M1 tank program was a disaster in its first four years, with terrible quality and cost problems: its price soared from a planned few hundred thousand to $2.5 million a throw. The situation was no better in the shipyards, judging by a U.S. Maritime Administration complaint that U.S. yards lacked thirty-nine out of seventy new technologies important for civilian shipping, which makes it easy to understand why

33

the Trident missile-carrying submarine program, for just one example, overran on both cost and time.

Worse still, this lavishly financed technology has often not worked, or not worked well. Very little has been directly useful in civilian markets, either; the real gee-whiz stories, such as Xerox or Polaroid in their heyday, or Apple and Intel of late, were private ventures. And even in industries that U.S. firms do still lead worldwide, such as chemicals or cars, the few technological advances have mostly been made outside America. American defense contractors, like government-financed firms everywhere, have stumbled over the myth of their own efficiency, forgetting that the marketplace is no respecter of legends.

Lockheed was so fabled a defense performer that its executives never conceived that they could flop over military projects or even make civil bloomers—even though their earlier Electra turboprop airliner, several years too late and accident-prone, was an awesome augury. The Cheyenne helicopter, SRAM missile, and Galaxy supertransport military disasters were promptly compounded by overstretching what was left of Lockheed's resources on the Tristar jet airbus. Almost from takeoff, the Tristar flew far behind in the vapor trail of its Douglas rival. Yet in beautiful downtown Burbank, Lockheed's directors seemed oblivious of onrushing financial doom. They could neither see nor admit that any management error lent a hand to the $2 billion (or 60 percent) excess on the Galaxy.

"We've asked ourself what we did wrong," said one executive, "and we concluded that there really wasn't anything." However rich Lockheed was in usable technology, blind conceit made it as vulnerable in management terms as any European corporation stuck in the fog of its between-the-wars mentality. Look down the list of prime American defense contractors—very few have made any significant new impact in postwar European markets. Where their technology was relevant, their cost structure was often too high. Until the 1960s, the Americans could trust greater productivity to offset higher costs, but that possibility was eroded long before the decade's end.

The realization has dawned that companies operating in highly unionized Megalopolis, U.S.A., have faced horrendous problems even in maintaining productivity, let alone accelerating its rise. Gigantic plowback of funds into new capital equipment was supposed to offset declining productivity of labor. Despite blatantly protective devices, such as "voluntary" import quotas, events showed, however, that, especially in comparison to the Japanese, U.S. plants had lagged fatefully in their modernization programs.

Countries with cheaper currencies had no real disadvantage against the armies of U.S. management—armies that sent ten men to do one executive's job. On imports of Japanese cars and steel, the United States' lack of competitiveness, just as much as the high valuation of the dollar, was responsible for the massive trade deficits with which the 1980s began. But these increasingly alarming figures were foreshadowed by developments a decade before. In 1969 and 1970, *Fortune*'s roster of the two hundred largest non-American companies showed sales rising by 16.2 percent and 16.7 percent respectively. Sales listed by *Fortune* for the 500 biggest U.S. groups showed growth of only 9.7 percent and 4.3 percent. Thus, as the 1970s started, the largest non-American companies were outgrowing the leading Americans by four to one. This was the first statistical proof that the American challengers were actually on the defensive, and that no managerial alchemy, taught at business school or anywhere else, could overcome basic facts of economic life, which have continued to rule the international economy ever since.

In 1982–83, true, sales of *Fortune*'s non-American 500 fell by marginally more than those of the Americans (5.5 percent against 5.1 percent) as the U.S. economy boomed. But the profit recovery outside the United States was stronger; the non-U.S. 500 clawed back almost all the decline of 1982 in a single year, while, that same year, the U.S. companies recouped less than half their collective setback.

By then, the threat posed by non-American competition, above all that from Japan, had become a cliché of American business journalism and management books. In a sudden access of inferiority complex, spurred by the clear evidence that, on many objective counts, when measured against Japanese competition, he really was inferior, the American manager went to excesses of imitative fervor; a centuries-old work on swordsmanship by a Japanese master, of all things, became a best-selling text for U.S. managers in the search for Eastern salvation.

The obvious truth is that American executives share all the normal human qualities, including incompetence. Where their own myth had made them overconfident, they proved just as vulnerable as Europeans wrestling with their far longer-standing managerial inferiority complexes. All the same, Europeans have found this hang-up hard to shift. Whatever the growth figures, isn't American business still more profitable than European? And don't American subsidiaries in countries such as Britain tend to earn more than the local bumpkins? Aren't Japanese growth records distorted by protection, cheap finance, and government manipulation of markets and money?

On the first point, accountants' ideas on profits vary across the Atlantic, which makes comparison tricky. Moreover, for a long time, U.S. levels of return depended on the cheapest money rates in the world (no longer, though, not by a long shot, which was another reason for the fading of the American challenge). Even the margin between the U.S. invaders and the locals has been narrowing, too, as American satellites became more mature and less able to live easily off the technology and output exported cheap or free by their ever-loving parents. These Americans, by definition, are offshoots of the more aggressive, better-heeled, and better-equipped U.S. corporations. It would be shameful if they couldn't outperform the mass, or gloomy average, of local industry. Yet some U.S. subsidiaries don't even manage that. Few records are as grim as the then newcomer Dow Chemical's $43.3 million write-off on the Phrix joint venture in textile fibers with Germany's BASF. Dow, in its despair, even asked an American competitor what production standards should apply to the Phrix operation. "We don't know," came the answer. "We've never seen a plant that small." That collapse was only the precursor of several American chemical comeuppances, culminating with such traumatic events as the total withdrawal of Gulf from the European market.

Both newcomers and veterans provide examples of mediocre performance. Quaker Oats has been in Britain for eighty-four years, yet in the 1970s it achieved (or didn't achieve) what one writer tactfully describes as "gentle volume decline," not just in one bad spell, but for an amazing seven or eight years. Hoover is a more awful case in point. While the annals of British marketing are littered with lost causes, few are more heartrending. Once upon a time, Hoover was as invincibly generic as Frigidaire (another collapsed cause—and also Anglo-American). The company's one-time reputation rested, not just on its vacuums, washing machines, or steam irons, but on the belief that here was an urgent example to the rest of British industry: market-oriented, export-hungry, low-cost, and profit-conscious—and, of course, U.S.-led. What went so wrong?

Over the 1970s, the company's net income came to only 3.5 percent of sales. Between 1975 and 1980 profits disappeared altogether, reducing the outfit to the point where the American parent (no great management shakes itself) had to pick up the shattered pieces. What can possibly explain so extreme a failure? No less a person than Professor Ted Levitt, whose marketing myopia thesis shaped a whole generation of marketing thought, argues that Hoover was weak precisely where U.S. companies were supposed to be strongest—the marketing concept.

Faced by inadequate home demand and limp exports, the Hoover men asked themselves the classic marketing question: What do the customers want? Unfortunately, the permutations and combinations were simply too many to provide clear answers, and features of the market itself didn't actually fit either the pattern of consumer preferences or what Hoover proceeded to do.

In Levitt's view, Hoover's mistake was not to offer a "simple, standardised high quality" automatic machine at a price between the market extremes. As it was, though, Hoover got the three critical pillars of marketing—price, promotion, and product—all hopelessly wrong; not just once, moreover, but for the best (or worst) part of two decades. Similar tales of marketing ineptitude abound in U.S. business—at home and abroad.

Still further convincing evidence lies in the blowing up of the conglomerate. The conglomerate was an American invention, founded on the supposed supremacy of modern management, nurtured on business-school graduates, fueled by theories such as "the free-form corporation" or the effective use of high debt. Non-Americans watched in awe as the conglomerate star rose, but didn't draw the obvious moral as it sputtered and exploded. That passage through the corporate heavens was symbolic of the whole American challenge. It was founded, not on real managerial, technological, and financial supremacy, but on passing circumstances, myth, and the infinite capacity of people for self-delusion.

By the same token, the comeback of American management in the 1980s, especially its strong leadership in the new industries of electronics and biotechnology, doesn't result from any innate human superiority. Rather, it reflects the innate vitality of an economic society that reacts rapidly to challenge, dearly loves an opportunity, and abounds in the human and material resources needed to seize chances like these offered by the large-scale integrated circuit and recombinant DNA. Leadership in these industries, though, isn't founded, like the expired and exploded American challenge, on the massive weight of expensive installed capacity. The new leadership rests on technology and still more on its application—and this is an era when economies of scale, thanks again to technology, have come to count for less. These days passing circumstances don't just pass. They change drastically overnight—and managers, American or not, who think otherwise are victims of the most dangerous myth of all.

That applies in spades to managers who attribute superior Japanese performance to anything other than superior management. This isn't because the Japanese government doesn't aid and abet Japanese business with all the guile it can muster—it does. It isn't because the Japanese banks don't extend credit to business on highly advantageous terms—they do. It isn't that there are no bad managements and no bad managing in Japan (there's plenty) or that Japanese social strengths don't help—of course they do. The reason for taking Japanese managerial success at face value is simply that only by doing so will American managers be driven to raise their own standards higher—without raising excuses. Give a manager an excuse for bad performance, and he'll take it; and that's the last thing an ostensibly chastened and recharged U.S. management can afford.

4

Marketing Make-Believe

The last two management decades have been vastly influenced by one question: What business are we in? The question was put by Theodore C. Levitt in a *Harvard Business Review* article, "Marketing Myopia." He cited the U.S. railroads, which chugged off into penury under the delusion that their business was railways, not transportation. And there was a buggy-whip company that went bust because it, too, had defined its business by the product, not by the market.

Levitt's thesis sounded plausible, although it did raise certain questions. Would dumbheaded railroad proprietors have been any brighter at managing truck companies or airlines? And what if the buggy-whip firm had decided that, instead of being in transport accessories or guidance systems, it was in flagellation?

But executives love a new panacea; so companies all over

the world chugged off, as the American railroads didn't, into the business of defining their businesses. The bigger the company, the greater their pain—because large firms, like rocks acquiring barnacles, build up an encrusted deposit of unrelated activities over time. In the United States, for instance, the biggest conglomerate in the sense of operating in the most different markets was not Bluhdorn's Gulf & Western or Geneen's International Telephone and Telegraph or even Ling's Ling-Temco-Vought. It was good old General Tire, one of the unselect few among America's leading companies, be it noted, whose earnings per share in 1983 were actually lower than a decade before.

The search for definitions led off in strange verbal directions. Of all odd results, one engineering outfit had the most alliterative and meaningless—*metal manipulation.* This fine phrase can cover everything from the tubes that provided most of the group's profits to hairpins, which it didn't make; but the company's products did include some that used no metal, and others, such as gas heaters, in which manipulating metal was about the least important factor.

Dunlop, deeply influenced by the McKinsey & Co. consultants, who are in turn high on the marketing concept, came up with an equal beauty to explain its confusion of activities. "What do rubber and its successors do?" asked the chairman of the day rhetorically. "They absorb shock. They cushion. They grip. They bounce. What binds us together is the extension of these kinds of things."

A binding that grips mattresses, tennis rackets, antiskid devices, and slippers is not tight; nor did the definition help Dunlop to absorb the shocks delivered to its rubbery system by its own incompetence—shocks so severe that in 1983, en route to final dissolution, it quit forever the European tire business where it had begun and (once) prospered.

Any diversified giant's business is seldom logical. It is

nearly always founded on one basic well-defined market—such as tires, which made up roughly two thirds of Dunlop. The logic of Levitt, if strictly applied, would lead here to one of two conclusions. Either everything unrelated to the cushioning and care of transport equipment should be dropped as time-wasting diversion, or Dunlop should be treated, not as homogenous, but as a bunch of different and unrelated businesses.

Neither course is attractive. Company directors never (or hardly ever) voluntarily reduce their imperial sway; failed conglomerates have been slow to reduce their mass, or deconglomerate, even under acute financial pressure. If a big company does dump a major interest (as GE and RCA did with their computers), there are usually only two explanations: either the disposed fragment was losing money in floods, or the trustbusters (as with ITT and Avis or AT&T with its regional phone companies) have forced the issue.

In the 1980s, the tune has changed somewhat. Although many of the businesses being dropped, in the greatest fire sale in corporate history, were indeed losing money, some were less mistakes than misfits, businesses bought in the era of conglomerate diversification, which, in the new age of concentration around so-called core businesses, suddenly seemed out of place. Some of the most spectacular offloading came from disenchanted conglomerates (the disenchantment being shared by managers and stockholders alike).

No case was more remarkable than the selling spree on which Gulf & Western embarked almost immediately after its creator, Charles G. Bluhdorn, was killed in a plane crash. What man had wrongly put together, it seemed, man must take asunder—and better had if the corporation wanted to meet any goals worth having. At Consolidated Foods that meant the management's selling *half* an astounding bundle of 125 businesses.

At the bankrupt AM International, the seven companies

put on the block in a dying spasm had mainly only just been bought. Just as Consolidated has reshaped itself to six distinct core activities, so AM was struggling back to life with three. Separate and strengthen, divide and conquer; whatever the description, the principle is hard to gainsay and makes much better sense than the old principle of join and justify, which so often ended up with the junction showing no justification at all.

The record-breaking surge in divestment, of course, has been battling against an equally unprecedented wave of mergers, ranging from routine multimillion-dollar buys (of exactly the kind that bloated Consolidated Foods in the past) to billion-dollar bonanzas (bonanzas for the stockholders at the receiving end, that is). These megamergers of the 1980s have provided some new and instant episodes of divestment under duress. Having paid a barely believable $2.8 billion for Esmark, Beatrice Foods was forced into a sell-off program to a total value (even less believable) of a billion dollars in a single year.

But mostly the duress is that imposed by inadequate results. That explains, for example, why Bowater's North American newsprint interests, long the very heart of the corporation, were set adrift. The company had two horses pulling in different directions on opposite sides of the Atlantic. No doubt, the split played a part in the grisly, 13 percent inflation-corrected decline in earnings per share per year over the decade to 1982.

Even in a bad American paper year like 1983, Bowater made just over half its trading profits from the West—and in 1982 the figure was a thumping four fifths. But while the split-up was spectacularly successful in market terms (as sell-offs, significantly, often are), the British management back home couldn't escape from one basic problem: its remaining interests were still highly diversified—that is, a ragbag.

Most executives are no happier accepting the fact that they have a ragbag, which cannot be managed as one company in one way by one group of top men. They have mostly risen

43

through the one homogenous business that makes sense for the company. They used to manage that business positively, by day-to-day involvement. In the 1960s and 1970s, they would not admit that their skills were of little help to the companies clustering around the mother planet. So they interfered and produced some concept of the company that lent rhyme and reason to their fiddling (as, in most cases, they still do).

The marketing myopia question thus inadvertently nourished a policy of widening spread, which is the antithesis of the marketing concept, although that is by no means unforgivable. Marketing has attracted piles of unenlightened prose. Its definitions wander into long, echoing sentences littered with the ugly word *orientation.* Marketing seems to mean finding out what the customer wants, putting on the market something that meets his need at a price the fellow is ready to pay, producing whatever it is for a cost that yields a fat profit at the price it is sold for, and knitting in the distribution and advertising with the marketing idea. All very sound and satisfying—until you ask what a nonmarketing company is up to.

Reversing the definition, that kind of company makes things whether or not anybody wants them, prices them any old how (except at the right price for the market), manufactures without any thought of the market, and distributes and promotes the result at random. Many companies are guilty of all these sins, but it isn't their marketing that is at fault. They need a new management.

Marketing's definitions end up describing every activity of top management, including even mergers, and stopping short only at personnel relations (on which top management spends too little time, anyway, except when there are strikes). If marketing equals management, and bad marketing equals mismanagement, why all the fuss? And why, if marketing is a nonexistent mystery, do companies hire graduates wholesale from firms such as Procter & Gamble that are supposed to have the knack?

Good books or articles on marketing are suspiciously thin. Except for recondite areas, such as the impenetrable equations of market research, there isn't much to write about—merely general management. One executive turned marketing professor, now retired, believes that marketing as a subject will eventually wither away, as executives finally master, for good and all, the outlandish notion that they have customers.

Marketing (not successful marketing, but marketing as the provision of bright ideas) is the easiest function in business management—which is why smooth-talking confidence artists have created such havoc. A former soap man, whose impeccable credentials included creating near-chaos in his first non-lather post, proceeded to tie up nearly all his next employer's working capital in the unsold stocks of just one division. The employer learned too late that any fool can produce a plan to capture 20 percent of the market. The excruciating job is making products that work at a cost that brings profits within earthly possibility. You can (the Germans did) successfully flog a well-made product for decades without having a marketing man or marketing notion on the premises.

But nobody, for more than the shortest period, can market mangled goods—no matter if every marketing consultant ever to wing the Atlantic is massed on his side. In a way, the old, despised production orientation had more logic. Any business has to be adept at its basic physical operations; without that, nothing is possible.

This is the lesson that W. Edwards Deming, the great guru of quality control, has been preaching to the Japanese (who lionize him) for over thirty years and to the Americans (who mostly ignored him most of that time) ever since the United States woke up to the threat of Japan's productive lead. Apply Deming's ideas on quality control and manufacturing organization and you get, not just lower costs, but better performance in the marketplace.

That, at least, seems to be the lesson of the Pontiac Fiero, said by *Fortune* to be, "the first U.S. car produced from scratch according to the Deming way," which has broken all U.S. sales records for a two-seat car. One of Deming's key principles is that companies should not choose suppliers on the basis of price alone, but instead should consider quality. In one extraordinary leap of faith in Deming, Pontiac chose a single supplier for each item it buys for the Fiero, without competitive bidding. By GM's internal ratings, Fiero quality is the best in the corporation, even though the Fiero plant has no on-line inspectors. Bad production, as much as bad marketing, is what let the Japanese in. What Western car companies, as opposed to their Eastern competitors, consistently got wrong were questions of engineering design, cost of production, purchasing policy, balance of productive capacity, manpower deployment, and compatibility of components.

In a period when British industry was being lashed for marketing lapses, its sins of production were far more heinous. Americans are (or were) more deeply indoctrinated in the arts of marrying engineering and manufacture to meet product and profit requirements. But the old black magic fled, possibly because, of all U.S. specializations, production is the least likely to lead to the top and therefore, presumably, the last functional area into which bright young things from Harvard will direct their pattering feet.

As the marketing thinkers and their disciples have taken over, so Americans have imitated British disasters—for instance, in the aircraft industry. Their problem was not designing an aircraft that the market wants. The trouble has come mostly from failing to get enough working planes or engines flying at economic cost, and at the scheduled time. As other industries, too, discovered that their ability to market was being sabotaged by their inability to produce (a discovery rubbed in by Japanese producers of all manner of goods), so the production expert rose from Cinderella to Princess Charming. Salaries and status have risen correspondingly. When companies are pouring belated billions into automation and improvement of both product and process, you can't entrust the investment to anything but the brightest and best. And they in turn can't give of their best unless, as in Japan, production and marketing work closer together than Laurel and Hardy.

Even the best-versed American companies have been coming to grief on these rocks. Thus, Ford Motor has long prided itself on understanding the interrelation between car manufacture and marketing, which isn't too difficult. You invest heavily to keep down manufacturing costs and to introduce new models; you engineer desirable qualities into the cars and so push up the price; you seek maximum interchangeability of parts between different lines; and you never launch a car until volume production is running smoothly and the dealers are stocked with the shiny new toys.

So what happened in Britain when Ford, in 1970, introduced the replacement for its biggest profit earner? Well after the launch of the new Cortina and before a crippling strike, the dealers had no cars, and the few thousands made had all been recalled because of a production defect. In 1983 a whole new brand was the favored answer to replace the last of the Cortinas, but the design was ahead of the market in one sense (going for a new look instantly christened the "jelly mold" or "jelly baby") and behind it in another—the car looked small externally, when the market mood, with gas going down in price, was moving in the opposite direction as regards size.

The Sierra consequently missed its targets so comprehensively that senior Ford men (those who survived the disaster, that is) could keep their chins up only by arguing that the entire market sector had shrunk. So it had—because of the Sierra's lack of appeal. Mainly, though, it's less mistakes of marketing than mishaps of mechanics that have crippled the car-makers.

At one point, the recalls of U.S. cars seemed to have reached epidemic proportions—and it was no coincidence that, while you could have called VW's Beetle ugly, noisy, uncomfortable, slow, and inconvenient (and, if you were Ralph Nader, unsafe), you could not, by industry standards in the Beetle's long day, say that the machine was badly made.

In a later generation and higher price bracket, much the same is true of the Volvo—an eyesore to many cognoscenti, and no great shakes in performance, either. But, as with the Beetle before it, the ugliness has become endearing to buyers who value the car's solidity, safety, reliability, and quality. The marketing man, of course, won't let that escape. Reliability, he will say, is Volvo's gimmick—in other words, whatever a company does right is good marketing, and whatever it does wrong is because its marketing is bad.

The marketeers have not only pushed production men into the cold but have also ousted the salesman. The standard sneer against "nonmarketing-oriented" companies is that they have merely called the sales manager a marketing manager. This is more sensible than importing a costly and expensively educated marketing manager and downgrading the little matter of selling. Just as you cannot market anything you cannot make, so you cannot market a product you cannot sell.

Selling, like production, is one of the grubbier aspects of management. Instead of hitting machines that break down, you come up against people who say no, or maybe. The great marketing companies were all founded on nothing more elaborate than the hard sell—3M, National Cash Register, Procter & Gamble, Coca-Cola, Shell, and IBM. IBM's acolytes would sing, of Thomas Watson, Sr., "He is the fairest, squarest man we know. Sincere and true, he has shown us how to play the game. And how to make the dough." The further they drift (like the men in head office aeries) from the hard base of making dough by selling, the more ineffective the companies become in the marketplace.

What business are we in? may have helped in brooding about the future and about the delicious directions that the company could or should take. But even that is dubious. Every single large company that diversified into computers had excellent reasons, based on realistic definitions of its business, for adding computer capacity. Yet every single one suffered untold grief as a result. They failed not by misunderstanding what business they were in, but by not seeing what business computers were in—and that, overwhelmingly, was the replacement of punch-card machines, and replacing them, at that, in competition with IBM.

The first real marketing question is this: How do we truly make our money? The answer, even in the largest conglomerates, usually comes down to that one basic area, established since its time began, in which the company is the lord of the market; in IBM's case, catering for the data-processing needs of the corporation and the corporation man. Defending and extending this position must have the overwhelming priority. The next two marketing questions are How can we improve the key products and their manufacture? and How can we improve our selling?

The major asset of any business is the expertise acquired over time in its fundamental activities, and that is defined not by broad markets but by specific products. The U.S. railroaders would have made a mess of road or air transport because, lacking equipment and experience, they would have failed to understand unfamiliar technologies of selling or operation. The moral is not "Look after your production and selling, and your marketing will look after itself," but simply that stuffing the company into a bag marked Marketing Concept makes not a whit of difference to its myopia, arthritis, constipation—or any other of the diseases to which corporate flesh is heir.

The proof of this vital proposition is evident from the performance of that most successfully market-oriented—or, in its own preferred phrase, *customer-led*—corporation of them

49

all: IBM. Suggesting to an IBM executive that he's not a marketing man is like asking Jack Nicklaus if he plays golf. Successive managements have worked back from the sales orientation of old Tom Watson all the way down the line through production to R & D. That's why a young executive starts a project at the development stage, is joined by people from manufacture during development, and stays with his baby right through its manufacture and marketing worldwide, and the development of its variants and improvements.

The customers around which IBM builds its business are defined as the market, the whole market, and nothing but the market. In the pursuit of every dollar going, though, IBM has never forgotten the essential paradox, which is that you never succeed unless the company is entirely oriented toward its markets, but that you can't achieve that orientation unless everything else in the company, everything that doesn't carry the marketing label, is as good as, or better than, the performance and attributes of the competition.

Sure, IBM lives by the marketing concept (and in the case of the PC jr died by it, when the product fell short of customer expectations and was finally killed, in April 1985, despite an apparently successful revamp). But that's simply shorthand for the concept of the whole corporation. Nothing less will do.

5

Big Business Blues

Everybody knows that the bigger the company, the sloppier its management, but everybody is wrong. The big company has the best managers, the best management, and generally the best technology, the best products, and the best production equipment—because the big company has the big money, and all these pleasures cost plenty. True, the large corporation can easily become tongue-tied, muscle-bound, spendthrift, and overweight—doing all it can, via these disadvantages, to outweigh its assets. But the mammoth's strengths give it an invaluable asset—staying power.

Large corporations are as durable as Old Man River. The whiz-kid companies come and go, rise and fall, but even a rudderless vessel such as U.S. Steel goes rolling along forever. It takes prodigies of mismanagement—usually in thorny industrial forests such as aerospace, into which many a man has disappeared without trace—to break a large company. Short of mislaying its trains (which it did, too) the Penn Central had to commit every folly in the book to sink into bankruptcy, yet there it was in 1983, 151st in the *Fortune* 500, still alive, if not exactly kicking, with a net income of $19.7 million, which represented less than 1 percent on its enormous, $2.5 billion of sales.

The received view, which looks at the failures and fiascoes of the leviathan rather than its strengths, requires correcting by what an American writer nicknamed the "Lestoil syndrome," after a once obscure New Jersey detergent firm. Expounding the Second Truth of Management, that *all good management is merely an expression of one great idea,* Lestoil broke out of obscurity by bottling the heavy-duty detergent that it sold to industry and offering the heavenly liquid to housewives as well.

Television advertising, cautious at first, bolder as sales soared, quickly shifted Lestoil out of New Jersey and into the New York big time. The highly salaried managers at Lestoil's massively larger competitors, Procter & Gamble and Lever Brothers, had (as is their wont) totally missed this opportunity, despite their massed brainpower. In the end, however, the mammoths reacted with multimillion-dollar force, swamping Lestoil in a sea of green bubbles. Hence the Lestoil syndrome —and it happens all the time and to anybody—even in an industry with unlimited growth prospects, even to the man who practically invented it, like one Joe Engelberger.

Before he literally said "Let's make a robot" in 1956, there was no robotics industry. By 1983, when Engelberger's creation, Unimation, had sold 6,800 robots worldwide, it had also, alas, chalked up a first quarter loss of $558,000. At that point, Westinghouse Electric, for a mere $107 million, swallowed the lot, including the "granddaddy of American robotics," the pioneering Engelberger.

He lasted only a few months on a battlefield now dominated by U.S. giants (as well as Westinghouse, GE, GM, Cincinnati Milacron, and so forth) and by Japanese superstars. As a writer for *Management Today* soberly observed, after quoting a Cincinnati executive to the effect that "Robotics is a very expensive club," it is "safe to bet that the only members of the club will be the big corporations" by 1990.

It has been commonly observed that more innovations by far come from small companies than from big corporations. It has been far less noted that the small company generally loses, not just its smallness (that is inevitable, if its innovation succeeds) but its independence, which shouldn't be inevitable at all. The main safeguard against these events in the United States was the trustbusting fervor that once suffused the Justice Department—and stopped the giants from swallowing everything in sight. In the new era of corporate sexual permissiveness, though, anything goes, and many companies have therefore gone, companies that, in previous decades, would have survived.

IBM, for instance, would never have been allowed to build its capacity in telephone exchanges by purchasing the up-and-coming Rolm, one of a myriad of smaller, new companies that, in the burgeoning world of microelectronics, have produced better products first and marketed them best. But that's where the writing appears on the wall: enter the Lestoil syndrome. In the usual situation, the giants retaliate, the competition intensifies, the growth levels off, and the stock falls.

Even a fantastic growth company like Tandem can suddenly look vulnerable. Born only in 1974, with the brilliant notion of building a computer that would never stop working, never go down, Tandem never grew by less than 90 percent in any year to 1981. The next year, its expansion was positively feeble—a mere 50 percent. Even 1983's crawl (only 34 percent) looked like lightning compared to 1984's rate of less than a quarter. Because IBM and others were trying to scramble on

Tandem's slowing bandwagon, it's no wonder that the stock collapsed from $45 to about $16 in a mere eighteen months—and this, remember, was a company still growing at a pace that, by any standards save its own, was remarkable beyond the dreams of avarice. The smaller company has its hands full simply to prevent the working out of an ancient management maxim: if you can't beat 'em, buy 'em.

This has its tragic aspects: little David hurls his stone against Goliath, who takes his bruises and then, with ridiculous ease, plucks up his adversary. But the tragedy is inherent in two facts. First, the Davids are worse managed than the giants, and this is hidden behind the smokescreen of their success. Second, an essential ingredient of the little guy's success is the somnolence of Goliath. Outside every big, fat company there are sectors of the market waiting for a lean competitor to thrust his way in. No corporation, no matter how rich and superbly staffed, can preempt every possibility in the market or in technology; and the wealthier the company is, and the more massively entrenched in its chosen sectors, the harder it may be for its directors to react—for reasons of economics as well as pure inertia.

Gillette's initial failure in the stainless-steel razor-blade war was not simply its refusal to accept the fact that a little British sword company called Wilkinson could provide serious competition. Gillette could compete technically—it made stainless blades for the Swiss and Swedish markets before the word *stainless* ever dropped into Wilkinson's consciousness, and Gillette even owned the patent for the critical PTFE coating of Wilkinson's wonder blades.

But Gillette had a huge worldwide production apparatus geared only to make carbon-steel blades, which, because they became blunt quicker, were bound to sell in larger quantities and at lovelier profits than stainless blades. No wonder Gillette didn't want to know about the horrible things. But in management you can't (though executives do it constantly) shut your eyes and hope the competition will go away. Eventually Gillette was forced to compete, after losing significant slices of a seemingly impregnable market in country after country.

Believe it or not, though, Gillette proceeded to make the same mistake again, only this time in concert with Wilkinson. While the two were slugging it out, with Gillette's double-blade and swivel head taking the technological lead, both took no notice of the arrival in 1976 of the brilliant Baron Marcel Bich, the French ballpoint king. His Bic disposable razor reached the giants' consciousness in what one Wilkinson executive recalls as "a very odd way. The patient thought he had a minor bruise. Two years later he found he had lost a leg." In eight years disposables cut out 60 percent of the entire wet-shaving market. Two companies hiding happily behind high prices and high margins had been wrecked by "the guy who comes in with quite different aims—maximum brand share and no regard for profit."

The oil countries, like the oil companies before them, have been forced to learn similar hard lessons about the difficulty—actually, the impossibility—of having your cake and eating it: both monopolizing the market and maintaining high prices and profits without reducing sales. Any high school economist could have told OPEC that this would never work. True, many graduate economists, even some with Nobel Prizes, couldn't see that Milton Friedman, almost alone, was right: that either oil prices or oil sales were bound to fall—probably both, as duly happened.

Every time a fat monopolist, whether his name is Sheikh Yamani or Nelson Bunker Hunt, tries to exploit a dominant supply position in some market (Yamani in oil, Hunt in silver), their Achilles heel is quickly exposed: that both demand and supply are elastic—that is, they can move in either direction, up or down, which is how the Hunt speculation lost $1.5 billion.

The days have long gone when the oil companies could fix world prices, in Europe and all points East, on a cozy formula linked to the free-market quote in (of all places) the Gulf of Mexico. The logic was only slightly stronger than fixing the price of beef in Chicago by that of yak's meat in Siberia. Under this umbrella of artificially high prices crawled the first cut-price independents; these tiny folk made handsome profits while charging much less. The big companies faced a horrid dilemma. Did they cut prices to cut out the independents, and sacrifice profits? Or did they maintain their profit margins and forget about the new competition? In the end, the issue was settled for them: the independents made such fast inroads that, thus getting the worst of both worlds, the majors lost market share and still had to cut prices. In the end, after much painful loss of profits, the Lestoil syndrome came into play and the independents were bought up—at the traditional premium prices.

The harder a leviathan is hit by small-fry competition, the more likely it is to undergo the whalelike upheaval from which its progress mostly springs. The leviathan can bask for decades at a time before some terrible shock (like the great lumps that Wilkinson carved out of Gillette) makes it shoot out of the water on a sudden, usually brief career of high-speed perform-ance. And it is easier for giant companies, despite their inertia, to react to challenge than it is for the little challenger to meet the awakened giant's attack. For the challenger's deficiencies are the mirror of the champion's strengths.

The sudden growth star normally has one or two thrusting and forceful personalities at the top—entrepreneurial types who lack interest in the routines of administration and organi-zation. Below these leaders are few, if any, middle executives able to plug the gaps. First, the needs of the company rapidly outgrow the capacities of the men on board at the start of the upward trajectory, when the company was much smaller. This calamity hit even the Italian domestic appliance-makers, long after they had become incredibly rich by flooding Europe with their refrigerators and washing machines so efficiently that even the mighty Philips, the giant of European electronics, was forced to surrender. The rot reached so deep into the Italian industry that in 1984 its flagship company, Zanussi, awash in debts of $615 million, was forced to accept a takeover by Electrolux—the Swedish giant whose boss, Hans Werthen, had proved, by multiplying sales twenty times since 1967, that the fault lay more in the Italians' management than in their markets.

Second, people with high management talent tend to go where it is most recognized and best rewarded—and that generally means not the up-and-coming growth company (which usually underpays) but the heavyweight corporation. Any investor, or any takeover bidder, who buys a second-rank growth company for its management is flying blind. The management looks good only through the distorting glass of the boom-type profit record.

Some challengers do make it to the top—more in America, where risk capital is relatively abundant, than in Europe, where the established companies have a hammerlock on the available financing. Xerox and Polaroid are the two stimulating examples of challengers turned champions, riding new technology that the giants wouldn't touch. Even when both companies were riding at their highest, though, their two biggest competitors—3M and Eastman Kodak—were prospering mightily all the same. Both achieved relatively good annual growth in earnings per share during the Polaroid-Xerox wonder era (3M's annual rate was 9.27 percent from 1960 to 1970, Kodak's 12.21 percent). Kodak's figures, however, were less significant than its reactions, however belated, to the technological challenge.

In fact, the Polaroid apparition galvanized Kodak into producing, in the Instamatic camera, its first great marketing innovation since a couple of concert pianists turned up with Kodachrome—just as Gillette was stung by Wilkinson into marketing the Techmatic razor, its first improvement in basic wet-shaving technology since the royal days of King C. Gillette. Both the challenger and the challenged continued with a string of counterinventions and innovations (with Gillette keeping so close an eye on Wilkinson that both of them, as noted, failed to spot Bic coming up fast on the outside).

It's interesting to speculate how much of this technical and marketing advance (if any) would have taken place if Kodak and Gillette had preserved their too cozy monopolies. It's fascinating, too, to note that Polaroid and Xerox, as they and their markets matured, showed exactly the same inertia in the face of competitive challenge, and have likewise been stimulated, after overlong delay, to dig into their pockets and their labs for the flood of new goodies that are the attacked giant's best, indeed only, means of defense—and which, with luck, as with Kodak's innovations in snapshot cameras, can actually strengthen the threatened monopoly.

A benevolent circle produces these wonders. Because they are relatively well managed and exceedingly rich, the leviathans attract most of the new talent, which helps to soup up their management horsepower and to make them richer still. But the managerial talent of larger companies differs from that of growth stars. Its quality is shown in the effectiveness of formal systems, in the recognizable ability of individuals deep down inside the organization, in consistent performance over the years, and in this very power to regenerate.

Royal Dutch–Shell is the biggest example that Europe can offer of this, as of everything else. Its managerial reputation was once so potent that *Time* magazine fulsomely lauded Shell's superiority over the American oil majors. It often happens that the summit of pride for a corporation precedes a fall. When the profits stuck fast shortly thereafter and the McKinsey & Co. consultants were called in, Shell was revealed as another overweight bureaucracy that could be cured only by painful slimming at the managerial fat farm. Recognition of its own defects is an excellent therapy for management. Shell led the oil majors into the giant tanker era and prospered accordingly; its pretax margins went up by no less than one fifth, which on a turnover in the billions has a perfectly marvelous effect.

Because it builds up so much blubber over the years, a large corporation is relatively easy to pare down: great lumps of fat can be sliced away without any visible effect on corporate efficiency. This is the lesson of Lord Weinstock's calculated surgery on the General Electric Company. Its net capital employed rose in three years by only $4.5 million, while sales galloped up by $23.6 million and profits by $10.6 million. As Weinstock wielded the knife, critics argued that the cutting would go too far, until the very heart of the old electrical giant would be chopped out. In fact, the amputation of superfluous offices, factories, and staffs left GEC so formidable that its two bigger rivals, English Electric and AEI, couldn't stay in the game. Both succumbed to GEC bids, while the bidder went on to prodigies of growth. From $2.3 billion in 1975, sales soared over threefold to $7.54 billion in 1984; earnings per share quadrupled as profits climbed to $886 million—a thumping 12 percent return on sales.

Cutting is not the same thing as creating—even though eliminating $1 million of running sores is just as effective financially as creating a new business earning $1 million. Loss elimination, moreover, requires no capital, and may actually free it, if the culprit can be sold off; new businesses always involve investing new money, a job at which large firms are worse than they know. The potential weakness of the big corporation lies, not only in the sluggishness and inefficiencies bred by long chains of command and entrenched bureaucracies but in inability to behave like small company entrepreneurs, no matter how it tries.

Big company managers are far better at running an ongoing, soundly based business. The money that Honeywell, for instance, has milked out of thermostats over the years could have bought up every small gee-whiz company along Boston's Route 128 and still left change. On this argument, big companies should give up the seldom successful effort to launch new businesses. If they discover bright, aggressive entrepreneurs in their midst, managements should encourage these rarities to go into business for themselves—and keep a slice of the equity for the good old company. Most of the offshoots, however, will fail. (Fear of failure within the big company is a prime cause of its entrepreneurial inertia; the key to making a personal fortune in business is to lose inhibitions about going bankrupt.)

Those breakaways who succeed can always be acquired in the big company's own good time. Cynical, perhaps; but it's the only way. Xerox provided clinching evidence of its own passage from entrepreneurial creation to established corporation in its first major diversification. It bought up Scientific Data Systems, a little computer breakaway turned sometime bonanza; and Xerox (behaving like an established giant all the way) paid far too much ($900 million) for a company that promptly lost much fine gold.

SDS had been purchased because the Xerox boss of the time saw, perfectly correctly, that an office-equipment maker of the future would vitally need computer capability. Unfortunately, Xerox bought the wrong company, managed it wrongly, and still ended in the wrong position—without the computer strengths required in the present for the office of the future. In this market (and others), despite such unpromising examples, Goliaths have kept on buying up Davids at prices which seem reasonable only by comparison with the purchaser's own mighty assets.

Thus the great GM forked out $2.5 billion for Electronic Data Systems in pursuit of its sudden desire to become to information processing what it is to autos. Whether doomed to failure or destined for success, the buy represented only a thirtieth of GM's existing wealth. A top executive put the best possible gloss on this particular deal to *Business Week:* "We're being more outward-directed, and we've stopped thinking that we're going to invent everything ourselves."

You could put that differently: that GM's bosses, as few corporation men do, have found the wit or psychological insight to concentrate on and refine what they can do well— running large commercial bureaucracies—and avoid the activities at which they fail. That quote, paraphrased, comes perilously near to admitting that "we're no good at doing new things; we'll let somebody else do it, then buy them up." Normally, corporate mythology has dictated, as much at GM as anywhere else, that, to quote a vice-president from du Pont, the entrepreneurial man who bucks the system is the man who makes it. Asked to give an example, the du Pont vice-president came up with a hero who started the company's antifreeze business—back in the 1930s.

In more modern times, plagued by a lack of entrepreneurs, du Pont pioneered a device designed to break any logjams. Called by the fancy name of *venture management,* this set up businesses within the business. One manager gets total responsibility for a new project. It is all his, to nurse to profitable fruition; all his, that is, subject to the normal limitations of corporate budgeting and policy restraints, which kill him.

A few large companies have realized the full extent of their disabilities in these respects and gone still further, by hiving off development projects from the main body of the corporation. The project team is separated not only geographically but in life-style: their premises, isolated and simple, are known as "skunk-works," and only when they have achieved success (in theory, far faster than would have happened back at the glass-walled ranch) are they brought back out of the cold. In this way the skunk-works are expected to crash or vault the big company's bureaucratic barriers.

There's the rub. The corporation's checks, changes, habitual slow, grudging reactions, and heavy overheads are exactly the forces that stifle entrepreneurial initiative. A new business may need new forms for its success; the old norms of a corporation may be deadly. For all du Pont's depth of resources, hefty research spending, and sophisticated techniques such as *venture analysis* (computerized assessment of projects, renamed *venture annihilation* by aggrieved managers), its flow of new riches has disappointed deeply. Its trumpeted Corfam synthetic leather of the 1960s had to be folded for a pretax loss of $100 million, after a series of marketing and manufacturing errors, in a notorious misadventure.

The tragedy of the new venture manager in the large corporation is what seems to be his strength—the fact that all the corporation's resources are behind him. The small men can't take four years to launch a product; they don't have the time, so they take four months. They can't install expensive engineering, because they haven't got the money—so they find a cheaper way to manufacture, which produces a cheaper price and so automatically builds in a marketing advantage. If guys like this save money, it's money they badly need. But if a corporation man is given a budget to invest, he spends it—for there is no personal gain in economizing. The small man runs hard because the bet is all or nothing. The corporation man is on double or quits. If the project comes off, he is a hero. If he is a Corfam-coated failure, he probably stays put. In the rare cases of dismissal, there is always some other job somewhere.

Yet it is possible to buck the system—not from the bottom, but the top. When former IBM chairman Frank B. Cary, riled beyond endurance by the fact that other people's personal computers were "stealing the hearts and minds of my executives," ordered the start of IBM's own PC project, he gave the team only eighteen months, instead of the usual three years, plus an override that bypassed IBM's elaborate systems and broke many of its shibboleths (like making as much as possible in-house).

The result was a triumph that has already passed into the Hall of Business Fame. So has Sony's Walkman—dreamed up by a junior Sony employee who could find only one man in the company to agree that the project was worth pursuing. As that one man was Akio Morita, the president, the Walkman went ahead, with marvelous results. But a young engineer named Stephen Wozniak couldn't get the same access to David Packard or anybody else at Hewlett-Packard possessed of Morita's power of decision, thought, and execution. Which is partly why Apple was born (when Wozniak teamed up with Steve Jobs)- and also partly why Hewlett-Packard is a panting also-ran in personal computers.

The big corporation that is really serious about innovating has to loosen the whole structure of checks and balances, reports and committees in which decisions are arduously taken and painfully executed. At the same time, the routine operations that go on for eternity are always a happy hunting ground for improvement. A great deal of work inside an organization serves only the organization; it has no direct relevance outside, which is the only place where the money is. All this work can be dumped without loss.

Large companies further compound the perennial problem of effective management of large numbers by overhiring. Far too many able executives sleep peacefully within those ample bosoms. As a former ICI executive once wrote, "If everyone in giant corporations of this nature who is earning over $50,000 a year were lined up, and the even numbers dismissed, not only would those left behind cope more easily with their tasks, but those dismissed would have a major impact on industry."

The paradox of too many competent executives, when (according to the complaints of most chief executives) there are not enough to go around, is easily resolved. The extant executives are used for the wrong jobs or pointed toward the wrong objectives by the kind of big company top management that (to quote a case) maintains a separate sales force to sell its own commodity to its own subsidiaries, which (naturally) are not allowed to buy from any other source. This particular company had imported bright, aggressive market-minded newcomers to run the businesses closest to the marketplace; but it offset the contribution from any of its ventures that survived pregnancy by losing all the money it could in older parts of the company.

Great companies would crash into these barriers less often if they saw themselves as they really are—not as thrusting, entrepreneurial commercial go-getters, but as bureaucracies with a tendency to domination by *apparatchiks*—people who have grown old in a company's service and traditions. The delightful chairman of one multinational jewel once said, "You can't turn a group like this upside down every eighteen months." That is the authentic voice of the apparatchik: if a corporation urgently needs turning upside down, even eighteen months after the last upheaval, inversion it must have. It is the apparatchik who stops the big corporation, time and again, from cashing in on its innate superiority. It is the anti-apparatchik who, time and time again, proves that the corporation can be freed from its self-imposed chains.

6

The Question of
Working Life

The work force of the West has suffered more change and threat of change in the past decade than in any previous postwar period. The oil price hikes shattered the dream of continuously rising prosperity and threw millions out of work. Hyperinflation destroyed savings and devoured purchasing power. Automation utterly changed the basis of production and reduced the number of jobs in industry after industry. Recession clobbered bargaining power so severely that, right across the board, once-powerful unions found themselves in broad retreat.

Yet, with rare and special exceptions, like the British miners' strike of 1984, industrial relations didn't worsen—they improved. It was hard even to remember that rebellion by the workers had alarmed managements all over Europe and North America as the 1970s began. That upsurge of unrest followed oddly on a decade in which, thanks to the blessings of behavioral science, the workingman's well-being had ostensibly received more nurture than ever before. Inventions in employee relations ran from the joys of job enrichment to the rewards of productivity bargaining. Yet the unions wanted still more—mysterious gains such as employee participation and co-ownership, as well as that simple, age-old need, more money.

Putting cash aside, labor felt unloved—which is strange, given that the leaders of big business cast themselves as leading humanists. Most annual reports contain ritual tributes to the labor force ("Again the staff distinguished itself by its team effort, its enthusiasm, and its loyalty. . . ."). Corporate heads are also fond of phrases such as "Its able and dedicated employees continue to be the company's most valuable resource" or "People are our most important product" or "our most important asset." How strange that those assets (or products) ever became increasingly prone to strike.

Actually, people are often less important than physical assets—companies sometimes move whole operations to new towns, leaving their labor forces in the lurch. Almost the entire New England textile industry shifted to the more pliable South, but its executives took care not to forget the up-to-date machines. Even if people can't be replaced collectively, they are always disposable individually. Against this background, too few managements—and this is a far greater cause of unrest than Communist agitation—pay a labor force enough attention until trouble actually breaks out.

Applied to machines, the same procedure causes instant chaos. But the labor force is not regularly maintained. It is treated as an asset, possibly, but as a fixed asset that requires attention only when the wages plumbing goes wrong or the pay boiler blows up in a strike. The failure is patched up (usually with money) by use of whatever conventional negotiating system is at hand; and most managements let their reactions to the emergency be dictated by external forces—the unions, the government, the law.

Look at corporate America's relations with its labor force over recent years, and in comparison Jekyll and Hyde are Tweedledum and Tweedledee. For instance, "quality of working life" (QWL) has been warmly espoused by, among others, Westinghouse, TRW, Northrop, General Electric, Honeywell, General Motors, and Jones & Laughlin, blue chips as ever were, all converted, apparently, to the gospel of quality circles and other forms of worker participation.

Consider, however, this equally impressive list of top American corporations: General Motors, Ford, Chrysler, Timken, Armour, Pan Am, General Tire. All these were among companies pressuring the unions, not for participation but for capitulation—giving up previously won conditions and wage levels under the threat of economic duress. Some givebacks are amazing: for instance, the meat-packers won a three-year wage freeze from their browbeaten union.

It takes an awful lot of quality of working life to make up for such quantities. So what was the true mood of American management? The strong arm or the soft touch? In reality, the name of the game was the same: to reduce labor's share of added value either by restricting wages or by raising output—or preferably both (as in the case of GM).

But the givebacks of the early 1980s give the lie to any idea that U.S. management has been suffused with new humanitarian—or even Japanese—principles. The pressure was not from the heart, but the pocketbook. Westinghouse, for instance, was, as John Thackray wrote in *Management Today,* "a company badly in need of some magic after disastrous acquisitions in the 1970s, coupled with a crippling $1 billion loss from fixed-price uranium contracts which were taken on as part of its nuclear reactor sales." It badly needed to raise "value added per employee" by 6 percent annually through a "productivity enhancing programme," heavily involving quality circles—those famous, Japanese-beloved devices in which groups of workers seek a joint solution to productivity problems.

But William F. Schleicher, editor of the *National Productivity Report,* is among several observers far from convinced by such efforts:

> Management is using smoke words—"productivity," "quality of working life," when really more than half the time the problem lies upstairs in the management suites' innumerable paperpushers, the excessive layers of management. When production scheduling is poor, or purchasing doesn't have the right components for manufacturing, management tries to cover up, saying quality circles will solve the problem.

When the need for better profits comes in the door, too, avant-garde ideas about permissive, progressive management tend to fly out the window—anywhere in the world. Thus Sandoz, the chemical giant, shocked the formal, conservative Swiss in the 1970s by banning the use of titles in-company. Flexible working hours, informal dress, attitude surveys, participation in decisions—you name it, Sandoz had it. But enter the slower growth and harder profits of the later 1970s; enter, too, a new managing director—and reenter nineteenth-century virtues, along with twentieth-century pressure for performance. Top Sandoz managers now have bonuses linked strictly to results; a euphemistically titled "overhead value analysis program" really meant a McKinsey cost-cutting exercise that lost 15 percent of HQ staff their jobs. The chief cutter, Dr. Marc Moret, noted that his ability to "eliminate nearly 1,000 jobs without damaging consequences seems to indicate the cuts were justified"—and that neatly sums up what happens to people when performance, as ultimately it has to be, gets put before participation.

Boards seem to regard the care and maintenance of the

labor force as a lesser function. In America, the personnel chief has as much chance of becoming president of the company as president of the United States. His status diminishes if the chief executive makes labor relations his own responsibility and knows how to manage them. Few do, and most wouldn't want to. The deterrent is that human beings in the mass are hard to handle; they are unpredictable, obstinate, demanding, intractable, and the wretches answer back.

Boards have preferred to mull over multimillion-dollar investment projects, negotiate large and comforting mergers, and compose optimistic five-year plans, rather than get involved with the messy events on the factory floor. This is a fatal error, precisely because manpower is not in reality an asset. It is more like a supply of raw material, changing but essential— the most important supply that a corporation consumes. Because this is so, the unions are a company's most important suppliers, which makes it all the sillier that boards of directors have so little contact with union leaders, either at national or factory levels.

In large tracts of America the necessity for unwholesome contact can be avoided by keeping the plants free of union contamination. This usually involves either locating factories in the equivalent of the Australian outback or continually keeping a jump ahead of whatever the unions might demand. The same gymnastic trick has been tried by American subsidiaries in Britain, and it works; moreover, it works for the right reasons, even if done for the wrong ones. It demands that management think how to bribe the worker. It means switching from passive management of labor to active concern with its desires, treatment, and satisfaction.

Even at the simplest level of forestalling strikes, no managerial effort can produce a better return on investment. After all, if the men don't turn up, no other resource, except the inventory, has any current value. Yet managements are constantly surprised, even hurt, when their own folly makes the men march out. At one engineering plant, where the loyalty of the men and the company's prestige were both taken for granted, the management was so shattered by a walkout that it called in consultants. They found that a complex pay claim had been submitted two years before—so complex that the management, unable to understand it, had never replied.

The late great A. J. Liebling tried in vain to persuade the American public that there are always two sides to any strike, that a deadlock requires an obdurate management as well as an obstinate union. The public, however, starts from the idea that the union is the protagonist, presumably because the men have to take the first active step by leaving the premises and posting pickets. Very few strikes are ever studied to discover who really is to blame; and the cause is often some abject management failure.

In one car plant, the men had been laid off during the week, were recalled at the weekend to make up a shortage of parts, and were to be laid off again the next Monday. They struck, of course. In another car crisis, two men accidentally got one another's pay slips—and the more skilled worker found he was getting less than a relatively unskilled man. Strike two.

It's questionable, though, whether these idiocies are any worse than the old tradition, in major American industries, of celebrating the end of a three-year labor contract with a huge strike, which used to be the only way, apparently, in which the two sides, labor and management, could bring themselves to agree on another three years of unarmed hostility. Britons used to regard this as an infinitely superior system to their own tradition of countless minor stoppages and short-term contracts. But it's become painfully clear that both approaches are so inferior to the Japanese system of cooperative, collaborative, strike-free working as to constitute major natural hazards.

Under the stimulus of recession, true, American companies, led by the steel and car giants, in winning large givebacks, have negotiated under duress the reduction of terms and conditions that tough and intelligent managements would never have given away in the first place. But that in no way takes U.S. industry toward Japanese levels of working cooperation, which are far more important in keeping down Japanese costs than lower basic rates of pay.

The relative all-quietness on the Western labor front as the 1980s began plainly didn't indicate any great rise in worker contentment. As to whether seething discontent lies beneath an untroubled surface, if you really want to know people's feelings, you have to ask them, and you get some funny answers. In one fast-growing company the men turned out to hanker after a long-lost mythical past: "We used to sing at the machines, and the buzzer at the end of the day was just an annoying interruption."

In all companies where labor and management *are* labor and management—that is, two separate and sometimes warring interests—it's the managements that are living in the past, and that will pay the price of doing so.

This isn't the same as a failure of communication, the usual scapegoat. Again, communicating (that is, putting out costly house journals, or some similar waste of cash) is easier than tackling real, tough problems. You can find out some of these by buying an employee attitude survey, an expensive goodie dreamed up by the sociologists. The risk of bringing the entire place to a standstill while unlettered workers wrestle with the questionnaire will be worthwhile if the results rub management's nose in the usual sorry truths; for instance, that the workers have taken amiss some pet managerial scheme for the advancement of mankind. The reason is not bad communication, but bad blood: workers distrust executives even more than executives distrust workers.

The ideal worker, from management's point of view, does

what he is told without argument; never makes mistakes; is punctual, clean, and tidy; produces maximum effort on a consistently rising scale; accepts any working arrangements his superiors ordain; and never demands more pay than the firm can afford (that is, the minimum that the management thinks it can get away with). The blue-collar paragon is expected to live a working life far more virtuous than that of the average executive—for that individual argues, makes mistakes, sometimes slacks off, always expects big annual increments (larger than a blue-collar man usually even demands as total salary), and though mostly clean and tidy, is often unpunctual.

And the executive, cosseted with fringe benefits to the limit of the law, looks forward to substantial advances in real wealth year after year on the long road to a heavily pensioned retirement. This gap—the true difference between Us and Them—has never been taken as seriously as it should be in the United States, where the mythology holds that any man (though, even nowadays, not any woman) can become president as well as President, and where informal relationships between boss and bossed conceal a classical gulf in corporate social status. The fact is that most blue-collar workers stay with blue collars; and even white-collar workers, supposedly more important and certainly more numerous with the explosion of the knowledge industries, divide sharply between the haves and (in terms of corporation privileges) the have-nots. The gap looms less wide in Japan, not just because of a different social system but because of a different view of the firm as a cohesive unit in which rank confers obligations as much as privileges.

All the men want the security of stable and predictable earnings, with a rising standard of living over the years. But they don't want any part of management's job. "Industrial democracy" and "worker's participation" sound well on a militant unionist's lips or on the brochure for an expensive management seminar. But it's hard enough to achieve democracy in any group of executives (or executive participation) in most companies; letting the employees into the act is impossible. It has been tried. One company had such elaborate consultation machinery that somebody once gibed, "Why doesn't it give up making bearings, and concentrate entirely on its joint consultation?" The effort didn't seem to affect the way the management managed, and nobody else has flattered its particular approach by imitation.

The executive at the middle level puts up with being frozen out of the big decisions because he feels that he belongs. Only in rare circumstances, and in carefully paternal companies, does the British or American worker share the same faith. In West Germany and Japan, the world's most strike-free industrialized economies, belonging is built into the social system, and paternalism cements the structure. Although the recipe is difficult to follow without the same social ingredients, that is the only way of making "the most important asset" *feel* important.

But paternalism is no panacea. Real paternalism doesn't mean that father knows best. Like everybody else, father is wrong half the time. The real need is to find managers who can look at the treatment of labor from labor's angle as well as their own. But this is not only hard work; it offends against the Third Truth of Management—*no manager ever devotes effort to proving himself wrong.*

Instead, companies prefer to try the newest device for satisfying the unsatisfied worker. Take *job enrichment,* a marvelous 1960s piece of word coining, because who can resist being "enriched"? It means asking the worker about his work and finding ways to make the worker's job more interesting and his performance more effective—the enrichers are peddling goods that sensible managements have always kept in stock.

The annals of enrichment are full of ripe successes. There was huge improvement in performance at one U.S. factory that completely altered procedures to give more initiative to the workers; one old sweat promptly recalled that "this was how the job used to be years ago." The old method had been abandoned to improve productivity, and now engines were being reversed for exactly the same reason and with exactly the same result. All changes that grab the interest of workers raise their performance—installing piped music or (preferably) taking it out; painting the walls red, white, and mauve; returning them to plain green; enriching jobs or taking out the skill element by mechanization; making the lighting brighter or changing its color.

Typically, the improvement in performance lasts for a limited period and then trails off; the workers regress toward their norm. They respond to the stimulus of somebody taking an interest, and backslide as the stimulus wears off. Executives lose interest too. Detroit Edison in the mid-1950s reorganized one thousand employees in the accounting office, proving that job enrichment worked—but the office has been reorganized several times since and everybody has forgotten about it. Similarly, workers whose operations are studied in an unchanged operation habitually raise their performance (unless the study is designed to cut their pay per job in a piecework system, in which case they naturally *lower* their speeds). But managers usually operate on the assumption that labor forces respond only to the one stimulus of money, hence the invention and brief flowering of so-called productivity bargaining.

This seed was first planted in Britain by American consultants working for an American oil company, Esso, at its Fawley refinery. U.S. firms find the refusal of British workingmen to behave like Americans peculiarly irritating; and the Fawley experiment could do little harm because the plant, like all oil refineries, employed few men. The Fawley deal in effect bribed the men to accept new working conditions, the theory being that improved productivity would pay for the bribes and leave plenty of jam to spare for the company.

Another U.S. oil company, Mobil, followed. Later on, manufacturers using labor forces of significant size climbed on the bandwagon—and sometimes fell off with a crash. Some paid bribes that greatly exceeded the initial productivity benefits, and then discovered (as did Esso after the original Fawley deal) that the process is subject to diminishing returns as new restrictions grow up like weeds, to be bought off in their turn. In one plant, the workers were shrewder than the managers. "They want more productivity," said one. "But all they will get is more fiddles."

Productivity deals are often uneconomic and hideously complex (cabalistic documents that only a union official, a management consultant, a labor lawyer, or a linguistic philosopher could understand); they also enshrine a hopelessly wrong principle—that you should pay people more to work sensibly, which means, of course, that up to now you have been paying them to work stupidly.

Unless all pay is reward for cooperative and intelligent working, total absurdity must result. For instance, at one giant tire plant, the new automated machines making radial tires were capable of outputs so high that the tire workers, all on piecework, stood to outearn the CEO. Only long and unbelievably tedious negotiations—altogether eleven and one-half months of talks with the unions were needed to evaluate 1,180 jobs—kept some of the productivity gains for the company. Management paid the price, in misspent time as well as higher wage rates, for perpetuating a nonincentive incentive system that made no managerial sense.

If you have a long-standing incentive pay system, perhaps the instinctive course should be to drop it for a day wage. If you have a day-wage system, however, maybe you had better try incentives. At least, in Britain at one period incentive schemes were going out of one factory while going into the one next door. On the whole, however, it is simpler and more dignified to pay a man a fair wage than to tie his pay to his output—an oversubtle task that is bedeviled by horrors such as the *learning curve* (labor costs reduce by one fifth with every doubling of output and without one liquid ounce of extra employee sweat). As a former president of Honeywell once observed, "It takes a very good factory management to make incentives work well. It takes outstanding supervision and if you have that, you don't need incentives."

He had a point, but you can make too much of it. Everybody likes to have a little more to go for; executives, after all, like to have a lot more—bonus payments that rise into six, even seven figures. Schemes like the Scanlon and Rucker plans, or the even newer systems that relate the bonuses to added value, have the virtue, not only of holding out the carrot of more money for more effective work, but of concentrating workers' minds on the fundamentals of the company or the plant. But any executive who thinks that those schemes will solve his labor management problems is in for the rudest of shocks.

So is anybody who gets carried away by some new nostrum, peddled by some enlightened manager or passionate professor, into believing that some experiment in human relations management in some other location will turn his business into a haven of light, love, and productivity. The annals of management are full of case histories that, on close examination, prove to be founded on circumstances so peculiar (a new plant on a greenbelt site employing hardly any people, say) that they have no application elsewhere; or on total misapprehensions (like the notion that the near-revolution at GM's Lordstown plant in Ohio was a rising by younger, better-educated, alienated workers); or on investigation so careless that there is no followup.

Where that does take place, the experiments often prove to have been abandoned, or the facts to be hopelessly wrong, as at Lordstown, where the cause of the uproar proved to be a good old-fashioned speedup, and where the cure was tough management, which took and won a strike—and then managed more intelligently than its predecessors.

As many observers have begun to point out, the same strictures must be applied to naïve beliefs that Japanese methods (whether in detail, like quality circles, or at large, like the whole paternalistic system) are the solution to American anxieties. The main lessons that the Japanese have to offer aren't those too deeply rooted in their culture to be transplanted, but those that can be learned by looking at any business or plant in America that follows good labor practices.

For instance, a good Japanese company like Canon will have the following critical elements in its personnel policy: (1) carefully controlled numbers, (2) good, progressive pay, (3) good jobs, (4) excellent training, (5) promotion by assessed merit, (6) continuous and effective motivation programs, (7) constant communication, (8) highly accessible management, (9) social equality within the company, (10) growth and constant change in products and processes, and so on. These are standard elements (or should be) in any company, East or West, that takes its labor relations seriously. But even they won't guarantee peace, quiet, and uninterrupted, bounteous production.

Like fighting wars, managing labor relations is full of disappointments—logical policies may not have logical results when you are dealing with human psychology. But illogic doesn't have to reign. Management must, following in the footsteps of Canon and its like, give its labor force a guaranteed acceptable level of earnings; give labor full consultation, but with management retaining the right to change equipment and methods; create a long-range manpower plan designed to provide steady employment; plan opportunities for promotion and good raises even for the unpromoted; give constant training throughout a man's or woman's career; and equalize fringe benefits between all grades of employee.

77

The dockers of Rotterdam were superbly treated in more or less this manner. For many years they were held up as paragons of virtue and cooperation and as standing rebukes to their London equivalents—tough, obstinate cookies, who, whipped on by the odd Communist, fought a running guerrilla war, breaking out in pitched battles, against some of Britain's most purblind employers. The London war culminated in a mammoth productivity bargain that notoriously achieved minimum productivity at maximum cost and has ended up with a more complete destruction of the capital's dockland than Hitler's bombers ever achieved.

They didn't manage likewise in Rotterdam. But for all their good treatment, the nice, undemanding Dutch dockers struck viciously over a pay claim one year, demanding gigantic raises, blocking the traffic, and using violence in a way unknown even to a London dockside militant. The moral is not that the Rotterdam employers were wrongheaded to treat their dockers well. The lesson is that the good employer does not practice truly good labor policies because he expects manna to fall from heaven as a result. It won't. He manages men humanely, generously, and thoughtfully because it is right.

BOOK II

Money Games

7

How Profits
Get Plucked

If management had a god, it would be Mammon—symbolized by a column of profits. Even in the deepest British backwaters, the most stagnant midwestern hinterland, the darkest Ruhr iron foundry, possibly even the most paternalistic sweatshop in Osaka, every executive knows that profit is the name of the game, the objective and the measure of managerial performance. But what is a profit?

In common-or-garden-variety life, the answer sounds easy: profit is the difference between what something costs and what you sell it for. Common-or-garden-variety ideas, however, become complex and slippery in the higher (or lower) reaches of business management. Sure, profit is the difference between costs and revenues, but what are costs and what are revenues?

In one vain fight against takeover, a $12 million profit

forecast for a financial year that had almost ended turned into a $5.4 million loss; and $17.4 million seems a hard sum to mislay. The essential point thus illustrated is that conventional accounting does not produce the one accurate figure by which managers are supposed to live. True, strange things happen in the heat and dust of battle. But odd things also occur in time of peace. The first spots of sickness at Lockheed broke out in 1968, when it added 50 percent to alleged profits by a switch in accounting for overhead on the government contracts that provided all but a tenth of its takings.

Even then, Lockheed's performance was distinctly earthbound, which added fiercer point to the vital question, Had Lockheed actually made that extra 50 percent or hadn't it? Even if the previous method understated "true" profits, could the Lockheed management take credit, in reputation or in pocketing bonuses and salary increases, for extra profits that had been "earned" by its accountants? Lockheed's example is made more glaring by the nemesis that lay in wait; but other managers all over the world constantly recook the books by which they are judged.

Thus Texas Instruments, clobbered with $660 million of home-computer losses, managed to keep its corporate deficit to a relatively modest $145 million by the neat device of putting all the tax benefits in its 1983 accounts—even though they weren't all being used that year. Then consider these findings of security analyst Thornton O'glove, quoted in *Fortune* magazine as citing

> the case of Union Carbide, which in 1980 lengthened depreciation periods for machinery and equipment, and started taking the benefits of investment tax credits into accounting profits in the year they arose instead of spreading the credits over time. Both changes increased reported earnings. O'glove figures the new procedures contributed 18 percent of Union Carbide's earn-

ings per share in 1980 and 15%, 28%, and 26% the following three years, but "did not affect income tax payments or cash flow," as the company stated in its 1980 annual report.

Then there's Allied Bancshares, whose treasurer

recently explained what Allied meant by special reserves: "When you are bumping along with such good earnings, you don't get any benefit by showing extraordinary increases. Some years we could have reported extremely higher earnings than we did. In fact, we were building our reserves quite high in late 1980 and early 1981. Our outside accountants, Peat Marwick Mitchell, began raising questions. 'Golly, folks,' they told us, 'as clean as y'all are looking, this is getting a little ridiculous!' "

The linen of these three managements was no doubt clean, their motives pure. But either before revision or after, Lockheed and Union Carbide must have portrayed an untrue picture of their lovely corporate finances. Strangely, or not so strangely, Lockheed, which ran into a financial setback shortly after its fine exhibition of dynamic accounting, was not alone in misery. Union Carbide, after suffering a 75 percent drop in earnings per share in 1983, ended up 13.43 percent lower than ten whole years previously.

Perhaps the plucking of profits out of thick air is a sign, registered in the conscious or subconscious of executives, that the real profits are drying up. For there is a real profit, just as there is reality behind the notion of capital employed. However, conventional profit is outstretched for elasticity only by conventional capital employed, and expressing one of these prize uncertainties as a ratio of the other mystery—dividing the profit by the capital to get a pretty percentage—cannot measure anything at all: that is, while the true ratio must be a vital indication of the true health of a business, what, as Pontius Pilate once asked, is truth? What is profit?

The question has become even more insistent in the light

of Richard Nixon's most important contribution to economics, and maybe to world history: the international monetary system in which currencies, instead of being tied to a fixed dollar, are free to float against each other. This poses a truly insoluble problem to accountants and to managers trying to use accounts as a management tool, for movements in exchange rates over which nobody has any control, and for which nobody is to blame, can make an almighty difference to profits.

Except, of course, that they don't. If a company has an affiliate in Britain earning £10 million on £100 million of capital, that is worth $24 million if the pound is selling at $2.40 (as it was in Mrs. Thatcher's finest hour). If the pound drops to $1.20 (as it did), and the affiliate turns in an unchanged performance, the numbers change dramatically: a $12 million profit represents a disastrous 50 percent decline. Moreover, the assets are theoretically, in dollar terms, worth 50 percent less.

Some managements were trapped in an exquisitely painful version of *Catch-22*. Their American overlords demanded that they make their financial targets in dollars—even if the dollar fell against their home currency. Thus (to use British figures again) an affiliate boss who had committed himself to a £10 million profit at $1.80 ($18 million) was expected to produce $18 million come hell, high water, or a $1.20 exchange rate. On the other hand, if the pound had risen, to, say, $2, he would still have been expected to hit the original £10 million target—and the extra $2 million would have gone into the profit column, no doubt to self-congratulation all around.

Businesses and heads of corporations don't earn profits: they earn money. Profit is an abstraction from the true, underlying movement of cash in and cash out. Any small businessman who has had trouble meeting the payroll knows the painful principle: without enough cash, you drown. Larger businessmen have learned the same lesson in the same brutal way; the mighty Penn Central in the United States ran out of hard currency; so did Rolls-Royce; so did a one-time textile star whose chairman once recalled to stockholders, "We were unable to pay the interest on the loan stock, or the wages on Friday, and already several checks had bounced." A big company's checks can rebound just as high as those of a little shopkeeper. But many top executives, even in sophisticated organizations, have been slow to master the truth that what counts at the end of the day is the cash in the kitty—not the abstractions in the books.

The object of the honest manager is to fit the abstraction to the reality as neatly as he may. Any managers who toy with procedures to invent a higher profit must search their souls long and harshly. Will the change paint a truer likeness, or will it obscure the truth? For high-technology companies, the dilemma is acute. They need, and badly, lofty stock market ratings to attract the capital for which they hunger, so they have high incentive to report high profits. Yet their spending on research and development has an unpleasant way of devouring any cash left over from financing equally voracious long-term manufacturing projects.

How such stars treat research and development, and how they value stocks and work in progress, determines their "profits" far more than what they actually manage to sell. When the managers of Rolls-Royce, as one later put it, "were having trouble showing a profit," the directors adopted a new magic formula. They assessed "the value of R and D recoverable from sales resulting from existing aero-engine orders." This lusty sum was not charged against the income for the year in the accounts (though it was paid out of that income). The money spent was instead counted as an asset, and Rolls (hey, presto) duly showed a profit.

This handy device has been employed by utterly respectable companies with the noblest intentions. But the money to be made from *future* engine sales was not the question that should have bugged the engineers of Rolls. The real issue was whether they could earn enough bread from *existing* business. The answer was crystal clear from its own books several years before the Rolls-Royce calamity. The company couldn't, and didn't, earn nearly enough.

Unable to cover its dividend, let alone all its R & D spending, from profits, the company raised £17.4 million from its poor benighted stockholders one year. In effect, they thus paid for their own dividends, which was kind of them. Rolls went on having trouble "showing a profit" because there was little or none to show. It was bad books, as much as the RB 2II engine for the Lockheed Tristar, that ran Rolls out of cash, unseated the chairman, and unraveled the company. If published accounts, with a little easy disentangling, can reveal hard reality to outsiders, there is no excuse for insiders missing the point. The harsher the truth, however, the happier executives are to hide it from everybody—especially themselves. The lives and ambitions of the Rolls-Royce men were bound up with building "the best aero-engines in the world." As the chairman put it, "We don't care whether you propel 'em with squibs or with elastic bands. We'll be up in front whatever the method." To admit that they could not be up in front at a profit would have negated their whole existence.

A misinformed executive is a doomed one. Witness one brave boss of a small company. He went after export business on a heroic scale at prices that covered only component costs and direct labor—and failed to take any account of increased overhead and indirect expenses. "Why didn't somebody tell me this before?" demanded the poor fellow, as they led him away.

The first fact of life that any manger needs to know is the likely cash effect of his decisions: what he must pay out, how that spending will be financed—including what income the firm will receive—and when. Cash-flow accounting excludes notional expenditures (items such as depreciation that don't represent physical cash leaving the premises) and also deletes notional income (such as the money that will be earned when, please God, somebody buys the inventory). It includes all real spending (such as research and development) and is interested only in real receipts (the safe arrival of somebody else's cash).

True, if company accounts were written only in this hard-headed way, a different distortion would follow. For instance, if the inventory is about to be snapped up by a screaming public, just counting its cost, without taking in any added value, must understate the lucky company's profitability. There was one building contractor who took in profits only when his bills were settled—and accountants thought him dangerously eccentric. As a matter of fact, he was, but not for the reasons advanced by his critics. As later events revealed, the arrival of profits in his accounts didn't take place until long after the work had been completed (especially since this particular financial genius garnered his profits not from the original contract but from the claims for extra work). This was fine as long as business continued to be good; but when, one far from fine day, it turned down, the grim reality of his trading experience was concealed by the profits being taken into the books from long years before. The first the world (and maybe the genius) knew of all this was when the company suddenly and comprehensively went bust—still showing a profit.

But are such distortions any more severe, or dangerous, than the folderols of conventional profit or loss accounting? That is a subject on which Saul Steinberg, the whiz-kid of Leasco Data Processing (now Reliance), should have interesting views after his costly tangle with a British publisher, Robert Maxwell of Pergamon Press.

The boy genius who invented Leasco by dazzling financial maneuvers (not least by switching into insurance and out of leasing computers before the latter business died on him) should have a good and twitching nose for a balance sheet. Yet

he accepted Pergamon's declared profits and forecast and compounded his folly by buying shares in the open market—an
escapade that eventually forced Leasco to write off some 10
million sorely needed pounds.

The balance sheet showed, to a casual but curious glance,
that in the year of a reported £2 million profit, Pergamon's cash
ran downhill by £2 million. That £4 million slalom should have
led Steinberg to ask some tough prior questions. As it was,
tough later researches—much too late for Leasco—turned that
£2 million profit into only £495,000, and that was before taking
account of stupendous losses on Maxwell's fatal effort to imitate the *Encyclopaedia Britannica.*

Books illustrate beautifully why a profit need not be a
profit. The highest point at which the publisher can value a
book is his own selling price. This assumes that the books will
all be sold. If they are not, the publisher has taken credit for
an unearned profit, and future losses lie literally in store. Books
can be valued at cost (which assumes, less hazardously, that
sales will at least reach the break-even point) and then written
down yearly. Or they can be valued as pulp (virtually nil),
which accurately mirrors the cash position, at the expense of
favorably distorting profits in future years. Of the two extreme
positions—stating current year's profits at the highest or lowest
possible level—the latter must be more desirable, less misleading to the honest publisher, less tempting to the dishonest.

Always select the most conservative accounting portrayal
that is consistent with previous years and with the inexorable
reality of cash flow in and out of the business—and that puts
off paying tax as long as possible. Precisely when the cash
reality shows up is less important than the knowledge that, one
day, show up it will. One small company reported large
monthly losses although its bank balance was mounting sky-
high. The explanation lay in ultraconservative accounts (subscription revenue was coming in but being phased over a whole

year), and the prognosis was rudely healthy. The reverse situation—a business combining high, wide, and handsome profits
with a rapidly rotting cash position—more often than not leads
but to the grave.

With financial half-truths (or downright untruths) the
outcome is the same as with boxers: the bigger they are, the
harder they fall. Yet sometimes the "truth" produces absurdi-
ties on the capital side of return on capital employed. The
return (or the profit) is what executives choose to make it
within a latitude wide enough to cover most sins. But the
similar yo-yo characteristics of capital employed operate differently. For instance, should you value property at cost or pre-
sent-day worth? Because of the endless inflation of property
values, revaluation of a store chain could easily double the
capital employed. This is a more "realistic" and conservative
figure—yet, if you do revalue, the return on capital will halve.

Assuming (extravagantly) that profits are truly calculated,
which is the more accurate return? The conservative one may
be more misleading; it puts forward, as a realistic alternative
(it seldom is), the proposition that the properties could be sold
off en bloc at market value. You could argue that whenever the
property worth of a business rises above its value as a going
concern, the business should be folded and the property leased.
What's the point of sweating to make a profit if you can earn
the same in easy rent? Alas, on this criterion, half the businesses in the world would be forced to close.

There are sometimes potent reasons for revaluing your
assets, and rapidly. When the British government announced
that it would switch to a return-on-capital basis in working out
its price for milk, the dairy chains reached for higher valuations
as one man. That was entirely understandable. But the nonsense of accounts, in which disappearing or appearing tricks
can be worked with profits and everything else, was never more
fully revealed, and over many years at that, as when Anglo-

Saxon accountants bent their brains to the question of inflation. For decades the impact of inflation had been blithely ignored, even though it was perfectly obvious that conventional accounting, based on historic (that is, actual) cost, overstated profits—not because a dollar earned after 10 percent inflation was worth 10 percent less (although it was), but because the replacement cost of assets became higher than the original cost. It's the book-publishing argument all over again. If you use inventory in making a product, do you charge the price it really cost in dollars—or the price it will cost you to replace it?

The answer became of more than academic importance during the years when inflation advanced into double digits. Companies that were showing profits might actually be (were actually) failing to make a true surplus large enough to cover their dividends, quite apart from any other purposes. Worse still, they were paying taxes on profits that were nonexistent—blown away by hyperinflation. So the greatest brains in accountancy set to work on *current cost accounting,* a revision of the rules that, by reflecting the ravages of inflation, would give a more accurate, more honest picture of these profits.

This admirable effort, though, hit several snags. One of the most prominent is that companies gain, as well as lose, by inflation. Replacement costs rise, sure. But repayment costs fall too: that is, a company that borrows $100 million in 1985 won't repay 100 million 1985 dollars in 1995. It will pay back those 100 million smackers less whatever the intervening amount of inflation has been. The financial picture wouldn't be accurate and honest without taking that profit into account—except that it's a profit that has never been earned.

The conundrums of inflation accounting were predictably (I can say that safely, because I predicted it) still unresolved when hyperinflation subsided, leaving the accounting profession on both sides of the Atlantic still unable to agree on the cure for a disease that had largely disappeared. But every at-

tempt to make accounts more real (as many accountants joy-
fully pointed out) had only made them more fictitious. In the
real world, anyway, real managements and real corporate
finance men were continuing perfectly happily with fictitious
operations of their own, for real reasons: for example, the
beleaguered banks.

You would expect these institutions, keepers of corporations' money, to be the keepers of their financial consciences as
well. But under the pressure of their own misjudgments, the big
U.S. banks adopted practices that roused a distinguished New
York accounting professor, Abraham Briloff, to a high pitch of
indignation.

> But the essential process of gamesmanship with and within
> accounting still prevails. . . . One would have assumed, based
> on ordinary, logical reasoning, that the loss would inexorably
> have to be recognized when a bank picks up a property worth
> $1 million in exchange for a loan on its books of $10 million. And
> one might have expected a certain inexorability with respect to
> bank accounting when the banks were compelled to swap a $100
> million New York City bond for a new bond worth $60 or $70
> million.

In fact, to Briloff's wrath, the banks didn't adjust their accounts at all. Profits that really have crumbled, it seems, can
stay intact as magically as profits that never existed at all can
be conjured out of thin paper.

A favored wheeze for companies losing money on favorite
ventures, borrowing a leaf from the aerospace accountants, is
to call it *development spending* and capitalize it (that is, overstate profits by that amount). Lord Thomson, busy dissipating
some of the profits of North American monopoly newspapers
and broadcasting, in the doomed effort to turn *The Times* into
a gold mine, called his staggering losses (made for sixteen
consecutive years) "development" and treated them as such.

But the accounting treatment made the drain no less, as was demonstrated when the disgusted Thomsonians finally decamped—and had to write off some $40 million.

Financial gimmickry has nothing to do with managing a business; the company director is only playing with numbers. The trouble is that not only investors and financial writers get mesmerized by the number game, so do the directors themselves. And when the profits in the case finally crumble away, it is too late for the mesmerized director to wake up.

8

The Accountancy
Dodge

Whenever a company fails, or a management wakes up covered in financial mud, one relevant question seldom gets asked: What were the accountants up to? Every failed management was advised, hectored, and helped by its own accountants, its auditors' accountants, possibly those of its favorite money-lender. Accountants are highly trained professionals in the management and recording of financial transactions. Yet collapse and calamity reveal them blithely or blindly accepting figures (such as the Rolls-Royce forecasts for the RB 211 engine) that would set alarm bells ringing in a half-trained mind.

A whole series of disasters in the United States, from the Penn Central crash to the Continental Illinois crunch, has raised unquenchable doubts about the efficiency of audits—given such sights as the lack of resemblance between reality and the befuddled railroad's, not to mention the beleaguered bank's published reports. The Penn Central affair was only one of several early 1970s horrors—like National Student Marketing, Equity Funding, and Stirling Homex; names mostly long forgotten despite stupendous frauds and/or misrepresentations, forgotten to be replaced only by the next catastrophe, like the abrupt collapse of confidence at savings and loan growth star (or former star) Financial Corporation of America.

Here the regulators, stepping in where the auditing accountants had apparently feared to tread, decided that a $31 million second-quarter profit was in reality somewhat different —a $107 million loss. Such a sequence of disasters of such size calls into question the accountant's usefulness as a source of management information, as auditor of the accounts, and even as a reliable keeper of the financial score. But that should come as no surprise. The accountant is playing an elaborate game whose purpose is not to tell the truth (for truth is a chimera) but to obey the rules. The rules in turn are not designed to make managers more efficient, or to inconvenience crooks, or even to keep companies solvent. They are there simply to allow the game itself to proceed. That explains how accountants can try to wash their hands of blame or dirt when disaster strikes. They can nearly always claim that they played their game according to their rules. Unfortunately, management is a different game entirely: that of producing more resources than the ones you started out with.

It's not the accountants' fault, moreover, if the executives they work for suffer from the widespread malaise of good old financial ignorance. Most executives, like most people, but more oddly, do not truly understand money in a personal sense (they handle their own financial affairs unintelligently) or in their business capacity, certainly in Europe, very possibly in the United States. It was in America that big business managers (even unto the sharp-eyed hawks employed by moneylender Walter E. Heller and the cautious corporate owls of American

Express) tripped over in their eagerness to become the victims of Billie Sol Estes, filler of phantom harvest silos, and Tino de Angelis, filler of phantom salad-oil tanks.

The problem is not even that managers lack the accountants' technical education in money—although that, too, can produce strange effects. One respected chairman of a family company complained bitterly when told that he couldn't finance a pet project. "What," he grumbled, stabbing at the left-hand side of the balance sheet, "about all those reserves?" Nobody had told him that reserves in accounting terms merely exist to make the left-hand side of the balance sheet equal the right-hand side. More often than not, however, guilty executives (assuming that they are also honest) are more innocent than unlettered.

A grim story about one crashed company reveals the distinction. One of its too-late rescuers put the corporate figures in a new presentation. The recast showed, sadly but convincingly, that the outfit could never make a profit, no matter what. He duly presented his findings to his fellow directors. "Your figures are wrong," answered one. "But they are *your* figures," said the outsider. "Well," remarked the inside man, "that's an interesting way of looking at it." Financial genius, fortunately, is not required of the business manager. But managers, the uncrashed as well as the crashed, often possess the reverse of genius—blind refusal to see inconvenient financial facts or, if confronted with the revolting truth, to admit its significance. The results of their innocence (which in the case of artists in the company promotion racket may not be so innocent) are written all over their bank borrowings.

The essence of money in management is, first, that *Cash In must exceed Cash Out.* This Fourth Truth of Management is the Law of the Barrow—known in every sweatshop on Seventh Avenue. A cash deficiency is not solved by borrowing money from stockholders, from equally innocent financiers, or from far too friendly neighborhood bankers. Debt merely postpones the day of reckoning: sooner or later (and the sooner the better) there must be a cash surplus, and the more you borrow, the bigger that eventual surplus has to be. But like any small businessman sprinting for trouble, a great many top executives incur immense expense, and allow subordinates to pile up still more extravagance, without more than a misty idea of the monetary consequences.

One management consultant learned the law of the barrow by starting four businesses of his own. He saw two flourish, while two shriveled up. With a bookkeeper as chastity belt, he had watched over the cash of the two ripe successes like a jealous husband. In the two sour failures, the cash was left to look after itself. Yet a company director is under no legal necessity to know either the amount of his existing cash or its future availability (to make sure that he doesn't run out of the stuff). His accountants and auditors are also under no legal obligation to make sure that their client does discover these two indispensable facts. Accountants, while they are often called in as undertakers, know more than anybody about the life-or-death importance of cash. But as auditors they habitually certify accounts, referring to events long past, though they don't know (and are in no way expected to know) whether or not at the moment of approval cash is pouring out in great lukewarm gouts.

The bigger the company, the more academic an audit becomes. The auditors (all three of them) for Royal Dutch–Shell presumably earn every pound, guilder, and dollar of their magnificent fees. But they can't do much more, in a company that gets through $61 billion of business each year, than approve the performance of Shell's own internal accountants, advise the directors on knotty points of tax law, do the odd spot check to see that nobody has run away with the company—and collect their enormous fees.

The notion that auditors are at arm's length from directors is, in any case, a blatant fairy tale of accountancy and management. The stockholders in theory appoint the auditors, but they do so in annual general meetings that are under the thumb of the directors and their captive proxies. Finance directors and auditors are in close and cozy contact. Even suppose an auditor does smell an accounting rat, he won't dream (except in nightmares) of making a public row. He will try to persuade the director to change his malodorous figures or, more commonly, the director will persuade the auditor that the inventory in Nicaragua really has doubled in value overnight. In the end the auditor almost always has to accept the business judgment of the director.

Sometimes, alas, it's not the directors' judgment that auditors must accept—it's their lies. The most conspicuous and unpleasant evidence of this was the revelation of bribery and corruption—"illegal payments" in the vernacular—at the end of the 1970s. The corporate miscreants, from Lockheed downward (downward being *le mot juste*), employed what John Thackray, writing in *Management Today,* called "varied and ingenious gimmicks" that "were all but impossible for outside auditors to detect."

According to one study, companies' "independent auditors were repeatedly stymied by corporate clients that entered the amount of the illegal or improper payment on their books, but misrepresented its real nature or purpose; or by hidden Swiss bank accounts; or by phony duplicate books, etc." The ingenuity at Schering-Plough involved eight different formulas in seven different countries—and over $810,000 in questionable payments. Reports Thackray: "These disbursements were variously listed as commissions, professional service fees, or cash discounts on sales, general office expenses, travel and entertainment and grants and consultancies, or a representation expense."

97

Accountants are thus unsure lie detectors, neither are they businessmen. (As one accountancy firm proved by going into a wine company, noting correctly that it was wildly over-stocked with one of red Bordeaux's greatest years and instruct-ing its customer to sell off those marvelous wines—now worth much fine gold—at cost price.) In the end, the accountant adjusts his fiction to the executive's version of the facts. Dis-honesty need not enter his head. Accountants know perfectly well that firms that gain a reputation for being uncooperative don't get audit work—and audit work is their main source of money, to which accountants are not wholly indifferent. The key is that they are free within the rules of their game to choose whichever version of the same truth they like.

That's still the case even though auditors should have been put on their guard, not to mention their mettle, by the increas-ing likelihood of facing lawsuits in the event of real or sus-pected dereliction of duty. As one writer was moved to observe, "There isn't a major auditing firm that has escaped public SEC censure or a barrage of costly suits in recent years"—*costly* being the word. When twenty-two financial institutions sued Touche Ross, alleging bum audits of United States Financial Corporation, the price tag was $30 million (though, as the author wryly noted, "it is the corporate clients and ultimately the shareholders who foot the bill, by paying, in the fee struc-ture, for more costly indemnity insurance").

The tale of two truths is an intrinsic part of "turnaround jobs"—of the company revival game. New management moves into a deadbeat, loss-laden company and turns it around, as Lee Iacocca famously did with Chrysler (turned around once be-fore by an earlier management as it happens), or as a host of professional turnaround men (like Hicks Waldron, whose work on Kentucky Fried Chicken propelled him onward and up-ward into Avon Products) have done with America's legions of battered businesses. But the key is more easily turned than appearances suggest. If the past conduct of the company has been paralytic, doing better is no terrifying test of the new men. The accountant, moreover, can help to make the turnaround man look more beautiful than he is.

The technique is to examine the corporate patient coldly from top to bottom. Every loss that could or should be taken is written back into the accounts, thus flatly contradicting the previous accountants' version of events. If the sick business has only rudimentary financial controls, every cupboard will be full of old bones; simply installing a sensible system ensures that no more skeletons will accumulate in the subsequent year. That year, the first of the new management, inevitably shows an inspiring improvement because of the absence of the previous year's bumper write-offs. This only heightens the optical illusion that arises in all turnarounds, even if the accountants lean over backward not to gild the new man's lily.

Penn Central is a case in point. Compared to the financial chasm of 1973, when earnings per share reached an abysmal *negative* figure of $119.33, almost any subsequent management performance would have looked good—and a number like that of 1982 (a positive $3.02) must seem like a miracle. Innocents (the turnaround executives, as well as investors) often look at the before-and-after figures and beam broadly, but what about the absolute figures? What about the real strengths of the company? In 1983, Penn Central reverted to type, losing 48 cents a share, yet management could still claim that the much-changed company was performing vastly better than ten years before.

Turnarounds should always be compared, not with the bad old days, but with present standards of good performance. Even a phrase like "present standards of good performance," however, leaves an executive in the helping hands of accounting conventions. The profit that an executive shows is "after depreciation." Many British executives believe that the withering away of depreciating assets is real. You can, of course, go too far the other way. Back in 1926 (which shows that the more things change the more they are the same), Armstrongs, the famous British defense contractor, showed a profit "conjured out of optimistic depreciation figures" when on its way to the slaughterers.

The distinction is between profit and cash flow. If you buy a machine for $1 million and it has to be scrapped after ten years, it makes evident sense to knock off 10 percent each year; but in the process a fiction is created—that the company has made $100,000 less money in the first year, $90,000 less the next, and so on. In fact, the directors get their hands on the "depreciation" money, to do with what they will, and the company pays less tax. The real depreciation, and its real financial impact, takes place only when the thing is scrapped.

The reverse analogy is that of a man who buys a house, reckons it will be worth twice as much in ten years' time (7 percent per annum compounded), and credits his income with the 7 percent appreciation each year. Clearly ridiculous. But the stockholder has no way of knowing whether the directors have allowed too much for depreciation or too little. Some accountants used to argue before hyperinflation set in that in the United States the amounts written off in depreciation over the years were excessive. In other words, higher profits should have been reported to stockholders—and higher dividends could have been handed out.

The boot, however, then moved swiftly on to the other foot. In 1979, *Business Week* worked out that, back in 1974, American companies had so far failed to allow for inflation in their depreciation policies that they paid 63 percent tax on their profits—and then paid out all but 1 percent of the remainder to their stockholders as dividends. As late as 1979, two thirds of U.S. companies were still using First In, First Out (FIFO) accounting for use of inventory: that is, they chose the method that maximized their tax and minimized their provision for the inflation of their replacement costs. Thanks to such self-defeating stupidity, the companies of America, so *Business Week* concluded, paid $17 billion more tax on 1978 profits than they should have. They also gave shareholders two thirds of the residue—much of it money that was vitally needed to repair the damage caused by the years of underinvestment then being laid bare by Japanese competition.

Tax laws have encouraged the stockholder to shun dividends, anyway. The net result, as Peter Drucker once pointed out, was to put more and more easy money into the hands of fat, old, established corporations and their executives, who, by every test, are the least adept at using the stuff. The inferior use of capital by big companies is self-evident even from the accountants' figures. In 1969 the median return on invested capital of the 500 largest U.S. companies was 11.3 percent; in horrible 1970 it fell to 9.5 percent after tax; in 1983 the figure was still only 10.8 percent; and that, too, can't have left much nourishment for the future. Given that invested capital, as noted in Chapter 2, is a flattering base for comparison with profits, it's clear that, even in a period of greatly reduced U.S. inflation, many companies had little or nothing left over to create new resources for expansion.

The annals are full of cases of giants that have failed to earn enough to cover the interest charges on big, long-term borrowings. One director in such a fix explained that a business of colossal size, doubling every seven years, can't hope to generate all its capital internally. But if the cost of capital exceeds the rate of return, a manager can't hope to generate any income at all from investing the new money.

Directors don't deal in concepts like the marginal cost of capital. So they gladly borrow long-term money at going rates of interest when they have existing businesses earning below that mark—unless they have the fortune to find and listen to an accountant who spots their folly. Far better to close or sell the corporate drags to finance the new and hopefully more rewarding ideas. Yet most executives, because of their fond attachment to what they manage rather than to its results, insist on retaining interests or products that run the gamut from poor profitability to aching loss, without understanding that even a low-profit business is a tax on the company's good apples.

Even more amazing, great companies purchase others for prices that appear to demand the financially impossible. Thus, to justify the $7.3 billion price tag on Continental Oil, the purchaser, du Pont, would have had to achieve an average 28 percent on equity for two whole decades; and that necessity compared with an actual return of only 22 percent recorded by Conoco in a period of stupefyingly high oil prices, which nobody expected to recur.

In cases of great merger misfortune, such as Dunlop's union with Pirelli, which promptly ran into horrendous Italian losses, the accountants may kindly arrange to have the losses put outside the company's accounts altogether. That, however, doesn't truly dispose of the losses, which were real enough to burden Dunlop with $50 million of write-offs, starting it on the path of mounting debt and declining effectiveness that led to virtual bankruptcy.

Financial figures are not the be-all and end-all of a business. Far from it—accurate money statistics are valuable only as a universal way of portraying physical reality. Profit is the *result,* not the objective of efficient management: it is the outcome of selling, pricing, producing, distributing, and organizing effectively. If the figures are terrible, it is always because the directors have failed in more tangible areas than the books. The books, as an index of performance, serve as weapons to control, as guides to make physical efficiency less inefficient—provided you have the will. One tasty little financial graph produced inside a big company showed a line plunging down right off the graph paper; it was a chart of the downward *variance* from budgeted losses. In situations like this, accounting has ceased to have any relevance to management. Control means taking action when the instruments give their warning. It's no good sitting helplessly in mission control, like many accountants and their bosses, while the company spins off forever into financial outer space.

9

The Inflationary
Sing-Along

Nobody has taken a tougher line against inflation down the years than the big business executive. Nobody deplores high-wage claims with greater fervor—or greater self-interest—since nobody else faces these monstrous demands. Nobody has applauded right-wing, anti-inflation politicians louder or backed their parties, Republican in the United States, Conservative in Britain, more willingly or with more cash. And nobody was more baffled when, in the 1970s, as the right tried to damp down inflation, sales fell, profits crumpled, orders melted away, stock prices slid, and money became hard to find and ruinous to borrow. Corporate man never paused to note that of all the beneficiaries of moderate inflation, nobody had out-benefited the corporate boss.

Every executive knows that the ultimate proof of corporate success is growth (a few suspect that profitable growth, while tougher, is far more meaningful). The blue chip that doubles sales in seven years, assuming that some profit cream goes with the jelly, can reckon to earn the thanks of stockholders, the warmth of stockbrokers, and stock options for the brains in the boardroom. For the leviathans, more dazzling progress looks pure pie in the sky: to double every five years, a $2 billion monster must find $300 million of extra sales in the first year alone.

Short of acquisition, there is little hope of reaching this nirvana, and acquisition is not true growth. Of itself, a $2 billion company's ability to pay $300 million for somebody else's sales says nothing about the purchaser's managerial quality. Even a self-generated (or "organic") growth target of only 10 percent a year must be a definite stretch: at least, most corporations can't seem to reach that mark without the benefit of inorganic acquisitions.

Remember those figures, quoted in the first two chapters, showing the poor performance of the *Fortune* 500 over the decade 1973–83? In the 1960s, in an era of rampant pursuit of growth, only 38 percent of the 500 doubled earnings per share, measured in inflated dollars. While that decade saw serious and accelerating inflation rates, those figures were laughably low compared to what lay ahead after oil prices exploded in 1973; yet the proportion of the 500 doubling this vital statistic in the decade to 1983 was still a mere 43 percent.

In other words, the great majority of large U.S. companies, despite organic growth, despite wide diversification by product and geography, despite a raft of acquisitions, not only failed to keep pace with inflation, they fell behind it to a huge and alarming degree. True, three quarters of the companies had stockholders who doubled their money between 1973 and 1983. But that, of course, again meant a massive lag behind inflation for capital worth in the stockholders' hands. On the record, *real* real growth should dangle in front of stockholders' eyes like a vision of the earthly paradise. Only 16 percent of the *Fortune* 500 quadrupled earnings per share over this latest decade—and that was much more like the standard required.

In many companies, real growth—of the physical variety—has been all but invisible. Physical output as an indicator means nothing in a large diversified company, and that definition fits almost every significant firm. But unit sales of vehicles in the big car companies do mean something, and they have grown by significantly less than their cash results. GM sold only 102,000 more cars from its U.S. factories in 1983 than two years previously—a miserable 2.5 percent rise. But its American automotive sales were worth $16 billion more—a thunderous surge of 35 percent. In U.S. industry generally, as *Business Week* noted in 1984, "historical-cost sales for the average large company have grown at an annual rate of 10% for the past five years—but there has been no growth on an inflation-adjusted basis." Company directors fail to see that general inflation makes their money growth much easier only because they share a common delusion of people throughout the world.

Next to depression (which nobody believed in, except John Kenneth Galbraith and Eliot Janeway, until the oil-price shocks), inflation is the dirtiest word in economic jargon. Enormous ingenuity has gone into discussion of cost push and wage pull, of spirals and equilibrium levels. However, economic expansion is a good thing for nations, companies, and individuals alike—right? Now, the faster a market or an economy expands, the more demand will press against supply and the more prices are likely to rise. The only big exception is when (as in the United States after Eisenhower or Carter) a yawning reservoir of spare capacity is waiting to be filled. Once that has been done (as under Johnson), prices usually gallop away; politicians reach itchily for the economic reins; and the complaining voice of the housewife is heard in the land.

Consumers, like executives, have been brainwashed. They

think of money as a constant measure when (as they constantly complain) the measure constantly changes its length. If the value of money is falling, it means little to say that prices (or sales or profits) are rising by that same sinking criterion. The man whose $75,000 house sells for $150,000 seven years later claims that he has doubled his money—though he should know that, because of the inflation that pushed up the price of the house, his $150,000 is worth nothing like twice the $75,000 of seven years back. Managements know just as surely that a $50 million profit is not worth twice the $25 million of 1974; but that won't stop executives from boasting that profits have doubled, or from being applauded for their splendor.

The executive has also personally exploited the hidden truth about inflation. It isn't what you can buy with your pounds or dollars that counts, but what you can buy with your time. Expressed in these terms, most prices have fallen substantially—and as much for the executive as for lesser hired hands. That's true by definition—otherwise living standards couldn't have risen over the years. The reason the American worker can afford to buy a better car today, even with a higher price tag, is that it represents less of his annual pay than a worse car ten years ago—and that goes for nearly everything else. How much the average executive salary has risen is a matter for debate, but it has probably grown at least as rapidly as any other man's; and that doesn't count increased fringe benefits, capital appreciation on his house, a share in inflationary stock markets, and all the other goodnesses of the good executive life.

That's not the end of the executive's blessings. If inflation reflects rising demand, sales must be rising, and rising sales (other things being equal) mean rising profits. New plant put in at today's lower capital costs, too, will earn profits at tomorrow's higher prices. Typically, however, executives do not rejoice over this fact; instead, they fret because the plant will have to be replaced at higher costs. But this may also work to the executive's joy. It implies that depreciation rates are too low, in which case current profits (on which the stock price and management bonuses depend) are being exaggerated to the benefit of the board. Even if depreciation rates are raised to the right level to compensate for inflation (and nobody knows what that is), the higher depreciation (if the Internal Revenue Service can be conned into accepting it) will result in lower taxes.

Most corporations, and most executives in their private capacity, are heavy borrowers, often over long terms at fixed interest. This, too, has a lovely result—or would have, if executives could curb their weird insistence on investing borrowed money at rates of return below the interest cost. The real cost of the interest payments declines as inflation rolls onward; and the final repayment is worth much less in real terms than the original loan. So the opportunities for exploiting inflation are always there. If executives fail to cope with its problems, the reason may lie in their own weakness.

The executive is pulled in opposite directions by self-interest and by conditioning, which includes the belief that corporate actions should be in the public interest. Self-interest dictates that directors should charge the highest price that the traffic will bear. The public interest dictates (or is thought to) that prices should never rise at all; but since rise they must, should do so by the merest smidgen. So administered pricing creeps onward and upward like lichen.

Prices are not treated as they should be, as the most decisive element in the marketing and economic mix. They become a fixed base to which inflationary increments are added from time to time. The cost-plus mentality takes over: firms fix their prices by costs plus a percentage and accept increases in costs as some God-given plague to be passed on to the consumer if at all possible; if not, the costs get handed over to the stockholder in massacred profits, slashed dividends, and tumbled stock prices.

In bad times company after company blames miserable profits on unprecedented rises in wages and other costs. In the 1970s, the rises really were unprecedented, but exceptional cost pressures were not so unreservedly to blame as companies liked to maintain. Take some of the worst losers in the period 1978–82, as charted by *Business Week:* steel (profits down 11 percent), automotive (17 percent), tire and rubber (17 percent). Although excessive wage costs, the results of previous inflationary settlements, took much of the blame, the truth is that these excesses were the responsibility of exactly the same managements that perpetrated such admitted howlers as the fatal lag behind Japan in steel technology, the poor quality and productivity levels in U.S. auto plants, the failure to follow the radial revolution soon or fast enough in tires. Had there been no world recession and no world inflation, these and many other gratuitous follies would have cost the companies dearly. As it was, inflation simply disguised the full extent of the folly—thus, the auto sector's profits, after allowing for inflation, would have been down, not 17 percent, but a thumping 29 percent.

The worst embarrassment that a company can contrive is to get caught in its own private deflationary spiral in an inflationary era; and it happens, more often than not, because managers put expansion first and profits well behind. This folly has severely stained the once pure growth records of the chemical companies of West Germany. They, too, blamed wage pressures, though labor costs matter much less in chemical plants than in car factories. Price weakness was a far more serious cause, and much of it resulted from their own errors of capacity planning and pricing policy, which have gone on blighting chemical profits on both sides of the Atlantic, with only intermittent relief, ever since 1970. After correcting for inflation, U.S. chemical earnings actually fell by a quarter between 1978 and 1982 (against the 1 percent growth figure reported). Whose fault was that?

An American chemical executive, coming into Europe from the lush green home pastures where companies know a pretty price when they see it, complained, "There is awful and unjustified price weakness in Europe." The Europeans cut prices to keep the Americans at bay; a self-defeating gesture, because the Americans, being richer, could better afford to give away their goods. Not that the Americans are blameless. Every executive in synthetic fibers knew that the amount of nylon-making plant being planned would eventually flood every nook and cranny of the market, but knowledge never stops a determined expansionist. American executives went on buying their way into Europe at prices that became still more ruinous as the backwash of the world surplus hit their cosseted home market.

The airlines showed with equal thoroughness how to create your own private deflation by overordering jumbo jets, just as they had overordered 707s a few years before. If capacity had only been balanced with demand, prices could have been slashed and yet profits would still have risen. A glut absolutely guarantees that prices will slump at the same time as operating costs soar because of the heartbreakingly low use of capacity. At this point, executives customarily institute sweeping cost-reduction programs, laying off employees on all sides, without reflecting that the costs being cut must have been inexcusably fat before.

Inefficient use of labor is endemic in industry. Whether the men put down tools for tea breaks, as in Britain, or stand guard around the Coke machine, as in the United States, or get sick with suspicious regularity, as in Germany, or are kept in full employment when they can't lift a finger, as in Japan, the results are the same. Their companies don't reap the full harvest of their new equipment; and they don't get maximum protection against the impact of inflation on their wage bill. To take just one example among myriads: there's a plant in the

British paper industry that faced almost every threat a management could wish not to face—including recession and ferocious price competition from the much-better-placed Scandinavians. It was producing 80,000 tons of paper a year with 1,500 people when the management finally gave up the ghost. The plant was taken over by an American company, which proceeded to manufacture 150,000 tons a year—with 400 employees.

Companies waste more than men; they also throw away expensive material. It's estimated that American and European manufacturers may waste as much as 25 percent of raw materials in the production processes. Since the usual spend on these essentiais ranges from 30 percent to 80 percent of turnover, that's no mean waste. But executives look through the wrong end of the telescope. Budgeting first in terms of sales, and setting targets in terms of profits, they pay too little attention to costs. Even when stringency and crisis force them to carve away at everything in sight, they choose the soft targets, such as advertising budgets, first, rather than the hard target, which is the corporate incompetence.

Excessive costs arise, not only from maladministration but from bad equilibrium. The deliberate creation of excess capacity is only one example. Another is making too many products and offering the excessive lines at tempting prices that are bound to yield amazing losses. If their cost accounting is weak enough, the executives may not even know that the losses exist (in disaster after disaster, the mortician's diagnosis is the same: "inaccurate costing and lack of financial information"). But higher prices will weed out losing lines that can be dropped forever, preserving only those for which the customers are prepared to pay; and the results can be delectable. One new management, anxious to escape from big unprofitable contracts in an underdeveloped country, but also anxious to keep face, elevated its tender (twice) to a level that looked certain to lose. It got the job (and might even make a profit).

In mythology, the executive is a rapacious creature who charges as much as he can as soon as he can. But the robber-baron spirit of John D. Rockefeller seldom rides in the great corporation. Its executives charge prices that are too low (that is, unprofitable, and less than the traffic will bear) for too long —and then make bad worse by offering discounts on the listed price. The sales side, in particular, has to be heaved away from a natural lust for low prices: no commission-crazy salesman ever willingly accepts any change that might, by any stretch of his imagination, make his selling task harder.

But price increases and discounts often have only marginal effects on demand; and the price increases, or saved discounts, then flow through as pure, pretty, and undiluted profit. The former boss of Mars in Britain agonized for months over whether to raise the Mars candy-bar price by little more than a cent—the hardest decision he ever faced. He never regretted the plunge for one sweet minute.

Those who argue that inflation is a destructive economic force are bound to oppose maximizing returns by maximizing prices; and many managers likewise miss the management logic. "You can't charge that much" was one sales manager's anguished cry. "It cost so little to produce." Anti-inflationists ignore the economic damage of underpricing. For years Jaguar managers labored under the delusion that their spiffy cars had to be cheap, starting at under $2,500 in the U.K. home market. This outlandish value for money produced a vociferous pileup of unsatisfied, waiting customers—many of them Americans, who wait for nothing. The lost income robbed the company of the resources needed to raise its production capacity to something near the level of demand. As a result of Jaguar's self-denial, BMW, whose prices have never been restrained by scruples, stole the market. It was making more cars in a day than Jaguar did in a week, and still is.

Executives find it just as hard as governments to leave the

correction of prices to the forces of the market. The pressure of governments anxious about inflation has greatly reinforced the businessman's own fear of public reaction, his own instinctive sympathy with the irrational feeling that there is a "fair" price that results in a "reasonable" return on capital. Words like *fair* and *reasonable* are purely emotive. For instance, suppose that General Motors earned twice as much on its assets as Ford. Would this mean that Ford's prices were fairer? Or that its products were better value than GM's? Or would it mean that GM was managed more effectively?

Then take supermarkets. In 1983 K-mart had a return on sales of 2.7 percent, getting on for three times the Safeway figure, and more than triple that for Kroger. Did this mean that K-mart's prices should have been lower? In fact, its success is founded on discounting—the higher margins result, not from higher prices, but from lower costs. That's the key to successful exploitation of inflationary and noninflationary times alike—to make higher profits than the other fellow at lower expense.

Companies that have offered progressively higher quality at relatively low prices are considered leading fire fighters against inflation. In point of fact, everybody's price levels have risen steeply over the years; the moral is that, even at higher price tags, the successful company's goods are well within the customer's vital willingness to pay—and its returns on capital will be much higher than those of competitors less effective in offering the market a high perceived value for money.

The company that gets inflation on its side will rush past those who are content to be its victims. After all, when all prices are rising, it's easier to put up your own without anyone noticing. So long as inflation is publicly execrated more than deflation (a process that is much nastier), wise directors may have to hide the fact that they charge the maximum price—not simply the price that covers the movements of costs and the competition. But even if a management manages badly in pricing and everything else, inflation, with luck, will partially conceal its failure, upgrading executives who would otherwise be downgraded professionally—and (far more painful) in their own pockets.

10

Why Mergers Make Mayhem

Business history is festooned with amalgamations. The mightiest manufacturers in the United States and Britain, General Motors and Imperial Chemical Industries, were created by merger artists. The colossus of Europe, Royal Dutch–Shell, arose from another bout of corporate love fever. But merger as a fine art got elevated to the upper reaches of the management stratosphere, stamped with the seductive, scientific-sounding word *synergy*. Ostensibly, this means a magic process in which two and two make more than four. More properly translated, synergy means that the deal makes no financial sense, but (please, God) something will come out of it in the end.

Most mergers are created in pious hope; their guiding drive is not financial or industrial logic but, in various forms, the urge to aggrandize. Yet a merger is nothing but a straight financial investment. One company pays cash, or stocks (that is, the right to participate in future cash earnings), or some hybrid security for another company's cash potential. The maneuver is no more sophisticated fundamentally than an investor's phone call to his broker—except that only a consummate sucker would pay a broker twenty times earnings for stocks selling in the market at a multiple of ten.

Industrial companies, however, play the sucker all the time (none more so than Britain's Midland Bank, which paid $820 million, or three times the market price, for only 57 percent of the Crocker National Bank—and then sat impotently by while this awful West Coast purchase lost $178 million in a mere six months). The more cunning conglomerates, in their formative years, at least avoided this trap. Their key deals were planned to elevate earnings per share, never mind whether the morsel was worth eating for any other reason. (As time wears on, conglomerate executives usually grow careless; contrary to their own myths, they pick up the bad habit of buying companies for ransoms that dilute their earnings.)

Conglomerators, at their best, pursue only the financial goals of mergers, because money is their obsession, lifeblood, and governing lust. Others merge regardless of cost because, for all their pretensions, financial maximization—or getting truly richer—is not their object. Maximization is the name of their corporate game, true; but maximizing the corporation, not its effectiveness or its share price, is the mainspring.

In Europe, this urge for bigness has been reinforced from time to time by politicians who believe that economies of scale (that is, the unreliable idea that bigger equals cheaper) are required weapons for fighting the good fight against U.S. economic imperialists. Many ill-starred European mergers were put together under this strange banner—including Pirelli-Dunlop (tires), Agfa-Gevaert (film), and VFW-Fokker (airplanes). All were dissolved after failure at every level: strategic, tactical, financial—and human. The conventional wisdom has consequently reversed itself. Europeans have begun to learn, as did the antiheroes of so many American mergers, that the opposite of synergy is *dissipation:* that two and two can make less than four, and that sometimes they don't add up at all.

These awakenings have still left most boardrooms dreaming of glory. Bids and deals preempt more top management time than any other pastime—and to minimal effect. Every study has shown that polygamous companies grow no faster, in terms of earnings per share, than firms that stay resolutely single. *Fortune* magazine quotes merger expert Michael Seely, of Investors Access Corp., to the effect that "in the past decade only one-third of all mergers have enriched the acquirer's shareholders, one-third have been a wash, and one-third have ended up costing investors money—sometimes lots of it."

Marvelous benefits are desperately hard to buy, and grotesque losses too easy to pick up; and common sense tells why. For managers can buy only three kinds of company—good, middling, or bad—and in only one of two circumstances— contested or uncontested (that is, rape or seduction). The perfect combination seems to be the seduction of a truly beautiful company; but the seducer must usually overpay, because beauties are seldom bargains. He overpays still more in cases of opposed rape, which commonly results in an auction. Maybe the companies to buy are the raped, bad ones—the only ones likely to be cheap in relation to their assets (if any are left), the only ones whose potential (if any) is sure to be underexploited. Even here lies no certainty: bad ingredients make poor dishes. In general, logic stacks the odds against the purchaser—good companies come dear, bad companies are bad.

The Fifth Truth of Management also applies: *however high its level, management capability is always less than the organization needs.* The junior partner (or mergee) seldom brings in supercompetence. After all, the hotter its management, the less its reason for merging. So the merged marvel has a broader management span, but even less management capacity in relation to need. Worse still, the overstretched management has the new, self-inflicted, and often chronic anxieties that come only with managing mergers. And human beings, when faced with more problems than they can handle (like rats in a psychologist's maze), do nothing.

Hence the familiar unconsummated merger—two companies that sleep together in name only. When Pan Am merged with National Airlines in 1980, for instance, the big idea was that the international passengers would no longer be lost to Pan Am when arriving in the States; nor would Pan Am be forced to take its passengers from the U.S. interior off other lines before flying them to foreign parts. The acquisition proved so troublesome, though, that Pan Am's management didn't get around to merging the National schedules into its own, the rationale of the whole deal, until the middle of 1982, by which time terrible damage had been done to the combined (or rather uncombined) airlines' reputation and to Pan Am's finances. Since the merger it has lost money—and its Far East routes.

These virgin marriages are usually friendly mergers; and maybe they are doomed to relative failure. The senior partner, being amicable, can't pick up the mergee for anything less than a pretty price, which rules out any remote hope of financial bonanza. The pervading friendliness also means that nobody gets sacked, and no activity beloved of the mergee's managers gets dropped. So much for synergy. After a hostile takeover, unhealthy inhibitions are fewer. The opposing board of directors may even be forced to walk the plank without ceremony —and that, while crude, is not the worst way of making merger sense. You can't make an omelet, or sense of a merger, without breaking eggs, and the longer the egg breaking is delayed, the fewer the benefits will be.

But there's a catch. If the acquiring management knows nothing about the business concerned, it's not in much of a position to judge the performance of its managers or to step into their shoes if that performance is deemed unsatisfactory. By no coincidence, four of the seven worst mergers found by *Fortune* were of this know-nothing nature: two oil companies (Sohio and Atlantic Richfield) buying into copper, and so on, and torpedoing their 1983 earnings per share by 23 percent and 19 percent, respectively; another oil company (Exxon) buying into electrical equipment and utterly wasting $1.24 billion in the process; yet another oil company, Mobil, purchasing the company that, among other undesirable things, owned the Montgomery Ward stores—a 1974–76 buy that knocked 39 percent off 1983 earnings and then got put on the block.

Since mergers do bring problems that can't be solved without time, trouble, and sorrow, buyers should be doubly careful about price. But most bidders are doubly cavalier. They follow the advice of art dealer Lord Duveen to earlier American millionaires: "if you're buying the priceless, you're getting it cheap." For priceless, read desirable, and you have the formula for merger after merger. One avid finance director admitted that his latest buy had cost several million too much. He explained that the overcharge had kept his dearest corporate enemy from picking the plum. "We are paying far too much [it was over $20 million]," said a real estate man on another occasion, "but it fits into the pattern of our future development." If the second half of that statement was true, then the first half was false—and vice versa. In effect, the stockholders bet their money (or have it bet for them, willy-nilly) on the chief executive's judgment. He may be warped by vanity, or if a battle is on, by simple hatred of being beaten. "It became a personal matter" for one company chairman, "and he had to raise the bid twice before he finally won, the last time even against the advice of our financial advisers."

An expensive merger always exacts a heavy toll on the bidder's management, and mergers may expose the ghastly secret that the bidder has no management at all. The mighty Pennsylvania Railroad was popularly considered to be a whiz at running railroads, and at piling up money in side ventures. When it wed the New York Central, the Pennsy's Stuart T. Saunders said that the railroad was getting "a new type of manager." (He added, a little more realistically, "Our programs have pulled us back from the brink of disaster . . . but they have not rescued us from the financial danger zone.") Industrial logic was rapidly overtaken by the reality of two struggling managements that had to divert their inadequate energies to new struggles—many with each other, some with diversified nonsenses, most with the terrible illogic of trying to fit two distinct rail networks into one. By themselves, possibly, neither line would have gone bankrupt; together, they were doomed.

The Leyland Motor Company was famed for lean, keen, efficient management when it united with the British Motor Corporation. Since BMC had mislaid one fifth of its market share since formation (by another merger), its capacities for mismanagement were regarded with some awe. Leyland's high repute outlasted the merger by only a few months. The senior partner revealed many of the mergee's faults—in marketing, middle management, underinvestment, one-man decision making, aging product lines, and a vacuum instead of labor relations. As the British Leyland Motor Corporation, and then as plain BL, it therefore really completed the good work on market share—reducing it in all by a staggering half.

It takes a very bright executive to make a merger into a success; and a very bright executive often is too bright to try. The duller executive cannot see the problem (or solve it). When one large oil company starts paying billions for unrelated businesses, the others plunge in pell-mell; then despite the terrible errors committed in this phase, they switch back to oil buys, also for billions, of course.

Fashion continues to call the tune. Once upon a time, food

firms, almost as one, diversified away from food, because of its slow growth. Their efforts to find fast expansion elsewhere met with notoriously scant success. Then, again in almost perfect unity, they returned to base, guzzling other food companies with every sign of voracious appetite. The only matter on which the gorging giants seemed to disagree was whether to go for the big bite (like Beatrice with Esmark, or Nestlé with its $3 billion swallow of Carnation) or the strategic nibble. Even nibbles weigh in heavy on the financial scales. It cost Dart & Kraft, for example, $290 million to buy a single Chicago distributor—but that was only 5.4 percent of Dart's assets.

The tiny size of overpriced acquisitions against the bidder's own elephantine proportions is no excuse. A series of bad small buys rapidly reduces the chances of improving the return on a mass of capital, which is the prime object of acquisitions, or would be in an ideal world. In real life, power is a more compulsive force, conscious or unconscious. Just as too few executives will genuinely delegate authority (for that robs them of their power and manhood), so few throw away chances to add new realms. And history and their contemporaries will applaud them for their power drives. The titan J. P. Morgan, a wheeler-dealer manipulator of James P. Ling proportions in his time, won eternal fame for his bloated, stock-watered creations, never mind that lesser figures had to make the monstrosities pay.

In these unaltered days, there are even cases of companies buying others they simply can't afford. With $2 billion of retail sales in lumber and building supplies in 1980, Wickes looked able enough to pay $193 million for the Gamble-Skogmo department and specialty stores. The catch was that the purchased company had $1 billion in debt, which weighed down the buyer, especially in a recession, like a lead balloon. After losing $400 million in fifteen months, Wickes had to go into Chapter 11 bankruptcy.

At that, Wickes survived, achieving some strange kind of

glory by becoming the largest U.S. business to emerge from bankruptcy, thanks to the heroic efforts of one Sanford Sigoloff (though even he lost over $1 billion of sales in the survival process). Baldwin-United, on the other hand, cooked its own goose permanently by borrowing $1 billion it couldn't conceivably finance to buy the biggest home-mortgage insurance company in the States. In the catastrophe that followed (a $673 million loss in 1983), Baldwin's own sales in single-premium deferred annuities (and maybe the savings of subscribers to them) were destroyed; so was $44 million of Merrill Lynch money, as the mighty brokers were obliged to repay customers for their Baldwin losses.

Often all that agglomeration achieves is to set the scene for some future hero. The bigger the company gets, the more overburden, deadwood, or rubbish it accumulates for that hero to cut away, elevating the profits and price/earnings ratio simultaneously, to general applause. At Consolidated Foods, for example, when 60 businesses (out of 125) were sold off during its deconsolidation, net income, far from falling, rose by 70 percent in five years. At Continental Group (formerly Can), assets shrank by no less than 13 percent in 1983—a cool $546 million—as the forest-products division was sold, with the inevitable result that return on assets rose as their quantity fell.

A good conglomerator can provide textbook theory in how to merge, if merge you must. The only merger object is to enhance the capital value of the company; and the best buyers have always thought and bought big. A $200 million company rarely has any good excuse for a $2 million buy. The deal can't have any noticeable impact on earnings, and small companies fit uncomfortably into big pockets. Unilever paid several millions (less than 1 percent of its own capital) for a plastics growth company. The new business was unrelated to the rest of its oversized group; and the latter's weight soon crushed the golden goose's entrepreneurial character—and its eggs. Big guns shouldn't be deployed on too narrow a front. The conglomerates, of course, overplayed the logic of buying big: thus Jimmy Ling, eager to bust the billion-dollar sales barrier by buying Jones and Laughlin's steel, virtually busted Ling-Temco-Vought.

It is easy but wrong to conclude that electronics companies have no business in steel, an industry that steelmen themselves mostly mismanage. Ling's mistake wasn't made in the management, but in the original decision to buy. The weakness of most mergers is not that ignorant managers enter unfamiliar businesses; it is that the price is wrong, regardless. If the price is right, the synergy and the management can look after themselves. If not, it will take years to close the gap by the workings of *industrial logic.*

This overworked expression is usually no more than a posthumous justification. Cadbury and Schweppes, two generally healthy companies, one in chocolate, one in soft drinks, had very little in common; only the industrially logical lust to create a food combine capable of spitting in the eyes of General Foods, General Mills, and Nestlé. Neither company competed seriously with any of the three (except for Nestlé and Cadbury in chocolate). Their deal mixed up the high-premium, high-cachet business of Schweppes with a low-margin, low-growth bulk operation in confectionery. Either Schweppes paid dearly to get into chocolate, or Cadbury paid expensively to move into soft drinks. Neither of the two American five-star food Generals, Food or Mills, lost a wink of sleep as a result. At the last count, Food was over three times as large as the Britons, Mills twice—while both had four times the profits.

The corporate slumber lost through mergers is mostly within the merged company as managers try to put together what could logically always have been left asunder. Take Philip Morris, once the shining text for marketing professors because of its achievements with Miller High Life beer—raised from also-ran to number two by high-powered promotion. Riding high on this success, Miller paid $520 million for Seven-Up in 1978; half a dozen years later, Seven-Up had still to turn a profit as the cola giants continued to turn the screws. That wouldn't have seemed so ghastly had Miller still been doing its stuff, but the High Life brand peaked and, as it thereafter slid down the slope, so did earnings—and so did the value of a brand-new, $450 million Ohio brewery. The "disasters" moved a couple of *Business Week* writers to comment that Philip Morris would have been better off to purchase its own shares than to buy into beverages—alcoholic or nonalcoholic.

It's industrially logical to buy a business that takes you into an entirely new market. Aha! But it's also "logical" to buy one in exactly the same market—hopefully killing two birds for the price of one. This is the only form of synergy actually proved to work, in the negative sense of closing down one of two factories or two distribution forces (not in positive expansion of the mergee's business by the buyer's magic touch).

The conglomerates at their peak were much better at this negative synergy. In the game only for the money, they sold off everything surplus or movable on sight. One conglomerate executive even had a man standing by in Germany waiting to chop off a loss-making limb the instant the takeover was complete. This demonstrated absolutely sound tactics. Since deeper human motives than financial sense are always involved in mergers, you must start fast to make the best of what (more often than not) will be a bad deal.

The first step is to find out exactly what you have bought. In the worst circumstances, that discovery may end all further interest. Assuming that you do still want any part of the company, then decide what you want and don't want in assets and in managers. Mergees always have some seniors who shiver the spine, and some juniors worth their weight in silver dollars. Casting the former out (as generously as possible) and promoting the latter (at high speed) is the proper routine. As for unprofitable operations, close them, all of them, especially those where, according to the anguished cries of the incumbents, prosperity is just around the corner. These pets mostly go on eating profits forever.

Where the mergee's operations, brand names, distribution, and so on can be swallowed into the bigger company without any loss of business, do it, right now. When skeletons rattle out of cupboards, take the losses and write-offs at once. When executions have to be carried out, sooner is always better than later. Don't leave sentenced operations waiting interminably on death row. Of course, a merged company is no different in these respects from an unmerged one—executives are always putting off the evil day, especially an evil day that they themselves have created.

11

The Overcompensated
Executive

Most executives are badly paid, not in the sense that they get too little (many get far too much), but because they are paid in the wrong ways. Their take seldom has any true relation to their personal success or to the company's. Come rain or shine, their dinner pail stays full. This is less true in the United States than in Britain. But even in America linking an executive's efforts to his immediate rewards is more pretense than effectiveness.

The soul instantly rejoices when reading that in 1983, at a time when overall executive compensation in *Business Week*'s survey soared by 13.1 percent, the chairmen of Bethlehem Steel and Pittsburgh Steel both suffered pay cuts: both companies had negative returns on stockholders' equity, of 29.9 percent and 21.6 percent, respectively. But the pay cuts were tiny (2 percent and 5 percent) and, at $419,000 and $265,000, the two men were a long way from the breadlines. The chairman of U.S. Steel, having presided over the largest 1983 loss in the entire United States ($1.16 billion), was sternly punished with a 9 percent raise to $606,000.

Another oddity is the way multimillionaires tie their rewards to profits. Before the war, there was an electrical boss who gave himself a contract for a nice slice of the net. After the war, as one of the new breed of electronics tycoons, when the company profits and his own fortunes in stock were vastly swollen, he continued to grab so huge a take that average salaries for his directors were the highest in the land, entirely because of the greedy old boy's cut. Henry Ford II, while still in charge of the family fief, was another whose pay was geared to performance (one depressed year, his company income slumped all the way from $600,000 to $515,000). Thomas Watson, Jr., of IBM was no different when in the chair and the driving seat. For though their fortunes yo-yo around in the stock market in one day by greater amounts, magnates go through the solemn charade of pretending that their annual recompense in some way affects their performance as profit earners.

Nor are family scions averse to fat salaries. At Anheuser-Busch, for instance, Adolf A. Busch III earned nearly a million in 1983—and $431,000 of that was bonus. The eponymous J. B. Fuqua of Fuqua Industries (estimated personal worth, $150 million) allowed himself to draw a salary of $509,000 that year. Bonus payments raised that to the much more impressive figure of $1.5 million; and Fuqua, filled by sentiments of noble generosity or just plain shame, of his own free will gave up a 1983 entitlement to $554,328. The Houghton family of Corning Glass (collective worth, $400 million) also collects bonus payments on top of salary, while Bill Norris, the embattled boss of Control Data, enhanced his 1983 salary by half with bonuses —a nice, comfortable addition to his founding share stake.

You could argue that this is not only right and proper, but axiomatic, that what really determines any top executive's pay is the size of the organization in which he works. A law invented or discovered by the nineteenth-century Italian economist Vilfredo Pareto explains practically everything about business. (Roughly speaking, it says that 20 percent of customers account for 80 percent of turnover, 20 percent of components account for 80 percent of cost, and so forth.) His law shows that all organizations build a pay pyramid. The broader the base, the higher the summit of the pyramid. I learned about Pareto's law on pay from research inside the personnel department of Rolls-Royce. Maybe this work had some connection with the pay raise, of £9,000, which the chairman got in 1969, shortly before his company completed its crash—one of the weirdest illustrations in history of the poor correlation between pay and performance.

The mythology is that superior U.S. corporate performance is greatly stimulated by stock options, cash incentive awards, and the like. But studies done before these goodies became all but universal revealed, among the top hundred U.S. companies, no distinction in results between managements that granted themselves every financial stimulus under the sun and those tiny few that bumbled along on straight salary—except that, by performing no better than the straight salary managers, the carrot danglers got much richer. The argument about whether or not these financial inducements are effective has thus become entirely academic, because no executive in his right mind will work for a company where the loot is less.

The stock option is in truth a device to enable a manager —generally a hired hand, not somebody who owns the company—to get rich—really rich, easily and without risk. Climbing up the ranks of a great American corporation can lift a man to dizzy heights of wealth, and it isn't even necessary to run the corporation successfully. If that sounds too good (or bad) to be true, it isn't: *Business Week* lists seven executives whose stock-holders saw their investments decline in value between 1981 and 1983 by amounts ranging from 9.8 percent to 67.2 percent. Collectively, the sorry seven hauled in $20.8 million of pay and other emoluments for 1983, making an average of $3 million per failed manager.

If a man is actually successful, like William S. Anderson, the hero who turned around a dilapidated NCR, the take becomes truly phenomenal—in this case, $14.5 million. Anderson has protested that (a) he deserved it, (b) it isn't really one year's reward, but a decade's, and (c) because of the compulsory six months' wait before selling, under U.S. law, he might never see the full $12 million of stock options that accounted for the bulk of his booty. He could well end up, Anderson opined, with a mere $9 million.

In fact, Anderson earned more straight pay than John R. Opel of IBM, in one of that company's palmiest years, and was entitled to five and a half times Opel's total remuneration. IBM had eleven times NCR's sales and nineteen times its profits. Equally odd, the president of superchip-maker Intel, Andrew S. Grove, got a million dollars more than Opel; yet IBM has a large stockholding in Grove's firm (which must have helped make its stock options still more valuable). The anomalies are legion. No fewer than three Ford Motor men figure at the top of the 1983 pay league, but none from General Motors—even though its chairman got a richly deserved 171 percent raise that year. All these funny figures prove only one thing: who earns what in the United States has become a matter, not of who did best for the company, but whose hand delved deepest into the honey pot.

The American situation has always been bizarre. By 1968 fully seventy-three of the one hundred largest companies had both stock options and incentive awards; another seven had incentive awards only; seventeen had stock options only; and three languished in the outer darkness of straight old-fashioned pay. Fewer than two fifths of the goodie-stuffed seventy-three bettered either the median performance of *Fortune*'s 500 largest companies for ten years' growth in earnings per share or the median for profitability in that particular year. The seven companies with incentives, but without stock options, did barely better. The less directly a management's pay was tied to the company's profit performance, surprisingly, the worthier the performance became. Stock-option companies with no incentive awards did very well on growth—88 percent were above the median, and 59 percent beat the median for profitability. All three of the benighted straight pay companies, however, outdid the ten-year median growth rate; and two of these three were abnormally profitable.

Some of the possible conclusions are too obvious to be true. For instance, growth-hungry investors would have been rash to charge into companies with generous option schemes before discovering which came first—the options or the performance. Often the executives, finding themselves onto a good thing, smartly arrange to share the bonanza. But incentive awards, unanswerably, seem to have no discernible incentive effect. The reason lies in the logic (or illogic) of incentive schemes. Honeywell, which employs greedy, hot computer salesmen as well as the average executive, found that 30 percent of pay has to come from incentives before "other guys get the driving get-up-and-go of the fellows in the Brooks Brothers' suits"—but what would the other 70 percent be paid for? Occupying the office space?

Management by objectives looks like a solution: work out an executive's objectives with him, then relate his pay to his success in hitting the target. But here, too, there is logical trouble: the man gets much of his pay for *not* meeting his objectives. You pay him for failing, and reward him with more for doing what he was hired to do in the first place. A manager is hired, and should be paid, to do a job that *includes* meeting a set of objectives and producing profits that can be reported to stockholders without sackcloth and ashes. If he excels himself, he is enriched, anyway, in a sensible company. If he fails, through a fault of his own, you may not want him at any price.

Incentive schemes have other snags, notably making sure that profit-linked bonuses really do reflect managerial merit. Head office can contain a bundle of superannuated dodos whose main contribution is, by all means in their power, to prevent the divisional directors from earning large profits. If the latter triumph against the odds, guess who collects the largest bonuses. And how do you distinguish between an executive who shuts off a $10 million loss and his luckier colleague who, given the company's plum division, raises its profits by $5 million?

Until you near the pay stratosphere, what's more, you can rarely cut an executive's salary. A manager earning $100,000 a year can't take much of a slash—not so long as he has a wife, three children, and a mortgage to support. The incentive system tends to be all rewards and no penalties; that being so, it doesn't work. Systems of genuine incentives do exist; however, few boards of directors would dream of imposing this kind of straitjacket on themselves.

Pay in a deadly serious scheme starts from a base high enough to cover ordinary living expenses and no more. Part of pay above that level is linked to profit performance; part is tied to stock performance (which executives can fiddle less easily than the profit figures). The stock-linked element, moreover, carries a downside risk. The money is either in deferred earnings or in stocks held in trust. If the stocks fall, so does the money in the executive's hope chest. Contrast this with the typical salary position in a large company. Pay is determined by rank and rises gratifyingly year by year with time and seniority. With it, up and up goes the pension entitlement. The executive knows at the beginning of the year what he will earn over the next twelve months, which will be more than his juniors get and as much as his peers. Given a choice between this security and the razzle-dazzle uncertainty of true incentives, ninety-nine executives out of one hundred will plump for security.

As for the one hundredth, he won't stay long in a big company, anyway. For all their talk about the entrepreneur, about risk-taking, and about the golden lure of profits, the majority of executives are staid by talent and temperament. Their instinctive, silent reasoning must be, Why expose myself and my family to financial risk, when I can always find secure employment of much the same kind in a noncommercial bureaucracy? Because of this, pay systems in all companies—including stock-option schemes and incentive plans—gravitate, or degenerate, toward bureaucratic stability.

Executives have great difficulty in recognizing this desire for financial peace and quiet in themselves. Whenever conservative politicians cut taxes on top incomes, a supposedly clinching argument is that reducing the tax bite gives executives greater incentive to take risks, win orders, and generally sweat harder. The unexciting record of most big British companies after this notion was first applied dismayed the incentive advocates not at all. Obviously, the cuts were too small. Reduce top taxes to the American level, and British management would *really* show what it was made of.

In reality, tax rates seem to have little effect on effort. The Swedish economy, just as highly taxed as the British, has grown faster. And the tax argument cannot explain away the yawning gulfs between the performances of different managements whose members all pay much the same tax rates. You can't of course blame executives for arguing that they would work harder or better if taxed less, even though they lie. What they really want (and who doesn't?) is to pay less tax. High taxes, again, were blamed for the lush fringe benefits with which many British executives were cosseted before an aroused Mrs. Thatcher swung an ax at them—the chauffeured cars; the personal Rolls or Jaguar; the house and gardeners; the expensive public schools for the children; the executive dining room, butler, and wine cellar; the trips to South Africa in the winter; the flats in Mayfair or Belgravia; and so on.

We don't actually like having all these presents, ran the argument—the tax system forces them on us. Before the war, however, and before taxes became so penal, British companies had their grouse moors and their private trains, as well as today's popular treats. A survey by Shell once established that most of its executives pined for the life of a country gentleman—and among older British chief executives today country sports are far and away the most popular pastime. The British company traditionally provided its leaders with life as their more leisured grandfathers might have known it; and if American executives live lower off the hog, at company expense, that, too, is more a matter of social tradition than of the tax system.

Not that the American hates using company money for his own creature comforts. That soaring skyscraper in Wall Street, Midtown Manhattan, or Westchester County, that chairman's office festooned with rare art and furniture, may be good for corporate prestige. But they also do no harm to the executive's own ego. The Germans are more frank: they admit that the depth of floor carpet matters almost as much as the size of a German director's salary. Stock options have become roughly the same thing in the United States—part of the furniture, which the executive expects to find there, but which doesn't motivate him recognizably. If fortune shines on the company, he pockets the profits. If the stock slumps to the floor, that's the way the cookie crumbles—there are stock options in the most moribund of America's corporate giants.

There are still plenty of U.S. companies, though, that don't cosset their top executives with the good, corporation-paid private life. At Emhart, for instance, vice-chairman Stephen J. Ruffi actually boasted in an interview that "I pay my own golf club dues, I pay my own Clipper Club membership. We have no company country club. We don't have a company plane. There's no financial planning done for me or other executives. I fill out my own tax returns"; yet this is a high-performing company, which ranked seventy-first out of *Fortune* 500 companies in shareholder return over the decade to 1983.

Over a certain level, pay always loses its importance. This is the weakness of commission systems. Once a salesman has earned what he reckons to be adequate, he is much less interested in earning more for the company. That level of adequacy varies between individuals and between cultures; in the United States the cutoff point is very high. But even one of the world's all-time selling champions, H. Ross Perot, after shattering all of IBM's records, stopped selling computers. With his own software firm, he then made more money in less time—on paper—than any man in history; next lost more in less time—on paper—than anybody, when his stock market bubble deflated; but finally cleaned up, to the tune of a billion real dollars, when General Motors bought his company in 1984.

The general theory of remuneration is to pay people their market value, pay them still more as their responsibility and contribution rise, and not to keep expensive deadwood around the premises. Only executives who are themselves incompetent keep on at $65,000 a year men whose services are worth half; only a misguided management congratulates itself on getting senior executives for $65,000 a year when the going rate is $120,000. For some reason, the proprietorial company finds this lesson hard to master. One multimillionaire took enormous exception to paying his new president, in a billion-dollar company, more than a marketing whiz kid would get elsewhere.

The fact that a laborer may not know his value is no excuse for paying him less. In Britain, where people are traditionally more secretive about money than sex, executive reticence helped to keep executives' pay before tax far below European levels. By 1983 the Swiss and the Germans had worked up to 100 percent more than their British executive counterparts, and both countries had caught up with, if not surpassed, American standards for upper-middle managers. An executive pay lag is one sickness that no country can afford in the new age of truly international and interchangeable executives.

Giving some pay, somehow, in the form of stocks is one right antidote, but not because it will produce superior corporate performance (it probably won't), and certainly not because a capital stake will make the manager more forcefully independent. A craven who won't argue with his superior because he's afraid of losing his job won't argue any more readily because he has a stock option. Executives should be deeply invested in their company's stocks for two different reasons: first, a man who devotes much of his life to a capitalist concern deserves capital himself; second, he also deserves to share the sorrows as well as the joys of the stockholders—when the stocks go down, it should hurt him, and preferably more than it hurts them.

But the corporate bureaucracy is most unlikely to reward its executives unfairly; and the unfairness is certain to get less and less the nearer the executive gets to the top. For top executives are in the happy position of fixing, or helping to fix, their own pay, as was demonstrated during the amazing explosion of executive fortunes in the early 1980s. When the golden parachutes and so forth floated gently down to earth, many and miraculous were the results. Among them, just two ripe and fine examples will do: in 1982, profits at Norton Simon, the dull and tarnished conglomerate headed by David J. Mahoney, rose by a tiny 4 percent. Mahoney collected $2 million for this effort, and then proceeded to reap a richer harvest still when the whole caboodle passed into the ownership of another and better-managed conglomerate. At City Investing, to quote *Business Week,* "a management designed plan of staggering generosity" offered chairman George T. Scharffenberger $16.4 million as his reward for taking the company into voluntary liquidation. Such bliss was perfectly summed up by a great *New Yorker* boardroom cartoon in which the table is surrounded by smiling faces and the chairman is saying, "Gentlemen, I think we can congratulate ourselves on voting these large increases in salary, thus ensuring to the corporation our continuing loyal services."

BOOK III

Board Games

12

Managing by Minion

The modern principle of decentralization makes enchanting sense. Simply split the corporate leviathan into big lumps of homogenous activities, then break down the homogenous lumps into individual morsels. Each lump and morsel has its responsible boss, and each boss has another boss on his back to bite him. Gone, or kicked upstairs, are the functional directors of production, marketing, engineering, or what have you —jobs so loosely defined that nobody could tell when they were mangled. In their place stand the divisional executive and his subsidiary executives and their subsidiary executives, each in charge of a distinct business. If the arrayed subordinates all perform according to plan, the chief executive and his summit sidekicks have little to do, except pat backs, collect pay, plan the future, and wait for a rich retirement.

With all this going for it, the decentralized company

should have soared into new orbits. It hasn't: decentralization has often meant deterioration. Du Pont is the daddy of all decentralized and financially motivated managements. In the 1960s its sales growth lagged behind that of other chemical giants. Its earnings per share growth was negative—a decline of 1.79 percent a year. Its net profitability fell to 9.1 percent. Even in 1983 the number was no better than 9.8 percent. Admittedly, the intervening years were more bothersome for the chemical industry than almost any other period—beset by soaring feedstock costs and by sinking prices (produced in part by its own addiction to overexpansion).

All the same, du Pont's stockholders had cause to complain: their total return over the ten years to 1983 had been a paltry 5.4 percent—and that thanks only to a surge in the stock price in the final year of the decade. Yet du Pont had decentralized down to the last digit long ago; British rivals even used to gibe that du Pont's board members were just a bunch of chemical bankers. Difficulty in recovering adequate loot from decentralized divisions is not confined to the bankers of du Pont.

Some companies even started to wonder whether they should reverse engines. "Recentralization is the word now," said one American executive gloomily. "But I haven't met anybody who's actually done it." The decentralization theory has no fatal flaws in itself. It just doesn't generally fit the real-life way in which companies work. The conglomerates fell foul of the reality. Some of them (some by accident) collected quite good companies in their stamp albums. But decentralization was their supposed essence. The conglomerator sat at the center of the spider's web, while, all around, the new acquisitions, separated by distance, organization, and the different natures of their trades, spun away. Very few big black spiders, however, could leave well enough alone for long—and the lust to interfere became still more irresistible when "well enough" turned to terrible.

At ITT, for example, the bright young men at HQ dreamed up the bright idea of dominating the business of contract cleaning for offices. So out went the ITT raiding parties to big city after big city, buying up the market-leading cleaners and making their deliriously happy family proprietors suddenly cash-rich. But the bright young men saw that their new properties were undermanaged. So they sent out other bright young men to tell the former proprietors how to run their businesses. The former bosses liked that so little that, one after the other, they left, taking their best contracts with them. ITT found itself competing against the very people whose companies it had bought—and competing, what's worse, at a terrible disadvantage. At that point, intervention became essential, but, of course, useless.

Another ur-conglomerate, Litton Industries, seemed to discover perfect decentralization. It kept the head office small; broke big units down to minimal, more manageable size; exerted strict financial control by fast, frequent, and elaborate reports, including weekly cash statements; placed able sharpies in charge of operations; and promoted them swiftly when they succeeded. And the top duo, the late Tex Thornton and Roy Ash, held strategy sessions at which, with the unit managers and the latters' group bosses, they belabored the questions at the core of any business—where it was going and how it was going to get there. One of the many Litton executives spun off into other careers has reminisced, though, that the strategy sessions were actually futile. Why? Because Ash and Thornton simply didn't know enough about the businesses to ask the right questions—not that this stopped them from trying.

So even at Litton the system failed, not because of act of God or national economic crisis but because of miscalculations and plain mismanagement in two of the new decentralized joys, shipbuilding and office machinery. No structural device (and "strategy sessions" are only gadgets) exists by which the head office can both manage and not manage. A clear choice has to be made, one way or the other, and you don't have to guess which way the head office manager will jump—into interference, with both feet.

Managing directors or presidents are possessed by ambition, power drive, and vanity; they have climbed many miles, over long years, to reach the top. Once arrived, they seldom breathe in, dock their highly polished brogues on the desk, and drop any desire to manage actively. The motivations that propelled their rise are just as powerful once they have risen. The decentralized corporation, with its profit centers, its corporate plans, and its group executives, becomes a labyrinthine mechanism to let the head office heads play at being executives—for in the end they cannot manage. Decentralization, even in quite small companies, is not a theory, but an inevitability.

Some executive, somewhere down the line, is in personal contact with reality—the customer who won't buy, the product that won't work, the machines that won't produce. The longer the rope between that man and the summit, and the more the men on Everest seek to know and influence what is happening in the far foothills, let alone in the valleys, the more the company becomes an expensive device for generating unused information. But modish decentralization rode over this truth, in the opposite direction. Turn everybody, it said, even the salesman, into an executive. Push responsibility further and further down the corporation ladder. Substitute individual initiative for central initiative. Achieve coordination through a common corporate philosophy plus common controls and common corporate systems.

Inhabitants of such wonderlands should consider a letter written in blood by one employee of an American group that is alleged to be a rare example of successful big-time management of diversity. Like most corporate fames, this one crumbles slightly if growth is assessed after deducting inflationary increments, or profitability by knocking off near-monopoly markets in the United States. But still, it was, relatively speaking, a good company and a lesson to everyone—or was it? The letter from its humble son, well down the scale, out on one of the European limbs, read:

> We have a very able sales manager who in turn reports to New York, but he is not able to see us very often. I have been told that I must be responsible for everything to sell my product—marketing, sales forecast, advertising, mailing campaigns, etc.—everything to enable me to sell my product better. I am completely inexperienced in how to do this.

Every day some decentralized employee, like this victim, is told, in effect and sometimes in so many words, "This is your business and your responsibility. It's all yours—run with it." But the man may not have the resources to run the department or the true independence that alone makes sense of the policy. The more important his operation, the more hotly his superiors breathe down his neck. The less important, the more likely he is to be strung up in that salesman's position—left alone, to hang himself, or to be hanged by some offended superior.

The organization chart won't reveal that somewhere in darkest Germany, stygian England, or murky France is a sales manager whose boss is three thousand miles away in Manhattan and whose own subordinates have all but forgotten what he looks like. That boss on Park Avenue is too remote and too busy with his own bureaucratic spawning of words and figures to understand the local business. Even if there is enough time to explain the business to him, is there really any point? The Sixth Truth of Management lays down that there are only two possibilities: *either an executive is competent to run the business or he is not.* In the first instance, leave him alone. In the second, move him. In neither case should another executive try to run the business through the subordinate by remote control.

Often the besetting preoccupation and sin of the distant superior is to demonstrate that he really is superior. The inferiors in turn become too preoccupied with the pressures from on high to avoid stupidities themselves—such as giving impossible responsibilities to unprepared salesmen. When the victims fail, the calamity is demonstrably not their fault; it's that of decentralization carried to its usual centralized excess. The whole idea stemmed from the exact observation that businesses had grown beyond the scale and scope of the center's ability to command. But responsibility can be pushed too far down. The Peter Principle seeks to prove that eventually all executives are promoted beyond their abilities. But incompetents are manufactured more often from above, by demoting responsibility below the critical point—the level at which it can reasonably be carried.

Many large groups have committed the sins of centralization and decentralization at once: they condemn their lesser executives to failure by this surefire method, while the abler executives waste oceans of time, initiative, and energy in preparing and discussing plans and reports and budgets with the allegedly detached center. Every westbound transatlantic flight transports the boss or subboss of a European subsidiary of an American multinational to Des Moines, or New York, or Pittsburgh. Briefcase bulging, he is on his way for the monthly or quarterly confrontation with his superiors. A common supplement is for the parent's senior management to go on a grand procession, like the doges of medieval Venice, around their satrapies, and nobody stops to query all this travel (which is easier and more enjoyable than work).

The reality of multinational decentralization, especially in companies with more or less homogeneous product lines, can only be experienced truly from within. In one multinational, for example, the downstream manufacturing operations had for years been regarded only as outlets for the group's base product, of which it was the world's most efficient producer. Unfortunately, the huge overcapacity of the recessionary 1970s made this less and less of an asset, and the strategy of adding businesses (any businesses) that used the base product came to look increasingly absurd.

Actually, it always had been, since the added businesses weren't evaluated at all on their intrinsic merits (if any). The decentralized subsidiaries around the world had been nothing more than centrally dominated funnels for product. Now, under enormous pressure for more profits, they were expected to change emphasis—and how. Businesses were to be market-led, not product-pushed, so the subsidiary managers duly and dutifully started to try and develop their own national markets.

Then they met the unpleasant realities: the unanswered memos to head office about market and product questions to which it knew the answer; the distant U.S. management hoarding information and experience that was vital to the development plans which Europe was desperately trying to form and implement; the European management, which regarded with suspicion and often obstructiveness the efforts of national managements to maximize their returns from national markets. And, of course, there was another problem: years of subservience had left the local managements themselves gravely short of experience at being what they were now supposed to be—real businessmen.

Yet the multinationals have (and always have had) the perfect setup to decentralize truly—if they want to. The local business is geographically remote and clearly marked out by national frontiers, often by national market characteristics. Its management, too, is largely separated by nationality and language. And the overseas businesses, mostly starved neither for capital nor for marketable products, are substantial economic powers in their own rights and own lands.

The parent's only vital functions are to watch and count

its money, to coordinate (that is, stop any one subsidiary from slaughtering the others), to soup up its baby's growth by providing any riches that the locals request from the American cornucopia, and to change the management if it fails. But the overwhelming tendency is to absorb the national company into the parent until decisions in Scotland, France, and the Midwest are homogenized into one bland whole.

The same thing can happen very easily, and with the same very dismal results, inside national boundaries. The giveaway signs are unmistakable. The center forces the supposedly decentralized operations to share common functions—not the essentially central control functions, like finance and law, but the inessential. Rather, it's essential for the good health of the affiliate that functions such as marketing stay where they belong—close to the market.

The results when they don't are visible from a *Harvard Business Review* study by Carolyn Y. Woo. She looked at leaders with high market shares but low returns on capital—in contradiction to the conventional wisdom (and common sense), which holds that high goes with high. Among various other masterpieces of mismanagement (like having heavier costs than lesser firms), over half the low-return leaders shared more than four fifths of the marketing programs with other lines of the corporation's business. That compared to 39 percent for the leaders whose returns were what they should be—high.

Over a quarter of the marketing channels were shared by two thirds of the low-return laggards; again, significantly more than for the high-returners. What the successful entrepreneur almost invariably does—to give carefully defined, separate businesses their own distinct marketing resources (meaning the armaments they need to sell effectively)—applies as a general rule, and often this simple act of separation has been the key to magnificent turnarounds.

Muddle up the marketing, or anything else, and you muck up the management. One of the key moments in IBM's postwar history, maybe the single most important step in creating the most successful multinational of them all, was the decision to stop making the entire product line in every foreign plant. Instead, each would concentrate on its own products—shared with nobody else. As Sir Edwin Nixon, the U.K. chairman of the time, recalled, "It was one of those management decisions which are absolutely right in retrospect, but which are quite difficult at the time"—"quite difficult" being, no doubt, a British, stiff-upper-lip euphemism for great pain.

Sometimes it's necessary, in the interests of a grander strategy, to combine operations rather than divide them up in IBM style. Much like the latter, Ford wanted to make collective sense of Europe—seen as a whole, rather than as separate territories. But to do so, Ford Motor turned its back on what had been apparently a triumphant tradition of European national independence.

Once, Henry Ford II's British pied-à-terre was brashly independent, with a large minority of British stockholders, a self-consciously tough Irish boss, and a creaking but tolerably successful product line. But the Americans from Dearborn descended on Dagenham. The minority stockholders were bought out, hundreds of millions were poured in to reequip the plants and revitalize the products, and American executives arrived in droves. At first their control lodged in a popular watering place for American executives, Brussels. Then the outfit, Ford of Europe, was removed to the same lush Americanized executive block as Ford of Britain, which came under the direct managerial control of the Americans, for ill as well as good.

The first, but not the last, ill was the choice of an American-style replacement for its largest Zephyr-Zodiac range—long-hooded, wide-wheel-based, gas-guzzling. It flopped, and one British director of the time believes, rightly or wrongly, that its mismarketing was compounded by production faults, in part because the local executives had no real faith in a project that wasn't truly and wholly theirs. But in what must have been a tough learning process for both the Americans and the Europeans, the successful coordination of the entire Ford apparatus continued.

As a result, nobody can now seriously pretend that the Ford managers in Britain (which had four managing directors in six years) are still the captains of the subsidiary's soul and fate—as they should be, in theory. But in practice the adoption of a European-wide policy for Ford, with production of European-wide models sourced in Britain, or Spain, or Germany as the European management decrees, took priority—and had to, especially after GM counterattacked with such force in Europe that two top Ford men in swift succession disappeared from their posts in 1984.

The difficult trick in these circumstances is to apply the still-relevant Sixth Truth of Management. In the simplest situation, if the locals say they know best what to produce, they should be left to prove it, and to pay the price if they fail. After all, if they can't be trusted on that, how can they be trusted with anything else, except the key to the executive washroom? But it's a difficult trick (managed with considerable skill by IBM) to achieve local autonomy and (just as important) the feeling of local autonomy while imposing transnational unity. If you don't achieve that combination (as Ford has found the hard way), product failures will follow in this country or that.

Cars are a special management problem in one respect: as trains used to, they turn almost any adult into a schoolboy. (A minor problem with middle-aged rail executives before the computer made the activity redundant was their passion for drawing up timetables.) But even if the products are less compulsive playthings, the urge to fiddle is omnipresent—partly because the chief executive likes to take personal credit for any successes (the failures he leaves to others).

Effective decentralization, however, means no fiddling and no meddling, except when mismanagement occurs. True, by then damage has been done, but the center often finds it doesn't have an early enough warning system, however elaborate. In one typical Litton case, its Hull factory in England was expensively geared up to manufacture typewriters that it could neither produce properly nor sell; this became evident from reports only when the company was already locked into disaster. The mistake was not lack of reports; it was the original, strategic decision, in which the Litton bosses had *participated,* to use their word.

In any big American corporation, the top executives participate all the time; that is, they hold endless meetings to second-guess the executives who are supposed to be in charge. Once you decentralize, you become more investor than director. You should act like a sane one. It's interesting how old saws of stock market investment apply to decentralized direction—Cut your losses, but let your profits run; or reinforce success, and never invest in failure.

One old-line board ignored both wise saws. It was notorious for inability to influence its largest subsidiary, which had decentralized itself right out of head-office orbit. When the offshoot's ideas and those of another part of the empire overlapped, both projects sometimes, ludicrously, went ahead. Both even developed their own computers. The correct answer, since the child went around the track much faster than the parent, was to back baby. But this would have meant downgrading another business over which the main board actually did possess day-to-day control. As the better managements of the 1980s realized, only when senior managers change their entire life-styles, abdicate the interfering habits of a managing lifetime, and substitute the fair but demanding standards of a

hungry investor, can decentralization be more than a myth—
and often an expensive one.

The relatively cheap and marvelously productive results
of true decentralization, though, have been demonstrated by
enough companies since the oil price shocks to provide proof
as abiding as there ever can be in management. Time and again,
the recipe's the same: decimate head-office numbers; make the
guy in charge at the decentralized unit into a real chief executive; impose fast-acting information systems, and use them to
squeeze out the top performance that, for the sake of his own
remuneration and ambition, the guy will want to achieve.

Set down like that, the formula sounds little different from
the one that, say, Harold S. Geneen used to peddle as ITT's
supreme contribution to the art of higher management. The
difference lies, though, in that head office. Actually, it's a
tougher trick to act as guide and goad, enhancing rather than
reducing motivation and management performance, than it is
to play the mastermind at the expense of your minions. For
that's what the old centralizing head office in the half-decen-
tralized company made of its managers: minions. And they
managed as if they were.

13

The Boardroom
Mafia

Boards of directors have an aura of sanctity roughly akin to
that of the College of Cardinals. The law sees them as they see
themselves: guardians of the stockholders' rights and the company's long-term future. A pungent *New Yorker* comment, at
the height of the Valachi revelations about the Mafia, is more
accurate. The cartoon showed a board chairman snarling at his
youngest and brashest director: "Perkins, will you stop calling
this company *Cosa Nostra.*" Perkins was perfectly right. As
senior executives in most corporations are both the dominant
directors and the controlling executives, the business all too
readily becomes Our Thing.

The board elects itself, reshuffles itself, congratulates itself. The directors are supposed to call the executives to account—and possibly did in ancient times, when the general
manager of the business was a lackey, like the doorkeeper.

Today the general manager is either chairman of the board, or managing director, or president. His first loyalty is not to the board as such, and certainly not to the unseen stockholders, but to an amorphous body of no legal standing, the upper management.

The Mafia-like aspect of top management coziness raises large, well-aired, but unresolved questions about the relationship between stockholders, directors, and companies. One question, at least as important, seldom gets any air: the relationship between the management Mafia and the efficient conduct of the business. This issue is most transparent in companies (meaning almost all of them in Britain) where the all-executive, all-supreme board is at its zenith, and where a handful, maybe only a couple, of nonexecutive gentlemen (almost never gentlewomen) are supposed to exert some kind of influence over the assembled gaggle of executives.

You might think that in corporate America the Mafia is under better control. A respectable midwestern giant like Honeywell, for example, had only three current executives on the fourteen-man board it maintained in 1983. Honeywell's eleven nonexecutive titans, too, are all businessmen, one of them a former Honeywell boss, which follows standard U.S. practice; British companies, in the local tradition, often favor out-of-work politicians. The American system looks more sensible, safer, and less Sicilian; but, as usual in American organizations, first glances do not reveal last truths.

The outcome, on both sides of the Atlantic, is remarkably close, despite the apparent contrasts. The most obvious of these differences is the position of the *capo,* the boss. In Britain's corporate families, the chairman, who is also chief executive and managing director, surrounded only by his disciple deputies, enjoys double strength. In the United States, the chairman's job of presiding over the company is normally distinct from directing its operations. Thus General Motors has long had both a chairman and president (plus a raft of more or less powerful committees, which needn't be chaired by either potentate).

But there are plenty of exceptions: like Kidde, where Fred Sullivan, as both chairman and president, allowed his board to pay him total compensation of $2.5 million in 1983, a year when the corporation lost $124 million. Managers have the word of none other than Harold S. Geneen, the architect of ITT, writing in his recent book *Management,* that the two-hat touch is wrong. Geneen should know; as he confesses, he "wore both hats in my day, and it felt great."

The question, though, is whether it felt great for the company, and that, in the light of some of Geneen's other admissions, is far from certain. The infamous disaster in Canada, where $320 million was lost on a wood-cellulose plant to which Geneen became personally and unstoppably committed, is one example. According to *Business Week*'s review of his book, "The resulting $320 million loss, he concedes, probably could have been averted if someone had just gone to Canada and looked at the trees—which, it turned out, grew to no more than an uneconomical three inches in diameter."

Keeping the chief executive in his place—one rung down —has its virtues. Or rather, the lonely summit has its vices. First, nearly all the capo's boardroom colleagues owe their careers to him and are used to his command, so they are less likely to challenge his policies—no matter how terrible—and when the emperor's clothes fade away, it takes them far too long to see him bare.

Second, the chair's formal and ceremonial obligations eat up hours. Any portly fellow can cut the ribbons and show around the visiting firemen. Running the company requires talent and time. Like everybody else, the capo has only twenty-four hours a day. After sleep, ceremonial and publicity distractions, he's lucky to find more than twenty minutes to attend to a reasonably important division—and this assumes that he is well organized. He is far more likely to devour available time with trivia that suddenly grab his emotions. Somebody should stop him, sure—but who? Certainly not cronies who owe their nonexecutive places to his grace and favor.

Hugh Parker, of McKinsey & Co. in London, has pointed out that the CEO's job is to press good performance from his subordinates, while the chairman squeezes the CEO. But if the latter doubles as chairman, is he going to put pressure on himself? The board can't pressure the man collectively, not if the members are largely those other executives whom the chairman is pressuring in his managing director role; his subordinates will stay subordinated. One major company had a mighty capo who loved flying kites—making and half-believing outrageous propositions. In the cold light of day, he leaked stories about how his fellow directors (none of whom would say boo unless ordered) had rebuffed him. The technique is that of the Dickensian lawyer who was always willing to agree but whose unseen partner (actually entirely somnolent) would have none of it.

Within the Mafia, too, a form of *omertà* applies: the code of honor lays down nothing but good about the capo until he is dead—or gone. After departure, the stories of the great man's weaknesses, foibles, and gross errors flood out. Not even Khrushchev telling tales on Stalin exceeds the relish of a successor executive recounting the sins of a predecessor (in which the successors were as deeply implicated as any Khrushchev). For proof, hearken to Hicks B. Waldron, the man charged with turning around the fallen marketing star Avon Products, delivering himself of a few well-chosen words about the true marketing skills of the predecessor regime: "They didn't have an understanding of any of the normal levers of marketing: like pricing and product positioning, segmented advertising. Although these were things everyone else knew, they didn't."

Just to rub in the incompetence of the old inhabitants of his new Kremlin, Waldron added that "there was a lack of professional management skills and a lack of attention to what was going on in the outside world." Yet, as John Thackray observed in *Management Today,* there's a little problem here —the fact "that Waldron and most of his team are somewhat implicated in the mistakes of the past. Waldron was an Avon director for a period of three years before he became chairman." It's evidently fair to ask what he, let alone the rest of the surviving management, had been up to all that time, while Avon completed the 33 percent slide in earnings that began in 1980.

The more collective the leadership, the more collective the clinging. The code is broken only when the leadership structure itself is cracking under extreme pressure; its breach is a sign of corporate disintegration and the first stage in the battle for power. The pressure has to be intense. Executives will dance the gopak for the boss, submitting to all manner of indignities —public rebuke, being kept waiting all day outside closed doors, even (in one case) writing out copies of the chairman's thoughts—and still they won't protest. Their submission is an inevitable part of the system when a Stalin has emerged.

The business can then become more His Thing than Our Thing—but only if he, too, obeys the unwritten law. He must preserve the continuity of the corporation, by which is meant the senior executive roles within it. The upper management's desire to perpetuate itself collectively isn't easily distinguished from devotion to the company: the directors' rewards and their powers rest on preserving and defending those of the corporation. If the capo threatens the survival of the management family, therefore, he is as doomed as Joe Colombo or the late, bullet-riddled Albert Anastasia.

That even a mighty capo can overstep the bounds was demonstrated by Harry J. Gray, a chieftain who, after his feats of supermanagement in raising United Technologies to $15

billion of sales, must have seemed invulnerable to anything—
save age. With his retirement looming as of December 1985,
though, the sixty-five-year-old Gray decided that even the
years should not stand in his way—nor would the company
president, his heir apparent.

In ridding himself of the latter, however, Gray so offended
the rest of the corporate Mafia that they talked openly about
ousting the capo himself. Given his outrageous high-handed-
ness, the fact that boardroom verbiage took so long to coalesce
into action indicates how powerful a hold the capo and the code
have inside the Mafia: two months after the ejection of the heir
apparent, there was the board expressing its confidence in Gray
—and there was *Business Week* reporting the following picture
of clearheaded determination among the lesser lights: "55 percent are conservative, 20 percent haven't made up their minds,
and 25 percent say the king must go."

What's extremely unlikely is that Gray's successor, or that
of Dr. Armand Hammer at Occidental Petroleum (another
famed dispatcher of heirs apparent), will have the same unchal-
lenged suzerainty. Both Shell and ICI, which had dominant
one-man control prewar, adopted explicitly collective management—Shell with a bevy of managing directors, ICI with an
array of executive directors, none possessing direct power over
operations. A rigid written code actually sought to ensure that
the ICI chairman never would exercise the powers of chief
executive, and ICI's directors resolutely opposed a McKinsey
suggestion that somebody else on the board should.

For a glimpse of the self-protective, self-perpetuating instinct at work, take this passage by a former chairman of ICI
(the capital letters are his): ". . . in a Company as complex as
ICI, it is extremely difficult for anyone, however able, to come
in as Chairman and be an effective head of the Company.
Inevitably, his lack of knowledge of the Company's affairs
would mean the appointment of a Managing Director, who

himself would have to be so well-informed of the Company's business that it would be just as well to make him Chairman and have done with it." This neatly glossed over the fact that ICI had no intention of having a managing director in any shape or form.

It is almost as if the management Mafia, after bruising and unsettling experiences of a one-man past, had collectively breathed, "Never again." Only in the 1980s, under the pressure of the worst trading conditions the company had ever experienced, did the ICI Mafia take its courage in both hands and entrust the chairmanship to an iconoclastic, executive-minded eccentric, John Harvey-Jones. With scant respect for the past, Harvey-Jones closed down the mammoth Millbank office (known to corporate jokers as Millstone House) and took the HQ weight off divisional necks. Under this stimulus ICI even found the gumption to exit from two huge businesses, polyethylene and bulk polyester, that it had originally launched on the world. First In became First Out—the result of putting first things (like effective business management) first.

Making collective managements work is no picnic, anyway. The company tends to move at the pace of the slowest director. But this drawback is less unpalatable to some corporations than the insecurity of a capo-dominated regime—especially in times when capos (just as in the real Mafia) are getting worse at their jobs. Repeated American experiments with "a president's office," with three or more persons forming a multiple chief executive, reflect this lust for collective security. It springs from the sheer difficulty, in the system, of developing the supermanager necessary to run, single-handed, corporations on this scale, although that's no greater than the difficulty of making one of these troikas run, or (still harder) cajoling harmonious music out of a managerial quartet.

Try as it may, the cult of personality cannot hide the fact that the typical U.S. executive is interchangeable and disposable. There is nothing wrong with this absence of idols. Business management in the supercompany is not an individual but a collective process. It must operate on the assumptions that somebody other than the leader may make the best contribution; that everybody's ideas are open to criticism, especially his; and that the leader is not a giant among pygmies, but a first among equals.

In West Germany the chief executive is actually known as "the spokesman of the management board," though anybody who thinks that this phrase circumscribes the authority of a supermanager like Eberhard von Kuenheim of BMW doesn't know West Germany: some German equals are much more equal than others. Similarly, anybody who thinks that the definitely dominant, giant-among-pygmies power of a Japanese president means dictatorial management doesn't know Japan. In both countries the appearances are deceptive; the reality, in the best companies, combines clear and decisive leadership from the top with strong contributions all the way down.

The Japanese even have a system, the famous *ringi,* for ensuring that every department, and every manager who is concerned, is involved before a decision is taken. That doesn't safeguard against mistakes—minor, middling, or calamitous. Witness Yamaha's attempt to catch Honda napping in the domestic motorbike market, which resulted in a bloodbath of overproduction and price slashing. The whole bizarre episode culminated in the near destruction of the Yamaha parent's finances and the swift expulsion of the motorbike boss into outer darkness. For in Japan, as in West Germany (where two VW chief executives in succession were ousted), the supreme responsibility carries with it the supreme sacrifice in the event of failure, absolute or relative. The United States, in contrast, has all too many examples of CEOs clinging to power, with the full support of the management Mafia, despite long erosion of earnings, or calamitous acquisitions, or both.

Executives won't take actions that are inimical to their own interests; they will always be tempted by decisions that directly benefit them, never mind the corporation. When one company proposed to merge fully with its own foreign subsidiary, a minor consequence was that the parent directors would no longer sit on the Paris company's board. At the meeting that discussed the merger, five and one half hours out of six were spent on this issue. One director protested that if he lost his regular lunches in Paris, "It will be the beginning of communism in this company."

On the Continent the system of dual boards (with the supervisors appointing the executives) is meant to purify this impure relationship. But the German supervisory board is just as feeble as the annual general meeting in Britain or America. The supervisors meet infrequently; nearly all promotions and appointments are from within the existing management; and the upper management of big German companies forms as heavy, impregnable, and self-respecting a body of men as an American pro football lineup.

Even at Krupp, where otiose mistakes ran the company into a horrible cash predicament, the top management echelon was hardly affected by the removal (through political pressure and the still more certain accident of death) of the last of the Krupps. By the nature of things, the upper tier of a two-tier board is seldom more than a gold-handled rubber stamp.

The Americans, technically ingenious as ever, have a two-in-one-tier system. The chairman, supported by the nonexecutive numerical majority on the board, is supposed to safeguard the long-term interests of the corporation (meaning, to establish corporate policy) as well as to cherish the stockholder. A finance committee, usually chaired by someone outside executive management, often grips the purse strings—especially the fixing of the directors' pay and perquisites, which is the most Cosa Nostra–like activity of the British boardroom. (One boss

maintained that a small nonexecutive knot on his board likewise ensured that executive fingers didn't wander into the
money box. Since the nonexecutives included his father-in-law,
he may have been right.)

The U.S. system seems to recognize and regularize the fact
that a company's executive officers develop a vested interest in
their own actions and their own status. The American board
is in theory designed to guarantee that the vested interests don't
jeopardize the interests of the company as a whole. Except that
it doesn't work that way. In the first place, the chairman is
often a full-time executive, previously president of the company, a charter member of the Mafia.

At least he knows and understands the business and the
men who run it (which is more than can be said of most
nonexecutive chairmen). But poachers seldom turn gamekeeper. Bitterness can creep in; but the president is usually the
chairman's boy, his protégé; and a president turned chairman
won't challenge the entire basis of the upper management's
operations and plans—after all, he was the genius who formed
them.

Nor are nonexecutives, however expert in their own rackets, in much of a position to question the wisdom and integrity
of the managerial elite, represented on the board by its senior
group. Realism dictates that nonexecutive directors are in the
hands of the top executives from whom all information comes.
Any moderately astute executive can fend off a nonexecutive
outsider (half of the latter's questions are likely to be silly, and
the outsider never knows which half).

This assumes, anyway, that the American company chairman or president, serving as a nonexecutive on another board,
wants to make life uncomfortable for the other boss who (very
likely) asked him to join. The invitee isn't a fool. He has a board
of his own, with the same situation, and he doesn't want to be
uncomfortable, either. Consequently, the you-scratch-my-

back-and-I'll-scratch-yours philosophy gets built into the corporate system, or you-serve-on-my-board-and-I'll-serve-on-yours. A wider management conspiracy, the presidents' and chairmen's club, gets superimposed on the narrower one of the company.

Managers get blackballed from the club and cast into outer darkness only for gross transgressions against the rules —and even then it takes time, and too much of it. Chrysler once had a boss who (like most Chrysler postwar bosses) wasn't very successful at running Chrysler and got involved in a scandal about his own business transactions with the company; it was a long wait before he was expelled. But really bad behavior is not the problem, because appalling misconduct will eventually break up the management Mafia, which (again like its criminal counterpart) can sometimes be exceedingly inefficient.

The real trouble lies in the self-perpetuation of the mediocre: of executives who are never brilliant and never atrocious, but whose use of the assets is less effective than the dumbest stockholder could manage for himself. There is no easy escape. The company is the upper management, and the upper management is the company, for as long as executives maintain an acceptable level of competence (or incompetence). Pressure rarely comes from inside because of the rare emergence of individuals outstanding enough to apply it. It can come from outside only because of a change or incipient change in ownership—mostly in the form of a takeover bid or, in other words, from the injection of insecurity.

Human beings clustered in any group will always seek security, and that is the enemy of dynamic business management. The fairy Blackstick in Thackeray's *The Rose and the Ring* wished the princelings "a little misfortune" as her christening present. It made them into excellent rulers. A little insecurity might do wonders for managements everywhere, for the idea that business life is short and nasty is an illusion sponsored by the Hollywood dream factory; most executives, though they talk and even think differently, sleep safe enough in their nests.

Anybody who doubts this should consider two exhibits. First, to quote *Forbes* magazine, "Some of the nation's finest businessmen were on the board at Continental Illinois. What were they doing for their fees?" The eleven worthies presumably sat there pocketing their $15,000 apiece without raising Cain while the bank slid into the losses, primarily on overly aggressive energy loans, that necessitated the biggest financial rescue in banking history: $7.5 billion. Second, an august witness for the prosecution states that "among the boards of directors of *Fortune* 500 companies, I estimate that 95 percent are not fully doing what they are legally, morally, and ethically supposed to do. And they couldn't, even if they wanted to." Why? Partly because "management does 90 percent to 95 percent of the talking. Outside board members, who are not part of the management, sit there and listen; then they go to lunch, and then go home and open the envelopes that contain their fees."

The writer is Harold S. Geneen, who should know whereof he speaks. As boss of ITT, his will was law. As a nonexecutive director thereafter, he is widely credited with having stymied efforts by his overburdened successors to lighten their load by selling some of Geneen's own bad buys. Had Geneen not been the former executive corporate godfather, of course, nobody would have taken the slightest notice of him. Poacher turned would-be gamekeeper, Geneen now wants to remove all management members, including the chief executive, from the board, which would have an "independent management auditor" at its disposal to "check policies and performance" in the same way as financial figures are already checked (though, given the high failure rate of the latter checks, this proposal shows truly touching faith).

The former ITT czar hopes that all this would result in "an informed board of outsiders, led by one of its members as chairman," with a "quality and intensity of board meetings at a level not seen for many years." Oh, yeah? The fact is that no company can be managed from the boardroom. The real changes have to take place in the executive suite itself. Executives who want to be insecure can easily arrange it. No contractual hiring, no compensation for loss of office, no golden parachutes or handshakes, all nominations to the board entrusted to a committee of investors, salaries and other financial benefits submitted for approval to the same committee before ratification by the annual general meeting, executive directors' stockholdings (and their families') held in nonvoting trust while they remain executives, and no chief executive allowed to double as chairman. Such conditions wouldn't guarantee the breakup of the management Mafia, but they would increase the chances of Our Thing being managed as Their Thing—"they" being the outside stockholders.

14

The Risk-Taking
Delusion

Management theory is obsessed with risks. Top executives be-
moan the lack of risk-taking initiative among their young.
Politicians and stockholders are advised (by directors) to make
directors rich, so that they can afford to take risks. Theorists
teach how to construct decision trees, heraldic devices of scientific management; and how to marry the trees with probability
theory, so that the degree of risk along each branch (each
branch and twig representing alternative results of alternative
courses of action) can be metered. But the measuring is spurious, and, anyway, the best management doesn't take risks. It
avoids them. It goes for the sure thing.

The greater the risk, very obviously, the smaller the case
for embracing the project at all. Risk-taking holds its pride of
place among the management virtues only because it's a sin of
which most managers are guilty. They need no urging to take

chances. The most purblind old buffer in the boardroom will cheerfully approve ventures of total insecurity. The monstrous chances that directors take with other people's money are often unwitting, but they are still risks. And executives who take great risks, whatever folklore says, are as dangerous to a company as a crooked accountant.

The great and fabled business empires, with hardly an exception, were built, not on outlandish risks, but on irresistible ideas of elemental simplicity. This is not just hindsight. From the Model T and the chain stores to semiconductors, instant photographs, and personal computers, the great entrepreneurs have taken available methods and married them to burning market needs. A peddler named Michael Marks decided to sell every object on his stall under one slogan—Don't ask the price, it's a penny. From that moment, the main lines of development of the Marks and Spencer chain were fixed: simplicity (the price limited the merchandise); control over supplies (if you wanted to sell everything for a penny, you had to buy everything for under a penny); value for money; and a uniform trading policy. Risk hardly came into the idea.

A marvelous, risk-free whim, such as Henry Ford's mass production to serve a mass market, can survive grotesque mismanagement. Ford lost $8.5 million in the 1930s, as Henry I bungled the challenge of Chevrolet, fell into the toils of the gangsterish Harry Bennett, and tortured his son, Edsel. He still died richer than Croesus—because sales went on proving, in their millions, that it takes a genius even more perverse than Ford's to ruin the commercial career of a great idea.

Terrible disasters (such as the oversized, overpriced, and monstrously designed Edsel car put out by Henry's grandson) likewise result from gross and elementary errors of concept, not from marginal mistakes in abstruse calculations like discounted cash flow. Yet intelligent men plump for one project rather than another on the strength of a difference of a few decimal points in the rate of return calculated over the next decade. All such mind-stretching calculation comes under the lash of the Seventh Truth of Management: *if you need sophisticated calculations to justify an action, it is probably wrong* (the sophisticated calculations, anyway, are all too often based on simple false assumptions). A rider to this is Shun any project that, if all goes according to plan, will just earn its keep. In real life, hardly anything follows the script. What sensible executives seek is the project whose margins are so wild that, if it actually works out, they can all retire to the Bahamas.

Most businesses meet only three classes of major investment decision—the inevitable, the optional, and the make-or-break. Only the last involves risk in the classic sense. The first category includes embarrassments such as new steel, paper, or cement works. Nobody interested in profits would build these expensive encumbrances today; but failure to expand in step with the competition guarantees slow atrophy in a business to which (because of its deadly concentration of fixed assets) the company is bound in perpetuity.

Factory extensions, modernization of machinery, even important product changes are usually fixed by market forces, not by managerial choice. The risk here is to do nothing—like Gillette when first confronted with the Wilkinson blade—or to do the inevitable at ruinous cost and delay, at which American steelmakers have proved adept. Gillette's forlorn hope that the stainless-steel blade would rust away was matched by the resolute conviction of Detroit car-makers that small-sized imports were a passing fad. The fad passed, all right: it passed into a permanent feature of the market, one that cost Detroit billions in lost sales, and billions more in a belated effort to catch up —not once but twice. Part of the effective executive's armory is a sense of when the rape of his profitability is inevitable.

The second category is where the company has a choice, and the decision, either way, will leave a viable business. This is where rashes of big mistakes are made—extending a product range into new markets, diversifying into new fields, merging with another company. The basic mistake is often not to recognize that any risk exists—for instance, in mergers, one of the most promising disaster areas. The error is usually compounded by refusal to cut losses. Sir Alexander Maclean, the toothpaste king, knew better. One of his associates recalled, "Maclean tried all sorts of things, but he exploited those which were successful and cut out those which were not." It's hardly a difficult technique.

By making really addlepated decisions in these optional matters, a corporation can even and very quickly disprove the original assumption—that the viability of the company will be unaffected. That was sadly true of the two companies mentioned in Chapter 10, Wickes and Baldwin-United, both of which castrated themselves by the purely voluntary purchase of companies they couldn't afford. Financial services have been a federal disaster area for big companies seeking to spread their risks, but succeeding only in making these risks vastly greater. What business does a steel corporation have going into insurance? Very bad business, if you take the example of Armco. In 1982 and 1983 its financial services added $181 million of losses on top of the steel horrors to produce combined losses of $1 billion. The financial flop was on an original investment of $270 million.

Over at Sears Roebuck the big push into financial services with Dean Witter turned the latter's investment banking operation, according to a former executive quoted in *Business Week,* into "a real mess. You could not have messed things up more definitively if you had tried." The cost of the mess? In the first half of 1984, $21.2 million. Unlike Baldwin-United, a $1.3 billion-profit giant like Sears, even a sick steel company like Armco, can take such reverses without much teetering. But in the process of committing their gratuitous follies, the big boys destroy or damage the perfectly good smaller firms that they bought.

More commonly, calamity follows from failures in the third main area of decision making, the make-or-break variety, where the entire company hangs on success or failure. In most of these cases, compelling truth lies behind management's mental processes. Chrysler had to widen its penetration of the U.S. car market to survive its near bankruptcy. When defense business seemed to be in long-term decline, only civil airlines offered Lockheed a growing market for its talents.

Coleco had to bring out an impossible computer package, with superperformance at a superlow price, to have any chance in a market dominated by the likes of Commodore and Apple. The loss when the Adam failed to appear on schedule and to specification was $7.3 million in 1983—devastating the year of Coleco's Cabbage Patch Kid triumph. To get back into a home entertainment market swamped by the Japanese and unable to compete itself in VCRs, RCA had to plunge into the rival disc system or else get out of its Japanese rivals' way.

Rather than do just that—get out—the executive, despite his alleged caution, goes for all or nothing; and nothing is often what he gets. Actually, RCA got far less than nothing —a write-off totaling $580 million when it had to exit, like it or not, with its chairman, Thornton Bradshaw, making the immortal remark to *Fortune* magazine that "No one's to blame. This is a risk company, and we're going to take more risks in future." The finest economy of scale, from the executive's point of view, is that size, like RCA's $9 billion of assets, can bury monumental mistakes. Divisions of Ford and General Dynamics both survived the two greatest commercial errors up to then, the Edsel and the Convair jetliner, because even losses of $400 million (especially after tax offsets) can be absorbed within empires whose assets total $9.9 billion or $1 billion. The stockholder pays the tab: Ford's earnings per share over the Edsel era rose by little more than 2 percent annually.

Even in big companies, whatever the Bradshaws of this world say, executives don't take brave risks. They make foolish errors. Like politicians, executives have a genius for compounding bad policies with worse execution. The Eighth Truth of Management is: *if you are doing something wrong, you will do it badly.* The reverse of this truth is that, if your decision is blindingly right, you will execute it well—or appear to do so, which is much the same thing. But any executive can massacre his own nonsensical project. The correct decision for RCA was to put all its resources behind joining the Japanese in the VCR market, rather than to try beating them—especially with a product that lacked the essential recording facility. In marketing the thing, RCA added mistakes in pricing and estimates of market size to its basic misunderstanding of what the customers wanted. The company never got even remotely near its targets (840,000 had been sold against 8 million VCRs when the plug was pulled). Yet its people continued to pursue the impossible like knights after the Holy Grail.

Similarly, nobody in the air industry believed in the original specifications of one bright new airliner, or in the fabulously low cost of its development, or in massive orders promised by its distributor. This little dreamboat was supposed to carry up to two dozen passengers. "Sure it can," grunted one competitor, "if they're all gnomes." Ironically, the company had some real-life orders, from the ever-ready Department of Defense, for the greatly changed, far more expensive model with which the company eventually and inevitably crashed.

Make-or-break risks can make it—as Apple had desperate reason to hope when it launched the Macintosh computer in 1983. Rapid acceptance of the new machine, with its far-easier-to-use technology, was the only way to ensure the very survival as a company of Silicon Valley's brightest star, the venture-capital triumph to beat them all—and which really did beat all predecessors in speed to the billion-dollar turnover mark. In Apple's case, the answers to a host of subsidiary questions turned out to be adequately encouraging.

Was the Apple name and image still strong enough to sell against the might of IBM? Had it retained enough market share, after being massively clobbered by IBM, to serve as a base for the new range? Could the company finance the project, including an advertising budget immensely beyond its previous outlays? Could Macintosh win enough sales fast enough to promise major profits (which meant, also, could Apple get the new product into production at the right time in the right quantity, with the right quality)? Was the market for personal computers likely to continue growing?

At Chrysler, too, Lee Iacocca had to pour everything he could beg or borrow into the K auto. A rise in sales, based on an entirely new automobile family, was the only way to ensure survival as a company: the successful wooing of the banks and the federal government was only the sine qua non of bringing that family into life. The subsidiary questions were perfectly clear too. Were the Chrysler name and image still viable? Could the company finance the project? Was the U.S. car market likely to improve in the years of the K model's life? On reasonable assumptions about demand, could the break-even point be brought low enough to yield a handsome profit?

These were not computer-bending problems. But the greater the primary risk, the safer and more careful your secondary assumptions must be. A project is only as sound as its weakest assumption, or its largest uncertainty.

Companies reach true make-or-break points only because of risky errors. Apple reached crisis point because of failure to anticipate the entry of IBM into PCs, failure to bring its organization and marketing up to billion-dollar scratch as its situation demanded. Lockheed had to go for broke, and in much less favorable circumstances, with the Tristar because of its flop on the Electra. It took years of mismanagement and bad autos to reduce Chrysler to the most parlous plight of any major U.S. company. RCA had a history of missed opportunities (failing to seize the dominant position in the color TV market it had long pioneered) and bungled forays into new areas (dropping another half billion on trying to live with IBM in computers).

RCA was not alone, of course, in thinking that, despite its lack of experience in business machines, it could breach the walls of Fortress IBM. These competitors saddled themselves with projects based on implausible assumptions; for instance: first, that the merits of advanced technology would of themselves sway the market; second, that the machines would get into production on schedule and work when produced; third, that if the first two assumptions were wrong, the company could afford the cash drain. Nobody has calculated how much, if RCA's and General Electric's computer losses are added to those of Honeywell, Bull, Burroughs, and so on, such risks cost the IBM rivals, but the number must be well into the billions, and all, remember, for a negative return.

If you seek to eliminate all risk, you risk something else —eliminating all enterprise and innovation. Nine times out of ten, this may be to the stockholders' benefit. But what about the tenth time? What about those unsung ghosts of American business—the IBM man who turned down the Univac computer, the du Pont executive who showed the inventor of xerography the door, the Kodak man who turned up his nose at Polaroid? Right back to the men who thought the horseless carriage had no future, business history is haunted by the memories of missed opportunities. But the unsung ghosts weren't frightened away by risk; like bureaucrats everywhere, they couldn't see the opportunity.

General David Sarnoff certainly could. He gambled, by the standards of his time, when he pumped $50 million into commercial TV. He took an equal gamble, apparently, in backing color TV in the 1950s, for $130 million more. But the odds were much shorter than they looked. Sarnoff's RCA was the only set-maker that could take the gamble because its NBC network could transmit (at a loss) the color programs without which, clearly, nobody would buy a set. And was color TV really a gamble? Color had taken over the cinema screen, and was as certain as anything in life to take over TV.

Sarnoff's only risk was of being too early—as he was, both technically and commercially. RCA still made a mint. But remember what happened in a virgin market where Sarnoff was not building on his know-how or his assets—those computers again. Just like GE, RCA had to throw in its hand: all its risk-taking had bought was a $500 million loss plus a diversion of corporate time and attention that lost the company the lead in these very markets in consumer electronics where the general's early, bold pioneering should have given Sarnoff's successors—and not the Japanese—the right rewards for the right decisions.

Faced with a decision, always ask one implacable question: If this project fails, if the worst comes to the worst, what will be the result? If the answer is total corporate disaster, drop the project. If the worst possible outcome is tolerable, say, break-even, the executive has the foundation of all sound decision making—a fail-safe position. Heads I win, tails I don't lose, may not sound madly adventurous, but that way, the executive always wins. As played in many companies, the game is Heads I lose, tails I don't win, and that is a pastime for idiots.

Many a tycoon has fostered his fortune by astute acquisition on the belt-and-suspenders principle. These canny fellows keep up their trousers by never buying any business unless the realizable assets (cash, the real estate, and so forth) cover their total cost, so the trading side is in for free. When BTR bought Dunlop's billion-plus of sales for £101 million in 1984, it was a comforting thought that the American tire business was salable —and a few weeks later, it duly fetched £104 million in a management buyout: making the net cash cost minus £39 million. Where tycoons make mistakes (and they all do), you usually find it's because they've ceased to obey their own rules —buying earnings instead of assets, say, or paying more than a dollar for a dollar of sales. Managers and magnates alike should stick to their maxims. In any business, remember that the object of good management is not just to maximize profits, or growth rates, or market share but to maximize them at minimized risk.

15

Serving
the Super Chief

Call an industrial chieftain incompetent, and he won't love you. Tell him he has laid a Grade A egg, and he will argue. But call his company a one-man band, and he will be furious—especially if it is. The natural tendency for powerful men is to dominate, and the natural instinct of those who serve them is to be dominated. One-man bands, moreover, are quick to spot each other—what they can't recognize is themselves. They are blinded by the received idea, in a democratic age, that one-man bands are a particularly heinous form of bad management.

When the ideal is the nebulous team, nobody likes to admit that he personally makes every decision—major, minor, or minimal; that his senior disciples, after years as yes-men, could never rule independently; that he lusts for supreme authority and would wither away without it. One such chief executive, whose brilliant dictatorship was as emotional as

Wuthering Heights, maintained less a headquarters staff than a court. The courtiers sat on long into afternoons or evenings listening to monologues that, although fascinating at first hearing, palled by the ninety-first. Yet the tycoon would never admit that his company had little top management, just him.

One day, when the master's behavior became too erratic to bear, the worms turned. Looking back on the debacle, the ousted chieftain philosophically admitted the truth. "The trouble was," he said, "that the company was a one-man band." In any company, and in any area of management, it's better to face the truth at the time when it hurts—and possibly helps.

There happen to be real managerial advantages for the one-man band, but self-deception can lose or offset all of them. The advantages are not in any textbook, because the reasons that make them great also make them nontransferable—they harness the working forces of a corporation to one highly personalized and identifiable driving power.

In logic and in fact, one man can't run a group of ten thousand, or thirty thousand, or eighty thousand, or two hundred thousand people—though some do try. There are chief executives who pass on *all* capital expenditure, right down to typewriters; others who approve all foreign travel; and others who operate a private KGB to discover what's happening before their underling bosses know it themselves. All this is totally illogical. But management is not logic. One unusual man can impress his personality on a gigantic organization, not only so that he knows, controls, and influences everything in the present, but so that for years into the future the company will live in his shadow.

This needn't be because of transcendent genius. True, the pervasive force of personality will also be generated by the abiding power of a transcendent idea—like Texan Charles W. Tandy's notion of combining a chain of radio and electrical stores, some franchised, with factories making the products they sold. Years after Tandy's early death, that inspiration was still the largest visible and invisible asset of the corporation he built.

Yet when the steam started running out of radio, hi-fi, and the like, Tandy was saved by something else—not by another flourish of the Great Man's genius, but by the combination of his personal power with an unplanned product: the home computer. At one point Tandy, through its Radio Shack stores, became the second-largest computer company (by numbers of machines sold) after IBM. It happened only because an engineer hobbyist in Tandy's employ had been playing about with computer kits. The manufacturing people got wind of this and decided to develop the thing into prototype form, just for the heck of it.

The resulting masterpiece was set up on the premises one day when Tandy happened to be passing through. After the computer had been briefly put through its paces, the Great Man said, "Let's make a thousand. If we can't sell 'em, we can always use 'em in our own stores." This was taken as the go-ahead. But when the management accountants worked out the costs, a thousand made no sense. So Tandy built 3,000; before very long orders for 10,000 had flooded in for the most expensive product the company had ever sold.

There's a reason why the aura of great men lives on after them, and not just in business. Thus the British Broadcasting Corporation is still within the aura of its first boss, Lord Reith, and the FBI won't finally escape from J. Edgar Hoover for decades. In business the great founder-entrepreneurs have the same supernatural impact—Henry Ford; the first Lord Leverhulme, creator of the British half of Unilever; or Thomas Watson, Sr., builder of IBM. The company is run as their personal property. The continued exercise of their property rights is founded on business genius, personal charisma, and family stockholdings. Such one-man orchestration is perfectly acceptable, up to a point.

If a mighty entrepreneur can raise the earnings and the stock price year after year, it hardly matters to stockholders that he also plays the dictator. It probably doesn't matter to his executives either. Many people love having every decision made for them, and executives are no exception. At least the one-man band makes the decisions, and usually at high speed. Delay makes a good decision worse and seldom improves a bad one. If the dictator is a genius, the decisions may even be right. The odds favor him more than the rest of mankind. He, after all, is the company, absolutely identified with its purposes and potential. And he has, by creating the empire, shown the energy that makes a good decision work—and can sometimes save a bad one from its badness. But no man's genius lasts forever, and the longer he reigns, the more seeds of decay get planted.

The travails of Texas Instruments, one of the most talented corporations in the States, are thus widely blamed on the founding management's reluctance to let go, and much the same song has been sung about Digital Equipment, Hewlett-Packard, and Control Data. Although the characters concerned were not particularly old, their industries are so new and moving so fast that age has become strictly relative; just as a 15-year-old dog is 105 in human equivalents, so a 40-year-old supermanager in electronics may be two decades older in real terms.

Few people now doubt that the supreme businessman/inventor of the postwar years, Polaroid's Edwin H. Land, hung on too long (into his seventies) for the good of the company. Discontinued disasters like Texas Instruments' ventures into digital watches and Tandy-rivaling home computers, or long-running failures like Polaroid's declining sales, are monuments to the dead, or deathly, hand of dominant heroes. Japan provides more constructive lessons—for instance, that of Soichiro Honda, who quit at sixty-three (quoting lack of competence in computers and insufficient appetite for saké and sex).

In his valedictory, Honda revealed that neither he as chairman nor his president had seen any executive committee papers for ten years. During all that time, though, the two men had guided their successors and the corporate strategy to ensure, as best they could (which was in high degree), that the corporation would outlive them—as Japanese ideology demands. In the West, too, the good that a great manager does should be interred in the success of the business he leaves behind—and that, almost by definition, means that he cannot be a total dictator.

Few really able men will work indefinitely under an autocrat. Those who do either lose the habit of making decisions or never get the experience: either way, there's no adequate succession. Anyway, dictators dislike having strong men behind their backs—though most, for some deep psychological reason, have an *éminence grise,* a longtime, shy associate whose special expertise, usually technical, keeps him out of power's way. (One tycoon, in a verbal use that would have delighted Freud, called his eminence his "day wife.") Another harmful quirk is that many one-man bands are also bullies—though, again, many executives like to be bullied. But victims won't turn into heroes after the bully quits; they are more likely to be punch-drunk or to follow willy-nilly too closely in the footsteps of Land or whatever other father figure used to rule the corporate roost.

A study of successful "mid-sized" American companies by a couple of McKinsey men, Richard E. Cavanagh and Donald K. Clifford, found that succession was a particularly critical issue: "The personality and drive of a builder chief executive are so pervasive and important that his loss and replacement can be a severe shock to the organization. Many of the ones interviewed suggested that no high-growth company has fully proved itself until it has undergone the transition to a new chief executive once or twice."

It's hard to argue with that thinking. Neither is it easy to contradict the general proposition that the best guide to a man's ability is that of his successor. The timing of the succession is decisive too. The presiding genius may be the last to understand that his best days are over, and terrible erosion can follow while he blindly hangs on. Many companies have known what it felt like in Nero's Rome: the decaying emperor fiddles while the city burns. In one case, the other directors were just alert enough to take evasive action. They got the founder-chairman to agree that a new executive committee would make all decisions before matters reached the main board. The committee was identical to the board—except that the chairman was left out. But mostly the decision to relax the iron fist has to come from the dictator himself, and this is the one decision he will not make.

It will eventually be made for him, if not by palace revolution, then by illness, fatigue, or death. Then comes the moment of truth. The autocrat has to pass the same test as any dictator (dead, deposed, or departed); does he leave behind an organization that—like Sears Roebuck after General James Wood—shows great continuity, flexible strength, and regenerative powers? Or does he—as in Ford Motor after Henry Ford I—leave behind a shambles, capable of losing $22 million in a single quarter?

The key is that men like Wood, for all their pervasive personalities, are so deeply interested in organization that their bands are orchestras. They express their egos through the systems they build; they have their eccentricities, but they don't manage through eccentric egos alone. The one-man band, in contrast, rarely has organizing ability. He convinces himself that he is an organizer, and easily convinces others—for arguing with success is even harder than admitting to failure.

But what looks like effective organization is the working through of that tremendous personal urge. Remove the drive, along with the person, or bring the drive up against some unexpected obstacle, and the apparently well-organized company tears apart. Maybe this is legitimate if the company really is the dictator's personal property. What a man creates, he is ostensibly entitled to destroy. But a great industrialist's empire can rapidly transcend the scale of one ego. Henry Ford I retained the power to destroy Ford Motor; he no longer had the right.

The proprietorial boss may well lack the ability to sense the destructive effect of his own management style on his own organization. There's a sad little story about Heinz Durr, who, according to *Manager* magazine, "was a successful Stuttgart manufacturer of paint shops for the motor industry when he was brought in by the ailing AEG [a vast and badly mismanaged electrical group] to kick it back into shape and profitability. He seems to have made a success of this assignment, but now has to worry about his own business, where things have been going wrong and various plants have to be closed." The proprietor owes too much to the executive colleagues and other workers who helped make him rich to neglect either the present or the future.

This applies far more to the professional director. The man who doesn't own the business has a particular obligation to follow the footsteps of Alfred P. Sloan, who created order out of primeval chaos at General Motors, and to shun the example of Henry Ford. As the paid servant of the company, the pro has no property rights. He must expect to be judged severely on short-term results (though he isn't); he must also demonstrate that he is *not* indispensable (which he isn't). The professional executive has no excuse for one-man bandmanship. But powerful forces push him that way; precious few countervailing forces hold him back; and who can resist an invitation to play God (the internal nickname of many a chief executive)?

The difference between proprietors and professionals is not really understood. The pro is expected to play the part of the founding genius, without having the latter's mystery ingredient X, which is his two-way identification, as owner and creator, with the company. True, the pro identifies with the upper management and with his own ego, but that's a different matter entirely.

The public can't tell this difference. It lionizes the management hero by instinct; it dangles before him the front cover of *Forbes* or *Business Week,* or membership on the president's blue-chip panel of business leaders. The public does this because it dearly loves a leader. This is the one argument in favor of the one-man band that its critics will accept. Everybody believes that leadership is a supreme human attribute—it even gets praised in school reports. But in management terms, leadership is a greatly overrated quality.

The British, with their long tradition of war, kings, aristocrats, and empire, have an innate tendency to fall down in worship before chairmen, headmasters, prime ministers, royalty, and commanding officers. The Americans are blinded by their recurrent desire for "a man on horseback" and by simple refusal to believe that anybody who has made millions, floated to the top of a large corporation, or both, can be an idiot. But at least Americans used to be quicker on the draw when the leader failed. The British often don't shoot until they have been staring at the whites of a failed capo's eyes for years, and sometimes they never fire at all. In high-technology traumas, lack of leadership has seldom been the agent of fate. If anything, the companies have suffered from an excess of being led. Under the one-man command of leaders who could have charged the Light Brigade into suicide, these companies, too, have headed straight for the enemy's guns.

The story goes that one ennobled, embattled, and really leading leader of industry was persuaded to spend three hours with a great and wise guru of real management. The guru emerged, shaking his head, and told the other directors, "It's up to you boys. I can't do a thing with him." One of them ventured in and asked the peerless leader how it had gone. "Very well," he replied, "he said the way I manage this company is perfect." As the highly led company gets bigger, and the high leader gets more heavily laden with outside activities and honors, he loses contact with reality. (Founder-entrepreneurs are more reluctant to take on outside commitments than professional one-man bands—another vital clue to the difference between them.)

Very easily, the dominating concept, the informing element, of all managerial work in the company becomes, not what is right but what will Mr. This or Mr. That agree to. This is only acceptable if the boss himself is consistently correct; but in eight cases out of ten, he will at some point become consistently wrong, and the consequences will show in the company's figures—not in calamity usually, but in mediocrity.

In the two exceptions, as long as the one-man bands are fit, in form and in situ, the company will run surprisingly, even magically, well. But even here their refusal to admit to their solitary power means that no action gets taken to prepare the corporation for their inevitable departure. This danger can only be countered by a simple rule: compulsory appointment of a new chief executive when the old one is sixty, compulsory final abdication of the old buzzard at sixty-five, and stick to it. Don't be like one formerly great food chain, where the retiring age of sixty-five was theoretical and "the older anyone was, the more theoretical it became."

In this sorry instance, the viability of the business became increasingly theoretical, too, and, mainly from that cause: aging, inept management. First dismembered, then disappeared, it merely provided bargains on which other, smarter managers fed. Never mind that the towering tyrant is still doing ninety sit-ups every morning and can outrun, outtalk, and outdeal any man in the room, the earlier he has to go, the more likely he is to think about the succession with an un-warped mind and to create some kind of organization to go with it. At Beecham, when the founding tyrant died, "All the performing seals got down from their barrels and began to fight," remarked one executive of the time. At another empire, when the elderly colossus finally came down off his plinth, there was no scrap—the old man had brought in a handpicked successor from outside. This, too, broke a simple rule: the more dominant a man is, the less he should be allowed to name his own successor.

For subconscious reasons, great men select successors who will not surpass the great one. Proprietorial one-man bands usually have this guaranteed for them by nature. Most have sons, nearly always inadequate copies of the master de-sign, ready to step into father's oversized shoes. There is an immortal (and doubtless unfair) remark about Robert Sarnoff, boss of RCA in succession to founder General David Sarnoff. The son, said some jester, joined the company at the bottom —but then his father took a fancy to him.

As in the case of the food chain, nemesis followed nepo-tism. The Sarnoff II regime was marked, and marred, by the massive losses incurred on computers before RCA capitulated to IBM; by destructive office politics, one of whose victims was eventually Bobby Sarnoff himself; and by the trail of consumer product errors that ended in the video disc humiliation. It says much for the strength of the general's creative power, if little for his son's, that RCA survived with $9 billion of sales. But the negative 1973–83 growth in earnings per share, and still more the fact that *Fortune* now classes the one-time giant of consumer electronics as a nonindustrial company, is testimony to the terrible damage that a badly managed succession can achieve.

Men cannot bear the idea that others will say of their successor, "Of course, he's done much better than old So-and-so." A Stalin chooses a Malenkov to succeed him, a Churchill picks an Eden. The man most likely to succeed is the man least likely to disturb his predecessor's legacy; yet counterrevolution, no matter how brilliant the past, is almost certainly a necessity at the moment of inheritance. This is true even where the ruler genuinely created a superb organization. Counterrevolution was badly needed for years, but not provided, at Sloan's General Motors, where the corporate constipation of the 1960s was already causing bad outbreaks of spots in overseas car operations (the Continent and Australia) and in the small-car market in the United States: spots that, although clearly visible in those far-off days, were allowed to develop into a near-deadly, debilitating disease in less than a decade.

The ideally wise one-man band would know these risks. So the third simple rule for producing discord-free corporate music is gradually to disengage—to reach the point of domination from a distance. You don't have to emulate the ghostly manner of a Howard Hughes (who, incidentally, was for a long time a highly effective director, even though he never saw, and seldom spoke to, any of his executives). But it is possible to animate a company brilliantly without day-to-day interference. The most successful of modern oilmen in the United States, some believe, is Robert O. Anderson of Atlantic Richfield, who only comes near the corporate headquarters twice a month and is sometimes incommunicado for weeks. Unfortunately, self-control is rare in self-centered successes; and absolute power tends, just as Lord Acton said, to corrupt absolutely. The essential weakness of the one-man band is that it establishes a closed circle, in which only the one-man leader can act against his vices. There is no way around this: his ultimate privilege is to be the first Gadarene swine over the edge.

16

The Eighteen-Hour Cynosures

The ethic of Western society dictates that to work hard is good. By extension, to work harder than anybody else is, therefore, to be better than everybody else. Since the only measure of an executive's work is the time spent, the hardest-working executive is clearly the man who puts in the longest hours: the eighteen-hours-a-day paragon. No normal executive would boast that he worked only three hours a day, no matter how superlative his performance. But corporate annals regularly feature the tycoon who (in the words of that great business musical, *The Pajama Game*) can hardly wait to get to work at eight. Hardly anybody worries about the abnormality (and sheer physical impossibility) of the eighteen-hour business jam session.

Once upon a time it made sense for the boss to get in first and leave last—then he could keep a constant eye on the till.

But in the great modern corporation, without a till to its name, the boss keeps shopkeeper's hours for one reason only—to satisfy his ego. In itself, there is nothing wrong with this hobby. A man who has clambered to the top of a business empire deserves some pleasures. But the pastime has unpleasant and sometimes serious consequences for the company and its other executives.

The eighteen-hour chief executive is unlikely to fancy working all alone in an empty office: he wants company. So secretaries and subordinates have to appear at the same unearthly hour, but for less good cause. One dynamo regularly employed two young management recruits as personal assistants. In theory, they were being groomed for future stardom; in practice, they served as early morning and late evening acolytes at the great man's altar, and later starring roles were supposed to be rewards for the service. It seldom worked out that way, simply because the brightest and best young men (or women) won't serve as anybody's lackey.

Young men are resilient and probably suffer little ineradicable harm; but older men, including the dynamo's directors, also get sucked into the same maw. If the chief executive summons a divisional manager to a breakfast conference or a 7:00 A.M. meeting, the subordinate may be man enough to refuse, but he will quail in his boots. Gradually, the whole working life of the executive suite revolves around the eccentric timetable of the perpetual motion machine at the top.

One personnel consultant felt obliged to tell a company chairman that the corporate organization could not survive in the same form after he stepped down. No conceivable successor would work the same punishing routine, starting before dawn had even cracked. Nor, judged by the results, would anybody want to. That chief executive was Daniel B. Haughton of Lockheed, which was about to sail into the Galaxy, Cheyenne, and Tristar disasters—the greatest triple threat in the troubled history of aerospace.

It doesn't follow that, if Haughton had worked on a saner regime, the company would have gotten its sums right. But equally, it didn't follow that, because the chief executive was a glutton for hard hours, the company would win success, avoid error, and fly into an ever-golden future. In management there is no correlation between effort and effectiveness, a fact so obvious as to be trite. But there may often be a correlation between excessive effort and ineffectiveness. This is foreign to the puritan ethic. Yet everybody knows the symptoms of ineffective effort lower down the management slopes—the departmental head whose desk is littered with pieces of paper that he endlessly shuffles as, piece by piece, he mentally sinks beneath them.

The eighteen-hour chief executive is the same breed of cat. Only, because of his power and because he has bursts of real effectiveness, the disease is not recognized by its symptoms, by its progress, or by its results. No man in any important executive position can find enough work to fill even ten hours a day, day in, day out, unless his operation is badly organized and/or he wastes time in what looks like work, but isn't.

The prodigious worker who headed one of Britain's former growth companies garnered most of its growth (and most of its profit) from an operation jointly owned with a partner, a joint goose that laid its golden eggs with little attention, apart from an occasional pat on the head. The rest of the company consisted of diversified interests, most added in recent years, which, like all mixed corporate baskets, included some rotten eggs. The company created its own problems by buying them; and its chief executive created his own work load by sending out a stream of memos, manufacturing at one stroke two pieces of paperwork—his own inquiry (which might or might not be relevant) and the reply (which might not be relevant either to the inquiry or to the business of the division).

In consequence, his in-basket was always one of the most heavily loaded in world business. His regime, not at all surprisingly, ended in uproar and debacle. The eighteen-hour menace hung on long after his retiring age, sacked his heir apparent in circumstances so scandalous that the affronted board secured the menace's departure as well, and left behind the ruins of a once-great company. A firm that in the 1960s had enriched its stockholders by 1,021 percent in ten years added only 83 percent to their capital in the entire decade to 1983.

It figures. The eighteen-hour day is often a symptom of deep psychic forces that drive their victim, not only to feats of magnificent empire-building but to destructive and ultimately self-destructive behavior. In *The Supermanagers* I chronicled the day of one high-technology manager: a mere fourteen-hour run, starting at 7:18 A.M. and ending at home at 9:00 P.M., it left him with almost no time at all for work with his papers or his colleagues. The description concluded with this prophetic (as it turned out) question: "At the time of writing the super-manager concerned is still alive, well, and doing reasonably well. But is his modus operandi good for him—or for the company?"

The answer to that is presumably written in the fact that the company failed to preserve its independence, despite the fourteen-hour days; while the hero thereof, shortly after the acquisition, was kicked upstairs into a post where three hours a day were more than adequate to perform his strictly limited duties. The truth is that, although superhuman hours will sometimes be needed to accommodate superhuman efforts, the organization and the human being cannot indefinitely accommodate themselves to the superhuman. More often than not, anyway, the inhuman hours continue long after the necessity for them has passed, with the certain result that inhuman demands are made on others than the menace himself.

Vicious circles of this kind are hard to break. One investment bank, notorious for long hours, adds to the burden on its bankers by the chief executive's memos: one vice-president alone found an escape—he refused to answer the memos on the grounds that he never knew what to say. The longer an executive works, the more time he has to dispatch unnecessary pieces of paper—and the more work he makes for the subordinates and superiors who have to deal with them. Some of the documents may be worth reading, but Pareto's law undoubtedly applies—80 percent of the useful transmissions will arise from 20 percent of the corporate paper flow, 80 percent of which will contribute virtually nothing.

But the paper proliferation is only a symptom of the disease. It usually reflects a deadly underlying situation: the executive who gets into too much detail concerning another executive's job is filling his own hours at the expense of the other man's effectiveness. There are other ways of achieving the same miserable end than flying paper darts around the corporation. The best-known and most heavily used device is the meeting. Nearly all executives spend a large proportion of their time in meetings (just as their secretaries say).

For example, here is one day's log for a manager in a red-hot, high-technology business:

8:00–8:30: Met with a manager who had submitted his resignation to leave for another company. Took incoming telephone call from a competitor.
8:30–9:00: Read mail from the previous afternoon.
9:00–12:00: Held executive staff meeting (a regular weekly meeting of the company's senior management). Subjects covered at this particular one:
  —Review of the previous month's incoming order and shipment rates.
  —Discussion to set priorities for the annual planning process (about to start).
  —Review of the status of a major marketing program (scheduled subject).

—Review of a program to reduce the manufacturing cycle
time of a particular product line (scheduled subject).
12:00–1:00: Lunch in the company restaurant.
1:00–2:00: Meeting regarding a specific product-quality problem.
2:00–4:00: Lecture at our employee orientation program.
4:00–4:45: In the office, returning phone calls.
4:45–5:00: Met with my assistant.
5:00–6:15: Read the day's mail, including progress reports.

The hero of this particular diurnal saga is Andrew S.
Grove, the president of semiconductor manufacturer Intel. In
his book *High Output Management,* the high-output manager
explains that

> in a typical day of mine one can count some twenty-five separate
> activities in which I participated, mostly information gathering
> and giving, but also decision-making and nudging. You can also
> see that some two-thirds of my time was spent in a meeting of
> one kind or another. Before you are horrified by how much time
> I spend in meetings, answer a question: which of the activities
> —information gathering, information giving, decision-making,
> nudging and being a role model—could I have performed out-
> side a meeting? The answer is practically none.

Maybe so. But note that Grove seems to equate one-to-one
meetings (with disgruntled employees or his assistant) with
meetings where more than one participant (numbers un-
specified) took part. The two things are not the same.

Simple logic dictates that the more people attend a meeting the less effectively the time of its average member is used.
If four people meet for one hour and talk for an equal amount
of time (an unlikely story), each is active for one quarter of an
hour and passive for three quarters. If eight people fill the same
time span, the active-passive ratio declines from one to three
to only one to seven.

In practice, the time taken expands to accommodate the
numbers present, rather than the subject matter. So eight

managers take two hours where four take one hour, and so on ad infinitum. It hardly matters whether the meeting is formally called a committee, or that the theoretical model is spoiled by all manner of incidentals, such as the proportion of those attending who are asleep (or wish they were). The principle is always the same—the more people present, the more managerial time consumed and the greater the amount wasted.

The eighteen-hour menace, however, introduces a savage twist as chief executive. His long hours and his detailed interference with subordinate operations imply that he is the dominant personality. The decisions taken at any meeting he attends will, therefore, be the ones he would have taken on his own. The other executives are only present like a claque in a Viennese opera house—paid to applaud the performance.

Usually, the most effective meetings *are* those in which one personality does dominate and which in effect simply endorse what he proposes. Hence the desultory nature of board meetings (a board is nothing but a committee) with nonexecutive directors present. Etiquette forbids dictation, so the conversation rambles on without direction, and the chairman often has to resort to standard strategems to get his way (like leaving the only important matter until ten minutes before lunch, or referring contentious issues to a pliant subcommittee).

Probably a company that pretends it is managed by committee, but isn't, is more effective than a company that genuinely is committee-run. Du Pont had the longest-running multiple top management, a nine-man executive committee that passed collectively on all matters of importance down to investments that are a mere bagatelle in the context of multinational chemical giants. The du Pont committee even voted. A very strong chief executive could operate this system as a rubber stamp; but if the president is both very strong and very good, what's the point of wasting time on endorsing his decisions? If he is neither strong nor good, there is even less point in continuing his employment.

Even the best and strongest executive needs advice and double checking. But not all the time. Part of a chief executive's essential equipment is to know when to scream for help and when not to; part of his duty is to be as sparing of the time of other executives as of his own because time is the one irreplaceable corporate asset. Physical assets can be replaced, financial losses can be recouped, lost production can sometimes be made up, but time passed can never be regained. No company is short of executives. The shortage is of effective executive hours. But what is effective and what isn't? The answers are culturally determined far more than executives realize.

Contrast this working routine, for example, with that of Andrew Grove.

> Mr. A. gets up at about 6:20 A.M. After light exercise and a shower, he breakfasts while reading the paper and watching the TV. His company car is waiting for his 8:00 departure; during the forty-five-minute commute, he continues with the daily news.
>
> Mr. A. spends three hours at his desk, checking paperwork, meeting with directors and section chiefs, and finishing the newspapers. During that time, he signs his approval to eighteen papers, representing the final stage in the decision-making process. The rest of his day, till 6:00 P.M., is spent in outside meetings with directors of associated businesses or banks, or with economic groups or industrial leaders.
>
> Three days a week Mr. A. returns directly home. Other days, he entertains business clients at dinner or for drinks. Reaching home, he bathes, dines, and watches TV, then retires early, around 11:00 P.M.

Not counting the entertainment days, Mr A. works for a mere nine and a quarter hours, only three of which are in-house. His meetings are not operational in the sense that

Grove's clearly are, and his approvals are plainly predetermined. In fact, they are the last stage in the *ringi* process. For this is a Japanese senior executive who has delegated a wide range of operational duties and powers and who is occupying a genuinely presidential (or presiding) role.

Where Grove is deeply involved day to day in how others do their jobs, Mr. A. is at a remove. That is the cultural norm in Japanese companies and that alone, not the real executive pressures within the company, explains how he spends his time. At first, and maybe second, glance, Mr. A. appears to be disposing of his time more intelligently. Indeed, any Western executive who examines his use of time and delegation dispassionately invariably comes to the conclusion that he is doing much that he ought not to be doing—and not doing much that he ought to be doing.

Unfortunately, executives have marked regressive tendencies in the use of time. Several studies have proved that, if the executive day is analyzed as above, large fallow periods pop out that, by self-discipline and changed methods, the good manager can promptly fill up with productive labor. Any follow-up, however, would surely show steady backsliding—probably to the point that as much time as ever slips away like sand through the fingers. Possibly, in some cases, the eighteen-hour executive, by spending twice as much time as normal in ostensible work, gets twice as much effective time. But this is the wrong answer: the ideal of summit management, and of delegation, is to reduce the job content at the top to the bare minimum. The boss who keeps his desk bare and his calendar empty, for one thing, is certain to be available when somebody really does need him.

Lord Weinstock comes close to this ideal. He turned a near-bankrupt GEC into the only profitable company in the electrical industry's Big Three (and finally turned the Big Three into a Big One) without any outward appearance of effort. Mythology had it that between mergers Weinstock could be found wandering around looking for something to do—and the myth contained a little reality.

The blissful state of always having time is easily achieved. First, the executive must avoid outside entanglements like the plague (most big-time executives, not content with squandering time on internal obligations, itch incurably to serve on outside committees). Second, attend internal committees only when strictly necessary, except for board meetings, which should be purely legal formalities anyway. The test of strict necessity for other meetings is whether the chief executive will save more time by being present than he will lose. The most important step, however, is to delegate—and mean it.

The dogma of delegation is simple—the Sixth Truth of Management again: either the delegatee is capable of running the operation successfully by himself or he isn't. This handy formula relieves the top executive of any responsibility except that of finding, supervising, and (at the appropriate time) moving the men who are doing all the work. He can then truly manage by exception: he does not get worked up over operations that are going well, but concentrates on the plague spots, where everything, including the management, is going badly.

But human nature is such that, the more wondrously smooth and rich a business, the more the head office wants to meddle; and the more dreadful and backbreaking a problem seems to be, the more prepared the head office is to abdicate to any potential savior—unless, that is, the problem is self-created and trivial. Such were the troubles an American chemical giant's European management made for themselves by buying two tiny and feeble businesses, one in Holland, one in Italy, for the sake of diversification—yet these mere pimples were absorbing most of top management's time in 1984, at the expense of far more serious sores.

Many years ago a company was well along the course of

its rake's progress toward a seemingly inevitable takeover by one of its own customers. In this emergency, it turned over its northern interests to a bright young director, who, in his own words, rang down an iron curtain between head office and the factories. Left to itself, without interference from HQ, the business turned around smartly; but as soon as profits were again respectable, the board started boring holes in the iron curtain. The director quit, and the company rapidly relapsed into its antigrowth trend. This tale is repeated again and again. The former boss of what was one of the fastest-growing big company divisions estimated that he spent half his own time insulating his executives from the interference of the multihour work glutton who chaired the holding company.

There are plenty of other ways to fill the workday of a management positively determined to get in eighteen hours— such as travel. First-class jet flights across America and around the world rapidly consume time; and the operation of the biological time clock, which gets thrown out of gear by even the small transatlantic shift, guarantees that few useful results will follow. Another device that combines maximum consumption of time with personal gratification is the business lunch or dinner. Hours can be eaten away in expensive restaurants or lush corporate lunchrooms on the excuse of conducting business that might take a brisk ten minutes on the telephone. Often there is no specific item of business to discuss, anyway—the engagement is purely social. But it still contributes its stint to the eighteen hours.

Work in these corporate circumstances is more realistically defined as absence from home. If real work is effective application to the purposes of the corporation, nobody has ever worked an eighteen-hour day. To the extent that they try, they merely create an artificial situation that can't possibly endure, and shouldn't. One American oil company prided itself on the superhuman hours its senior executives worked seven days a week. They argued that as they were no brighter than their rivals in other companies, they would outdistance the competition simply by putting in more mileage. In fact, the company did grow faster than any other outfit in the industry. But to what end?

Any corporation, looked at from one angle, is a club of senior executives who all have lives outside its frontiers. A breed of zombies can always be created; but the corporation is not an end in itself. The sensible company organization operates successfully within the framework of human (and humane) hours. In *Further Up the Organization,* Robert Townsend tells a revealing tale: "One of my colleagues once spent a twelve-hour night working on an undated document that turned out not to be the current draft." Townsend's point was always to date a memo; but the better point is that twelve-hour nights indicate gross organizational failure somewhere along the line.

If a man has this strange inner compulsion to spend the maximum time in the ego-boosting security of the office, there is no harm in letting him indulge the urge, provided that, first, he is effective, and, second, that he doesn't force saner men to adapt to his rhythm. The second trap is hard to avoid, if only because underlings will be tempted to emulate their boss (and grab his attention) by showing equal enthusiasm for the office. More often than not the maximum-hour leader explicitly expects to see effort matching his own. The corporate boss who calls the break-of-day conference, or who rings around on the squawk box in the evening to tell the executives they can go home, is asking for inferior performance: it takes an inferior executive to submit to what is little more than bullying.

Outside the entrepreneurial foundations (whose founding bosses often have a touch of monomania, or megalomania, in their genius) the eighteen-hour boss is a rarity. The corporation man seldom has this lust for self-flagellation. Yet he tends to work longer and longer hours as he gets older and more senior, as if the corporate executive's ideal was somebody like Harold S. Geneen of ITT or Haughton of Lockheed. The first named was once, probably, the most cogent of the conglomerate-makers. But neither his record, nor Haughton's, says anything for or against masochistic hours, and that was self-evidently true even before Geneen's creation ran into the calamities and errors that reduced its earnings-per-share growth to a miserable 0.64 percent in the decade to 1983. Nobody would dream of modeling a corporation after the life-style of a lazy genius, and there is just as little point in building the company in the image of an obsessive worker. But if you have to choose between the ant and the wizard, pick the latter every time.

17

Top Management's
Secret Vice

No management school runs courses in mendacity. They aren't needed—executives are to the manner born. Not the deliberate lie; that is reserved for occasional denials of financial deals or other forlorn suppressions of the truth. Not, usually, deception on the criminal scale, like that of America's recently convicted price fixers and bribers. No, the kind of untruth that is endemic in management, and potentially fatal, is self-deception. For example, it is well known that if five firms compete in an industry and all five are asked to give their market shares, the resulting figures always add up to well over 100 percent.

The American boss of a GM outfit in Europe was once asked about the miserable sales of his new family auto. "We don't think it's done badly," he replied. "It has 70 percent of its market." *Market* had been defined to exclude practically everything else on four wheels, except a few imports. Automakers are prone to wishful futility; the GM man was eventually moved, or removed, as his charge slid further down the scale of reality. This habit of gilding the lily, or the weed, is every executive's secret vice, and often his last protection. Executives usually quit after a "policy disagreement," or "for personal reasons," or even because of ill health—seldom for the real reason, such as that they have been sacked for incompetence. (One departed chief executive, said to be at death's door by his successor, turned up right as rain in an even tougher chief executive spot the very next week.)

The lies can be personal as well as corporate. *Forbes* magazine discovered one company president who "listed a B.A. from the University of New Hampshire, an M.B.A. from Babson College, and a master's degree in materials from the Massachusetts Institute of Technology—all of which were bogus." The culprit kept his job, though—no doubt because he founded the company and still owned 20 percent. The managing director of Korn-Ferry International in Chicago was less fortunate when his bogus degree was uncovered. He resigned, not surprisingly, given his employer's identity as a large, maybe the largest, consultancy in, of all things, executive recruitment.

Deciding when the secret vice is conscious or unconscious is for psychologists. When a Ford of Britain man said, "We don't believe they can sell the same car in Germany as we can here," when the company was about to do precisely that, was the untruth deliberate or instinctive? (Or did the American overlords simply forget to tell him?) Men who apply more or less uniform private standards of morality divide their commercial lives into areas of honesty and other areas (such as future product plans) of total untruth. Lying in the cause of commercial secrecy does little managerial damage (and little good for that matter, as competitors mostly know what you are trying to hide, even without benefit of industrial espionage). But damage comes when the truth, the whole truth, and nothing but the truth doesn't govern every aspect of the company's internal affairs.

The secret vice can spring from virtue. Enthusiasm is an essential component of the executive's survival kit. He has to believe in the product: If he doesn't, how can anyone else? But enthusiasm shades over easily into obtuseness. A top shipyard executive once denigrated Japanese competition as that of "little men with vacant minds," and his company objected violently to being told in public that the little, vacant men built ships far faster and much cheaper.

That same shipyard later on boasted that it would sign only profitable contracts, then promptly signed several that made losses in the millions. The excessive patriotism and the gross commercial error are two sides of the same coin. There is no ultimate escape from reality. The executive eventually must come to terms with his real blessings and curses. The longer he delays, and the further his fantasies drag him from the truth, the worse his danger.

The fall of Avon Products from a unique and shining commercial beauty to Wall Street dog, with its stock down nearly two thirds from the peak, is a typical tale of self-deception taken to extremes. Nobody in either cosmetics or door-to-door selling had excelled Avon's achievements in ninety years of nonstop growth. The method hardly ever varied. The Avon ladies determined what was stocked; the fortnightly catalogue stimulated the sales; the Avon representative delivered the goods on the next call—and wondrous profits were earned.

So where could weakness and the risk of self-deception possibly lie? The answer lay in the very core of the company —the sales force and the increase in its numbers, which had been the key, the only key, to overall growth. The crunch came in 1979, when the Avon old-liners predicted that the representative army, having risen to a stupendous 401,000 beings, would advance as always—that year, by at least 5 percent.

The chairman five years on, Hicks B. Waldron, explained what happened to John Thackray for *Management Today:* "Here we go again, they said. But they didn't get the 20,000 increase—they got only 7,000. The old system they'd lived by failed. And they didn't know what to do." The normal, logical reaction, you might suppose, would be to mount a crash course in learning or importing the unfamiliar and now suddenly vital marketing skills that Avon lacked. Not a bit of it.

The management deceived itself with the comforting notion that large increases in the numbers of representatives, despite the 1979 experience, were still available and would still generate all the growth that Avon needed. As Waldron noted, the forecasts of 10 percent and 13 percent in which some executives continued to believe were not only self-deluding but impossible. They meant that by 1991, every woman over eighteen in the United States would have had to be either a current or a past Avon representative.

The minor conglomerators all had to learn the same hard lesson. Their only talent was to stick together lucrative paper empires and personal fortunes by using fast, fancy, and modish financial glues. They couldn't manage anything or anybody (except Wall Street patsies), but they pretended otherwise. Even some major conglomerators managed to get seduced by their own myths. Jimmy Ling, who owed his apotheosis mainly to success with the military, had no aptitudes for most other businesses he shoved into Ling-Temco-Vought. All he knew was how to buy them (and sell them all over again to a doting public). Litton Industries, also basically a successful Pentagon contractor, kidded itself and everybody else that the corporate genius lay in civil high technology.

Just as Goebbels persuaded most of Germany, and the rest of the world, that Hitler's thugs and murderers were statesmen, so corporate publicity men, or external hired hacks, have often convinced the public (and the man himself) that a lucky wheeler-dealer is a superexecutive. The misrepresentation needn't be deliberate. Goebbels genuinely believed in Hitler and company, and this real faith made him a fearsome propagandist. Very likely, even Bernie Cornfeld, while leading the Investors Overseas Services mutual fund operation to fame, fortune (personal fortune), and collapse, sincerely believed in Bernie Cornfeld.

Self-deception flourished in more respectable surroundings than the sybaritic château of Cornfeld's IOS mob. The public relations directed from the Litton office in Beverly Hills (a former movie palazzo, furnished with low-technology antiques) cost plenty, but it worked wonders. Of all postwar companies in the United States, Litton was the most flattered and followed. Its emphasis on converting expensive space-age technology into commercial products summed up the ethos of the moon age; and its specialty of "systems" introduced a new and magical phrase into the salesman's sample bag.

Litton raised the pursuit of higher earnings per share, with the aid of heavy debt gearing, to an art form, starting off a nationwide chase that ended only with the 1969–70 market crash. Its stockholders got their dividends, not in cash, but in stock; its executives, too, got their kicks in stock options; the top two, the late Charles ("Tex") Thornton and Roy Ash, achieved their higher rewards in the rise of sensational paper fortunes. The whole Litton legend was built around the constant rise of the share price, though Ash said, predictably, in an interview before the crash, "It is not an essential or even an important part of our growth for the price of the stock to go on rising."

Like hell it wasn't. Self-evidently, keeping a high head of steam behind the share price in such situations is the bounden duty of the publicity machine—and everybody else. *Forbes* reporters heard the doomed Charlie Knapp, creator and near-destroyer of Financial Corp. of America, "screaming into the a phone: 'You're supposed to be my investment bankers. Why aren't you helping support the stock? You're off the payroll tomorrow.' " Institutional investors had dumped Knapp's stock for the good and sufficient reason that they were worried, and with better cause than they actually knew. As the magazine observed, before Knapp's crash, the "profit numbers," which showed a fifty-four-fold rise in half a dozen years, "seem too good to be true. They probably are. . . ."

The desire to match the price of the stock to the ambitions of the management is not confined to operators of the Knapp variety. Even an apparently high-minded company like IBM isn't immune from this mercenary objective. Anybody who thinks that the sudden, simultaneous appearance in major business magazines of stories lauding the new, aggressive IBM of 1984 was a coincidence is underestimating IBM. The stories resulted from a carefully orchestrated public relations campaign, planned largely to elevate the stock price—as it duly did. However, the stories were not untruths. At Litton, though, the truth, as opposed to the untruth, was that Litton as a company was (and is) very like an old-line mastodon such as General Electric. GE, like Litton, pioneered any number of new management concepts; its resources in high technology leave Litton lagging; and it, too, is heavily decentralized into divisions and departments, or "strategic business units" (observers once saw this as weakness in GE, although it was hailed as a strength in Litton, and is now regarded as a GE asset, too). This similarity extends even to normal measures of efficiency—except that GE always came out better. In 1970, Litton earned 2.9 percent on sales, GE 3.8 percent; and net return on stockholders' equity was, respectively, 8.9 percent and 12.3 percent.

The real difference between the companies was the behavior of the two stock prices. In its prime, Litton was a glamour stock, GE mostly an off-color blue chip. In other words, because people believed in Litton's story, they made it believable. After all, isn't any company that increases its stockholders' wealth tenfold or twentyfold in a decade a marvel of management, technology, and diversification? It ain't necessarily so. Litton's sheer growth in sales volume, half at least coming through acquisition, was formidable, but its profitability (the name of the real game) was never up to much.

Litton went on living its myth. At the nadir, Ash said, "I regard what happened as a stumbling in the search for growth." The stumble lasted so long that it qualifies better as a crawl. In 1970, earnings after pooling of interest were only 20 percent higher than in 1964 (on doubled sales). Would Litton's management have operated any more successfully over the earlier period if the myth had not been believed, internally and externally? If Ash and Thornton had not persuaded themselves (presumably) and the public (certainly) that there was some meaningful connection between building ships and making portable electric typewriters?

Since history can't be written backward, questions like this can never be answered. But when myths swell up in such huge bubbles, their eventual bursting makes a far louder bang. Even in 1971, when the Dow-Jones index pushed up to near the magic 1,000, Litton shares dragged along the ocean floor, at only a quarter of their one-time glory. And yet in many respects—such as the quality of its managers and former managers (the so-called LIDOs, or Litton Industries Dropouts)—Litton was truly admirable. Its trap was pretending to be something it wasn't. The only successful consequence was to drive the earnings per share down to so low a level—a barely visible 84 cents a share in 1973—that the subsequent decade gave Litton one of the best growth numbers in U.S. business; even though, at the end of the period, its returns on sales and equity remained strictly middle-of-the-road.

Inside every fat bubble there lurks a truth, though—maybe a big one. Knapp saw that there was a profitable gap between the interest rates charged on mortgages and the price an S & L had to pay on its own money—a gap that he could exploit more aggressively, although at the price of lending too much money too long while borrowing too much too short. Cornfeld saw unerringly that nobody was using American sales methods to tap the oceans of non-American savings; John King of King Resources, another battered hulk, noted that an entirely new (and ignorant) class of investor could be lugged into oil exploration by mutual fund techniques. All these ideas (like the inertial guidance systems with which Litton first made its way in the world) were strong enough to make fortunes for anybody who exploited them with vigor, whether the men were corruptible or incorruptible, organizers or hucksters, captains of industry or con artists.

Because of a basic myth of management (that success equals skill), the public makes no distinctions. But as the wonder idea pays off, the wonder boy's competitors—the big corporations who missed the beautiful force of his idea—run scared, act jealous, and retaliate. Their Cassandra-like carping, however, is always discounted by everybody, including the wonder boy. This is sheer folly.

Big established financiers, though more than capable of making mammoth boners of their own, really do know the loan and investment markets down to the last decimal of a percentage. And every time an upstart like Penn Square, or Equity Funding, or IOS appears to be running circles around them, the odds are overwhelming that the new boy is headed for catastrophe, just as the big-company Jeremiahs say. If Charlie Knapp is lending longer and borrowing shorter than other S & Ls, while reporting stunning rises in profit, the likelihood is not that he has found the philosopher's stone, but that he is taking greater risks with both his lending and his financing.

However, the hero is now so rich, so successful, and surrounded by so many flatterers, that he is convinced of his genius at management, as at everything else. He has a lovely growth record, a managerial myth, and money. Money has a magnetic attraction for other money; so the wonder man, bit firmly between his teeth, typically strays (just like Litton) into businesses of which he knows nothing, such as oil lands and banking (Cornfeld), or steel (Ling). The new areas rapidly strip bare the wonder boy's shortcomings, organizational and personal, in short and horrible order.

Organization-man types will protest that they aren't a bit like the failed entrepreneur. But then they shouldn't behave like it. Don't deceive anybody, especially yourself. For a start, listen to what competitors say about you, your company, and your products. Eight times out of ten it is more accurate and, if used properly, more constructive (and much cheaper) than the findings of a management consultant. What you believe about your own products and performance, eight times out of ten, is untrue.

Second, never trade solely on a personal reputation: observe that entrepreneurial stayers who leave enduring empires are usually as close with their mouths as they are mean with their money. And never seek to manufacture a myth. Myth-making can fuel a stock boom, making it much easier to raise money and buy up other businesses. But if the record of achievement is genuine, the stock price looks after itself, there are no cash problems, and acquisitions are optional. If the achievement is spurious or inflated, the stock price will collapse one day, the borrowed money will strangle the corporation in its inevitable downturn, and most of the buys, being compulsory, will be bad.

Third, never misrepresent the financial facts, internally or externally. If an old, old product is expensive to make, but looks cheap because there is no longer a depreciation charge, the management that keeps churning it out is being misled just as dangerously as the investor who thinks that a change in accounting methods produces a real gain in profits. Don't, like the $2 billion Engelhard Corp., follow a $35 million profit bonanza, achieved by treating nonrecurring inventory profits as operating income, with the shock announcement of a $63 million write-off—resulting from the closure of two plants, revealed in April 1984, which had actually been on the cards for months (in one case, eighteen of them). Even if you get away with it (although the CEO in the case didn't), the stockholders won't.

Fourth, act on the truth about products, services, and the caliber of colleagues. As a rough rule, if nobody tries to hire away a company's executives, they are not as good as they or their superiors think. A top executive who starts praising "the team" is usually concealing the fact that none of the players is of much value by himself. As for the product, it is not a world beater unless it is demonstrably beating the world. Moreover, every product and every service (like every management) can be improved, usually to a marked degree, and should be.

Fifth, never believe your own advertising (after all, nobody else does) or your own public relations (even if everybody else does). The public relations chief for a Swiss giant once said firmly, "Our top officers would like to get their names in the paper, but I say no." He could have been doing them a wonderful service.

Sixth, don't lie gratuitously. When asked, on leaving a secret conference with a company you want to buy, or that wants to buy you, whether a merger is on, don't deny it with your hand on the Bible—as Carnation did twice while negotiating its $3 billion deal with Nestlé, to the great joy of the smart money, which knew perfectly well what was going on, and to the deep sorrow of the dumb small investors, who were conned by the denials.

When a new product line moves from losing $1 million to dropping $900,000, don't say it's nearing break-even, either. And when you fire an executive for incompetence, or having his hot little hands in the till, don't say he is resigning for personal reasons or after a policy dispute—just don't say anything (which is what happened when the Engelhard president mentioned above vanished from the scene—about the only right move in the whole affair).

Finally, remember that the ultimate victim of self-deception is the self. Had Avon, for example, seen itself as it really was—no longer a red-hot sales organization with a magical growth formula but a company pressed hard by heavy competition that it wasn't fitted to tackle—it couldn't have missed the demographic changes in America: no mean miss, when everybody in the land knew about the increase in working women, smaller families, and so on. Discover what the company is really good at, and remember that there are no such things as technological strength or management depth in themselves. If these claimed assets are not being applied to useful purposes, the company is good at nothing. And if the company really makes its money, not by any real merit, but by fooling the suckers, forget it. You *can* fool all of the people, but you can do it for only some of the time.

BOOK IV

War
Games

18

Planet
of the Planners

In the 1960s big business found a new religion of planning that, with many subcults, culminated in the long-range corporate variety. This ultimate in techniques had to wait for its moment; earlier managers needed the long view, all right, but they lacked the computers, or the men to feed them. When a new breed of hardware and soft humans was born, corporations could at last cope. Before the computer, the task of gazing into the chasms of the future and juggling with its endless permutations would have chained every manager to his slide rule for eternity. Thanks to the computer, companies could now do their sums, right or wrong, in comfort.

The chances of getting them right, though, remained slim. Thus "a reassessment of strategies described in *Business Week* in 1979 and 1980 found that 19 failed, ran into trouble or were abandoned, while only 14 could be deemed successful." Among the fourteen "successes," what's more, the jury is still out on cases like American Motors, which has linked up with Renault in yet another attempt to find a role (and consistent profits) in the U.S. auto market; and Gould, which has shed all its traditional businesses in favor of high-technology operations without, so far, getting profits up to the same height as its technology. Note, anyway, that these "successes," along with failures like Campbell Soup's attempt to diversify away from food or Adolph Coors's effort to regain lost market share, are based, not on the crunching of numbers by computer, but on human judgment of broad strategy.

Corporations might have headed off in just such directions without benefit of the long-range planners. The latter, though, were following their own strategic plan. They embraced responsibility for strategy after the previous phase of planning's meteoric rise had fizzled out, again in a rash of disappointments. This first phase went hand in glove with the compulsively reasonable subcult of management by objectives. Of course, managers should know what they are trying to achieve; of course, it's fair to judge them by how far they reach their own objectives. Provided that the aims are realistic, and the man isn't proposing to outsell Chevrolet with a three-wheel minicar, this wraps up in one neat parcel the messy problems of appraisal and direction.

The trouble starts with the misplaced hope that the formality of the dance—in which boss and subordinate go through a fixed waltz of setting mutual objectives, and then assessing performance together—gets rid of the dreaded interpersonal conflict. You no longer give your subordinate orders: he gives them to himself. You no longer have the painful task of whipping him for his failures: he flogs himself before you. And if this smacks somewhat of the confessional, so be it. The Catholic Church hasn't found the guilty conscience of the faithful to be a useless management tool. But if a manager hates his boss to distraction, he will hate him no less because they have worked together on his objectives. The second pious error is to hope that all management tasks can be turned into objectives, or that all objectives can be described precisely. The great entrepreneur, for instance, often doesn't manage by objectives, but by instinct, and by riding his luck. He doesn't, above all, work on a system.

In the objectives system, the corporation's aims, or plans, are broken down into a hierarchy of lesser aims or plans; and the grand total of all those objectives adds up to those of the corporation. Then all the executives have to do is meet their planned and agreed objectives and—hey presto—the corporation does the same. Perfection in management, at last, has arrived, except that it hasn't and won't.

The golden years of planning have seen errors of strategy and missing of objectives on a macabre scale. Twice, massive overordering of airline equipment had jumbo jets crossing the Atlantic more than half empty; only the despairing support of their bankers kept the airlines aloft. Steel and chemicals have likewise veered between undercapacity and overcapacity the world over before settling down into seemingly permanent oversupply. In industry generally, plant after plant, computer after computer, has come in late and at grossly excessive cost, while forecast after forecast has come grievously unstuck.

After oil prices went sky-high in 1973, every planner in the oil industry proceeded on the assumption that scarcity would continue, and prices would go on soaring, forever and a day. Milton Friedman apart, almost nobody, from the CIA downward (or upward), foresaw that sharply higher prices would choke off demand, which actually fell, dragging down prices, when all those brilliant planners expected it to rise. In the computer industry, packed with brainpower, both human and electronic, the planners confidently expected the mixture to continue as before; they completely missed the overwhelming swing away from mainframes to distributed information processing, with a computer on every desk or bench.

Even the electricity industry, whose only business is to balance supply and demand, has run short of generating capacity or run into gross surplus at critical times. Annual growth targets have been missed by so many miles that companies have wisely forgotten all about them. One U.S. group, which formed the sensible-seeming, once fashionable objective of 15 percent annual growth in earnings per share, four years later needed a 170 percent jump in one year to get back on target. That's some objective.

None of this has disturbed the planning industry one whit. The long-range planners have been striving to establish themselves as a separate breed—technicians as essential to the corporate future as a competent accountant is to its present. Some American companies consequently found themselves with brilliant vice-presidents who spent half their year planning and the other half converting the plan into an action program for the next year. Which conveniently left them no time whatsoever for managing.

Among the top executives who pay the planners' bills, this gap between ideas and action couldn't pass without notice. GE, a pioneering force in the planning endeavor, found that "the staff-work did not make a good connection between environmental studies and the implications for top management decision or action," according to the company's own ace planner of the 1970s, Michael G. Allen. The staff was cut by around a quarter, leaving a mere 100-odd people to plan the future of this mighty corporation. That was in 1975. Move on to 1984, and *Business Week* reported as follows: "In a bid to return strategic planning to its original intent—forcing managers to take 'a massive, massive look outside ourselves' —GE chairman John F. Welch, Jr., has slashed the corporate planning group from 58 to 33, and scores of planners have been purged in GE's operating sectors, groups and divisions." *Plus ça change, plus c'est la même chose.* Now the cry is a capitalist version of "all power to the soviets." For *soviets,* read the line managers: they saw strategic planners seize authority from the line after the work of consultants like Boston Consulting Group and McKinsey & Co. had wondrously sold big U.S. business on a twin concept—that strategy is the key to corporate success, and that its construction can be made manifestly effective by the use of relatively simple tools of the consultants' trade. Now a GE man talks of "gaining ownership of the business," of "grabbing hold of it" from an "isolated bureaucracy" of planners, while a GM planning chief, not to be outdone, says that "planning is the responsibility of every line manager."

It may not be a responsibility they covet. *Business Week* also quotes managers at a midwestern manufacturer who still complete strategic planning forms that HQ had dispensed with. "You almost had to rip them out of their hands." It's easy to understand why. Taking action is where painful mistakes may be made and jobs risked, so merely thinking about what to do may be nicely to an executive's taste. Nobody is to blame for a plan that is falsified by events—for nobody can foretell the future, can they? After five or ten years nobody will even remember who drew up the original document. Like Lord Keynes and everybody else, the planner and the executive are both dead in the long run.

The long run, however, is only a series of short runs added together—and this is vital, as the directors of one big boiler company should know. Self-described as an unrepentant planner, its boss (its *former* boss) said, "The real benefits of reorganization will be tested in five to ten years' time." Within just two years, the company had run into a brick wall and disappeared by merger.

Such relatively primitive failures were supposed to have

been made less likely, if not impossible, by the new sophistication inspired by Boston. Since the consultants had identified
high profitability with high market share, it followed that corporations should seek to maximize the latter—but where? The
choice of markets was made gloriously simple by the matrix
that, judging businesses by growth rates and market shares,
divided them into stars, question marks, cash cows, and dogs.
You backed the stars to the hilt, tried to turn the borderline
cases into stars, milked the cash cows, and disposed of the dogs
—and, hey presto again, you had a corporate strategy, a
planned portfolio of existing businesses.

As for new ones (needed, of course, to replace the old dogs
and dry cows), you found those from a market matrix constructed on the same principles. Unfortunately, many managements found that high-share and high-growth businesses may
equate with low profits—and may even bring large losses, if the
competition is too intense, the price of entry too great, the
corporate experience inadequate, or (as often happened) all
three adverse factors operate at once—as when Exxon blun-
dered into office automation and electrical manufacture. Look
at this and the other nineteen strategic failures mentioned before, and you find the same story over and over again: the
strategy failed either because it was based on incorrect assumptions about the industry environment or because its implementation was mishandled.

In the case of industry environmental error, corporations
can do very little to guard themselves. Error is of the essence,
which is why the embattled planners have long seized on the
magic word *scenario*. Instead of committing themselves to a
definite projection on interest rates, winter weather, the supply-
and-demand balance for energy or cement or chemicals (to
name a few of the factors where gross mistakes made flops of
the unlucky nineteen), the planners now offer management a
choice of alternative scenarios (three, usually). The idea is that

the options force the manager to think for himself, in short, to manage; but the scenario approach has the not-so-incidental virtue of taking the planner off the hook.

He can also hardly be blamed for the operational mess-ups —like the fact that Coors' great drive for higher market share was vitiated by its lack of needed marketing strength. As in war, strategic success depends on tactical effectiveness, and no degree of planning can lessen management's tactical impera- tives. The first responsibility of the executive, anyway, is to the here and now. If he makes a shambles of the present, there may be no future; and the real purpose of planning—the one whose neglect is common, but poisonous—is to safeguard and sustain the company in subsequent short-run periods. Every executive should go to bed happy that no omission of his will leave successors with no new products in the pipeline, with no cash in the bank, and with an inadequate production plant crippled by crazy labor relations, as actually happened at the erstwhile giant of British autos. This kind of planning is only intelligent anticipation, extrapolating the trends of the business to deter- mine probable needs for capital, cash, new plant, product re- placement, and the rest, with a massive allowance for contin- gencies thrown in.

What goes wrong is that sensible anticipation gets con- verted into foolish numbers, and their validity always hinges on large, loose assumptions. After the first Suez crisis of 1956, the world oil industry, stacked to its eyebrows with planners, con- cluded that, without a major new pipeline across the Arab world, built at stupendous cost, Western Europe would run dry of oil. For the first and presumably last time in history, every oil company boss who mattered (and many who didn't) met, blessed by the U.S. trustbusters, at a London hotel. As soon as the moguls got back to their desks, they found that, because forecast growth in oil demand hadn't materialized in a single year, Western Europe was oozing with excess oil, a condition in which it has remained, with odd interruptions by Middle East politics, ever since.

The chemical company Monsanto, influenced by the Boston theories, made a large, loose assumption of its own: that, partly because leisure suits would stay in high demand, so would polyester fiber, making the number two spot in polyester a great place to be. As the CEO sighed to *Business Week,* "Our assumption that there was enough growth disappeared in a hurry." There's a confusion that appears in most planning. An exercise that starts in simple prudence—ensuring that you have the resources you need—becomes another gung-ho device for achieving superlatives of growth and profitability. Executives take their eyes off what is going to happen and think about what they are going to *make* happen—they manage, in other words, by objectives.

In the long-range passion, they even ignore real short-run happenings. Commonly executives, in the worst examples, start playing with their "rolling five-year plans" in the spring of the preceding year. At that point they can only guess the outcome of the current twelve months. Anything from cocoa blight in the Congo to a strike in Wichita or Upper Tooting may be about to hit them; yet they plunge into documents of immense volume and tiny detail. The translation-into-numbers defect smartly takes over. Once the basic assumptions are made —just as the corporate objectives can be split into atomized individual aims—the entire future of the business can be sliced up, right down to the usage and price of raw rubber in four years' time, or the sales margin on light bulbs in three.

This is tricky enough when executives are simply trying to predict. Better to heed the experience of the Beecham drugs-to-foods group. "We found a five-year forecast was pie-in-the-sky and it tended to encourage excessive expenditure. The forecasts were nearly always way out because one cannot legislate for failure." When executives are attempting to achieve, as well as forecast, the corporation has a potential tiger by the tail. Because the mercy of God is infinite, however, there is a self-correcting device. The executive soon catches on to the notion that, if he is being held to a plan or objective, the plan had better be one he can meet.

The Russians, though they lag behind Western management technology in every other respect, have pioneered in this subtle art. The only yardstick of a Soviet executive's performance is whether or not he makes his plan. So, not being a complete idiot, he spends most of his ingenuity on getting an easy plan. One Communist executive whose screw factory's output plan was set by weight, switched, clever lad, to making heavier screws. When the boss of a plan-happy American corporation says, "The numbers are getting better all the time," he cannot know whether the executives are improving as planners or as timeservers, Soviet-style. That quote came from Honeywell, whose own plans, anyway, can't have envisaged the merger with GE's computer side, which threw everything back into the melting pot—making Honeywell fight for its hard-won computer happiness all over again. Not that the effort was worth Honeywell's while. The plan to become a mini-IBM with IBM-style growth rates misfired to such an extent that management in Minneapolis decided to rebuild its strategy around noncomputer interests, instead of the other way around; yet a decade's growth in earnings per share to 1983 left Honeywell strictly in the middle of the road, with a 6.3 percent figure almost exactly half that of Fortress IBM.

Locking executives into detailed plans and objectives, self-fulfilling or not, has a saving grace. At least the executive is made to think about what he supposes himself to be doing and what the consequences will be. Companies part at the seams, not because executives don't plan, but because they don't think. Planning and management by objectives have their point as devices for compelling thought, so long as executives don't forget that any plan worth making is inaccurate; the longer a plan takes to write, the worse it is—just because of its consumption of time. And the more they change plans to suit events, the better they will manage—if you've made a mistake, you had better admit it.

Even businesses into which the long-range planners have not burrowed need these three lessons; even in such firms, unless they are stuck fast in prehistory, annual budgeting (really a one-year corporate plan) and capital spending approval (the crunch part of any planning activity) are bound to crop up. Even annual budgets are a postwar fashion in many companies. Plenty still have no controls worth the name on costs and none on revenues, and some quite large firms still strike the profit at the year's end. The surprises are occasionally pleasant—but that's about as rare as finding a capital spending plan that pays off according to schedule.

This isn't for lack of sophistication. Investment appraisal became advanced enough to generate worthy tomes on discounted cash flow, net present value, and internal rates of return. All of these sets of numbers rest on anticipations of the future that are so dubious that the use of the technique, according to some statisticians, is little more effective than picking projects with a pin. This won't worry most executives—for expansion projects are all but unstoppable. Boards of directors are always claiming that performance will be "greatly" (or "significantly" or "substantially") improved when the new wonder factory starts producing, in March, or August, or whenever. In case after case, it doesn't produce then. When it does, for month after month all that pours out is trouble and loss. The only thing that doesn't emerge is the promised rate of return.

If the board sets 20 percent or 25 percent as the minimum return on investment, the managers cook the futuristic figures to fit the target. Every company has beloved projects on which if prices had held up, if the contractors had finished on time (or finished at all), if the plans hadn't been altered, if the thing had actually worked, the planned return would have been earned. But since some or all of these calamities usually happen, any manager who neglects to allow for them is not planning—merely thinking wishfully. Desire for the project has, as usual, overtaken desire for profit.

Letting the wish be father to the accomplishment is only one route to a false objective. Another is to start from a false premise—say, that the company really can achieve some dazzling growth rate or return on capital. Like setting a subordinate a "stretching" objective (that is, one he can't reach), this guarantees failure. Managements regularly survive many years of missing announced targets without much damage, even to their self-esteem.

That's hardly surprising if John Thackray is right in saying, "Planning is, of course, first and foremost a security blanket of both practical and symbolic value. A great deal of planning is an occult and highly plastic activity. . . ." As always, though, executives who don't require artificial security, or occult aids, can make the most out of what weaker men misuse. These days, the best corporations, in Japan or the West, plan no further ahead than they have to. In the majority of businesses, that's no more than three years. Only the first of those years is hard and packed with figures—as it must be, because that's the annual budget. The whole three-year view, though, starts with objectives expressed in words, not numbers; indeed, a Japanese president wouldn't feel happy without an initial statement of the corporate philosophy—and never mind about cash cows and stars.

You couldn't have a sharper contrast to the once all but universal, inherently defective American game of picking on arbitrary figures and then working back. Take 15 percent annual compound growth in earnings per share; and forget, for the moment, that since earnings per share is a very funny number, it can be manipulated to produce "growth" from the wild blue yonder. Even if the 15 percent is translated into real, honest growth, what grounds are there for expecting this jacket to fit the corporation? And if it doesn't, what then?

The saner executive would surely plan and develop each component business according to its potential and settle for whatever group growth turns up. Then, as long as the business can coin the requisite money, growth will look after itself. If only it were so easy. That's the du Pont way, and the net result is that ICI, from its bogged-down base in the British economy, drove past du Pont for the heavyweight lead in the world chemical stakes. Du Pont reaped no harvest in profit terms, either: net earnings in 1961–70 rose by only 20.5 percent, which compared (almost unbelievably) with 176 percent for sleepy old ICI. Since then, du Pont has transformed itself only by the megamerger with Continental Oil—a gigantic strategic move that looked less and less wonderful with every downward lurch in the petroleum market. In consequence, du Pont stockholders didn't even double their money in a 1973–83 period that saw ICI's investors get a near fivefold total return on their money; thanks in part to a new regime at ICI that, picking up assorted goodies like the U.S. chemical business of Beatrice Foods on the way, pursued a corporate strategy that any Japanese, or any schoolboy, could understand: to be, according to chairman John Harvey-Jones, "the best bloody chemical company in the world."

How executives plan or what numbers they choose doesn't count; what does is the standard of performance they are ready to exact. The essence of any objective is that reaching it should be reasonable. The precondition is that you expect it to be met. But corporations settle on plans and targets with little idea of how to react if the objectives are missed. If the whole company undershoots its targets by the width of the Atlantic Ocean, the directors are unlikely to take the extreme step of firing each other. This weakens their position when it comes to firing others for the same offense—which consequently rarely happens, except in time of earthquake, when the system has already (and long since) broken down.

Every executive has one double objective, to do the most possible with the least possible. Don't concentrate on the first —the earnings—to the exclusion of the second—the capital. An executive who is being tyrannized by his boss into raising return on capital from 10 percent to 15 percent grows ulcers trying to lift profits by half. He can get the same effect by reducing capital employed by one third. Don't start from statistical objectives and work backward. Begin from the premise that whatever the company is doing could be done better, and start moving forward by making the improvements that are always waiting to be grabbed.

All companies use more capital than they need. Many firms, as they discovered, and corrected, in recession and in response to the Japanese example, are like the Pentagon or the army; they hoard inventory that is too hefty and slackly controlled; they let unnecessary fixed assets pile up; their forgetfulness about cash flow leads to regular and excessive borrowing; they tie still more money up in businesses that never have produced a worthwhile return, never could, and never will. Anyway, all capital generates costs, so cutting out capital must eventually cut expenses. Other things being equal, the capital cutter will improve profitability simultaneously on both sides of the hallowed ratio of return on capital employed.

The process, while as near as anything in business management to ranking as a golden rule, is less thrilling than planning a five-year future. The future, however, is pure uncertainty, limited only by the constraints of possibility. The manager must understand those constraints, and he can limit that uncertainty by thoughtful anticipation. But, above all, if you want to master the future, you have to find out what is really and truly happening right now—and to make sure that it is happening right.

19

The Motivational
Misfits

The most emotive word in recent management vocabulary is *motivation.* Those four syllables motivated boards of directors so powerfully that they shelled out plenty to have Saul Gellerman, or some other high priest, elucidate the mysteries of motives. And Gellerman doesn't even claim to be the original hot gospeler: the original is Frederick Herzberg, an academic consultant, who (as a founding thinker) is reputed to have pulled in $6,000 a day from some corporate admirers.

The high noon of these hero-thinkers has passed, but not before their ideas have become a pervasive, inescapable influence on management life—hardly surprising, given the sheer height of that noon. To quote John Thackray, writing in *Management Today,* "The allegedly humanistic psychologies of Douglas McGregor, Abraham Maslow, Frederick Herzberg, Chris Argyris and others [made them] the chief spokesmen for a liberal attack on traditional corporate authoritarianism and hierarchies." In their "promised land of greater voice and personal fulfillment for the individual" wonders would flow: "Participative management and 'enriched' jobs, they claimed, would foster worker happiness, and also boost productivity and profits."

The paradox is that, at the time when these comforting theories were being promulgated, in the 1960s, productivity and profits were not the besetting concern of U.S. management. They should have been; but when the crucial nature of the American productivity crisis was realized, under the extreme dual pressure of recession and Japanese competition, the ideas of the motivational sages mostly went out the window. The next most conspicuous school of thought (if that's the right word) sought to embrace the principles of JABMAS—the Japanese business and management system that had done so much of the damage to American pride and profits.

But motivation—like all spiritualism—contains its share of truths, or rather truisms. Its blue-chip acolytes basically got an insight that they could have obtained as easily (and much more cheaply) from peering into their own interiors: that money is only one of the forces that motivates people to work effectively. This truism burst upon companies like a blinding light because of their deep yearning for a universal key to unlock their everlasting problems. The "behavioral scientist" offered a kind of philosopher's stone, an explanation and solution rolled into one, with which to attack the irritating refusal of men (and now women) to act in the best interests of the corporation.

The late-twentieth-century executive feels his pains more than any predecessor. He is also more convinced, after being inundated by a Niagara of business theory, that cures exist for any corporate condition. Man, he believes, is a perfectible animal. So, if the management is not developing marvels of entrepreneurial initiative, drive, and speed, or if the workers, instead of churning out untold productivity, are militant, grudging, and alienated, the solution is plain. They all want (because all normal men do) to achieve: they are just not properly motivated—or so the gurus explained. Press the right motivating buttons, and the machine—at last—will whir off into beautiful action.

Even the language of business began to change. Companies don't "employ" executives anymore. In the now standard phrase, you "attract, retain, and motivate" them. In this Holy Trinity, motivation must loom largest: it's no use having a splendidly attracted and retained executive who won't jump up and *do* things. The behaviorists can show, which is easy, that management's approach to employees has been misguided and muddleheaded for decades. Better still, they can apparently show—"scientifically" too—how to get elevated results by amending the approach.

But anybody with elementary human insight knows that the question What are your motives? is embarrassingly subjective. The answer varies wildly from person to person and day to day, and men lie or are unsure about their motives, even to themselves. In the days when British scientific brains were draining across the Atlantic in flood proportions (just in time for the great aerospace and computer recessions), the departers never admitted that doubling or tripling or even quadrupling their living standards was a prime reason for going West. No, the confessed lure was always the wider scope, the richer research and development budgets, the more lavish scientific equipment.

Those disinterested scientists who would have emigrated to the United States for unchanged standards of living could have been comfortably hijacked in one small executive jet. But Western society considers it shameful to admit doing anything (even something perfectly respectable) just for the loot. How often does a multimillionaire allow that making still more millions is his dearest hobby and most pressing motive? That he simply loves to roll around in the green stuff? On the contrary, the money, he will say, is just "figures on a piece of paper." The man clings to those pieces of paper like a starving octopus.

Self-made tycoons are highly acquisitive and retentive: the proprietor with millions in the bank gets wild over wasted paper clips or secretaries paying for cabs with his cash; the professional executive, with little more to his name than a big mortgage, never minds at all. Greed is a great motivator, in all its forms, and you can't disentangle greed, for money or anything else, from nonfinancial motives of equal force, such as ambition.

No doubt Jack Tramiel, one of America's roughest and toughest entrepreneurs, whose ideas on motivation are allegedly closer to those of Attila than of Argyris, had strong emotional reasons for taking on the awesome mess at Atari—not least, monumental pique at being ousted from Commodore, the company he built to a billion dollars in sales. In trying to rebuild Atari to the same size, and in the same home computer business, Tramiel could satisfy his powerful personal drives—and prove to the world who had really made Commodore commanding. In the process, though, if Tramiel could pull off the Atari rescue (a tough trick, given its half-billion 1983 losses and battered market standing), Tramiel would mint money in equally ego-satisfying quantities. Which comes first, the money motive or the management drive, is exactly the same question as the old conundrum about the chicken and the egg.

The boy who sets out to be President of the United States is motivated by personal ambition, desire to better mankind, lust for power, and other drives. He also ends up rich, with a splendid mansion on Pennsylvania Avenue, an army of servants (and a real army too), *Air Force One,* a fleet of cars, a high salary, and after these delicacies are removed (by the voters or the end of his second term), a huge pension and rich book rights to his ghosted memoirs. The corporate man who wants to achieve is a bundle of powerful motives, which include desire for the personal benefits, in wealth, prestige, and their companions, that await those who reach the top. But that man's motives are of little interest or relevance. Motivating an ambitious, able executive isn't the problem; the difficulty is to retain him. The real agony of the corporation is motivating the vast majority, people who don't have any particular wish to achieve.

The large corporation is structured more for timeservers than as a springboard for the ambitious. Big companies have usually desired to offer a lifetime career to those they hire, still moist behind the ears, straight from the universities. Lifetime hiring means a steady progression on grounds of years alone from one rung on the ladder to another. The ladders would all come tumbling down if the corporation became a gymnasium for the ambitious, all vaulting over their seniors in a mad dash for the top.

This is a crunching problem that the gee-whiz companies of America's electronic belts have had solved for them only by the eagerness with which employees motivate themselves right out of the company. The spin-offs have acted as a necessary safety valve. The average age in a company like Apple is only twenty-nine. The president, previously with Pepsico, John Sculley, at forty-five, was ancient by these 1985 standards—and by those of the twenty-nine-year-old founder and chairman, Steven P. Jobs. The Old Man of Apple was no doubt right in claiming that "there's incredible interest by young people in Apple. . . . What we're finding is that we can take young people out of a university, train them, and put them in positions of great responsibility much earlier than was ever thought possible." That's hardly the most novel insight to come out of Silicon Valley. But what happens to the college kids when they grow up to Sculley's age? For that matter, what happens to Jobs when *he* grows up?

If a company opts for a board of go-getting, high fliers under forty, what age will the next tier of management be? If thirty-five (allowing five years before they high-fly onto the board), the next rung down will be thirty. What does the great and good company do with everybody over forty? Shoot them? And what about the forty-year-old whiz-kid directors when they in turn reach the rotten old age of forty-five? The big organization needs its medium fliers and even its earthworms; it needs them so that the relatively few high fliers can have somebody else to manage.

But there's bound to be a leakage; some of these low-voltage managers will seep through into the highest levels of the company. Having arrived at the top, panting and unprepared, they seek more motivation for the company, when they really need it for themselves—and the man who has to ask for motivation is not the most suitable case for treatment. Every force in the organization presses him into the conservative mold that his own temperament prefers. This long-service, low-volatility element dominates most large corporations: at General Motors, the chairman and president of 1983, Roger Smith and James McDonald, had soldiered on for nearly eight decades of service between them. Their Praetorian guard of vice-presidents are similarly distinguished by their long years of loyal service—to be precise, 32.6 average years per Praetorian.

In this pattern of organization, mere survival and the submerging of personal ambition into the corporate ethos set up the motivational norms. Managers such as Smith and McDonald at least have their public exposure and awesome responsibilities to stimulate them. But how does anybody motivate the equally long-toothed managers who lie secure lower down in GM's bosom? As the behavioral scientists have said, money alone won't do it, partly because these men earn too much, too easily, anyway. But nothing else will ever change them into human dynamos; dynamism isn't in their character, or in the corporation's prescription for their behavior. If a man is disinterested in money, he can't be made to be interested. If a man is unambitious, he can't have ambition thrust upon him.

The corollary is that, the more highly motivated a man is, the easier he is to motivate. If he loves money, he will try twice as hard to get twice as much. One danger of the motivational movement, however, is that the cardinal motivating importance of loot can get mislaid. James Thurber tells how Harold Ross, his great editor at *The New Yorker,* tried in vain to hire the old *Herald Tribune*'s star writer. Finally a new managing editor snagged the prize by offering the man three times his *Tribune* salary. "You're a genius," said Ross, "I never thought of offering him money."

Every man may not have his price. But corporations customarily pay the price irrespective of what, in performance terms, they are buying. If an executive is paid adequately for being adequate and loses nothing by being inadequate, money has very little chance to show its power. Don't think that material bribery will get you nowhere. Rather, unless the bribery is skillfully calculated, or the bribee (like some computer salesman) is highly bribable, it won't get you far enough.

Herzberg ("I am an achievement bug. I think the most rewarding thing is achievement.") distinguishes between the *hygiene factors*—a curious phrase that suggests brushing the managerial teeth—of the environment, such as pay, and other factors that have to do with the content of the job itself. The latter, according to Herzberg, are the motivators: achievement, responsibility, recognition, advancement, the nature of the work. But what if the manager's idea of achievement is to earn $200,000 a year by the age of forty? What if the recognition he seeks is a fat pay increase, a lavish stock option, or a more profoundly carpeted office? One man's hygiene is another man's motivation.

The motivation prophets also preach "You don't hire a thumb, you hire the whole man." But you can't activate one motivating factor, you hire the whole lot. You can only motivate the entire man, which means the whole complex of his personal drives. Equally, you cannot motivate him beyond the potential of the organization. Put a rapacious, ruthless egotist into most large companies—the kind of man who becomes a millionaire by thirty—and the organization will squeeze him out before he is twenty-five.

The key to motivation is not only the man but the company. Place an executive in a well-found company with whose objectives and style he can identify, and whose growth and drive create personal opportunities and challenge, and where the executive feels secure, appreciated, properly rewarded, and constantly under fair test—there you have the conditions for marvelous motivation.

By no coincidence, that description accurately fits a company that used to be a byword for conformity, IBM, but that has shown, particularly in the early 1980s, that neither size, nor market dominance, nor strong cultural norms need be an obstacle to creative management. In other words, the characteristics that give a corporation the stability that the organization man craves can also give it the foundations for discontinuous initiatives. The saga of how IBM stormed Apple's personal computer market, starting from scratch, by setting up an organizationally independent group with authority to override all the preconceptions of the tight IBM world, is already a chapter in the history of great business achievement. But the tale of the electronic typewriter is equally enlightening.

IBM makes mistakes. Missing the early years of personal computers was bad, but understandable. Making a mess of electronic typewriters was bad and inexcusable. That's exactly what IBM did in 1978, losing the electric customers on whom it had a stranglehold to electronics from Xerox, Adler, and Canon. But six years later, IBM had picked itself up off the floor, started churning out highly competitive machines from a \$350-million automated plant capable of 4,000 units a day, and looked certain to crack what had become a key market— just in time. To anyone familiar with Japanese companies, it was just the kind of comeback (like that, say, of Toyota when its first cars bombed out on U.S. highways) that has characterized their careers in world markets.

But, then, Japanese managers consider IBM a company that is very Japanese in many respects—including the personnel policies that underlie a devastating degree of motivation. It isn't the lifetime employment of a Canon or IBM manager that motivates him: the security, the corporate ethos, and the excellent conditions of employment combine with rotation around demanding jobs and a strong corporate strategy to produce an outfit in which the individual assimilates his own ambitions to those of the organization without really feeling that it's happening—or finding it intimidating.

The number of corporations fitting this description is small, partly because the two elements are in continuous conflict: security and appreciation in one corner, contradicted by challenge and testing in the other. Most top managements concentrate on providing the first couplet rather than the second; they have their own security and comfort at heart and they hate the psychological traumas of demanding good performance.

The typical executive, myths to the contrary, hates firing, does it rarely, and usually after long and pointless delay. He can't face the terminal interview, even though most candidates for firing know they deserve it, feel guilty in consequence, and can only have their guilt expiated (to their enormous relief) by being fired. If companies don't fire when firing is essential, they

233

do injustice to their other employees. They also lose a motivator almost as powerful as money: the stick, as opposed to the carrot.

Apart from firing, a company has very few canes in the cupboard. Cutting a man's pay or demoting him is tantamount to firing; he may quit and he is unlikely to be an effective servant of the great company after the act. The corporation is like a dictator who has only one legal penalty to control the rabble—sudden death—the difference being that most dictators are less namby-pamby than directors when it comes to capital punishment.

Hire-and-fire companies, in contrast, are run by neo-Nazis, not by namby-pambies; and their malevolent dictatorship usually has to be balanced by high pay. Too much benevolence and too little money are the worst motivational combination; but malevolence and too much money can work wonders. One company boss surrounded himself with well-paid weaklings who periodically had to be fired for their weakness. Over a long-drawn-out dismissal, the boss would sadistically strip the victim of his last vestiges of self-respect. Rebuking a man violently and cruelly in front of others never fails to demolish the current target and soften up later candidates. Finally, the victim would yearn for dismissal as a condemned man longs for the scaffold. The irony for humanitarians is that investors in this company multiplied their fortunes tenfold in a single decade.

As a rule, and for a time, hire-and-fire companies have disagreeably good growth and profit records. At first sight, this seems to prove that the stick can motivate more magically than the carrot; and it is true that, used alternately, the two produce a positively Pavlovian response to stimulus. The chief demon of one growth company, for instance, found this technique highly effective: he would wait at some highly paid subordinate's desk and go through the latter's papers; the sight of the dreaded boss metaphorically laying bare the executive's soul was correctly calculated to produce a quivering, malleable subordinate.

Even Saul Gellerman has called the carrot and the stick "the oldest management theory in existence," adding ruefully that "the rationale of the carrot and the stick is not altogether unrealistic . . . some people are motivated by the lure of wealth or the fear of being fired all of the time and all people probably are so motivated at least some of the time." But don't conclude from this that the neo-Nazi corporation has an advantage. That's the same mistake made by prewar commentators who ludicrously thought dictatorships were more efficient than democracies, because Mussolini made the trains run on time. Hire-and-fire companies grow, not because of their addiction to carrot-and-stick management, but in spite of it.

The carrot guarantees that they attract mobile, hungry managers; the stick, however, also produces a large quota of murderees, born victims who lust to be whipped by those to whom they act as yes-men. The sadism of the corporate führer eventually motivates his better managers to leave, as soon as they can match his pay in some more benevolent climate. And the sadism doesn't generate the growth; that's done by the sheer personal drive. Part of the drive is expressed in the autocrat's despicable personal behavior, but the two are not inseparable. Both the man and the company would be better off, if possible, to keep the drive and lose the whip.

The most you can say for carrot and stick is that a good executive heading into this variety of company has the self-confidence to accept risk, welcome insecurity, and be judged on his results. The standard corporation operates on a different philosophy: carrot and comfort. The executive who makes it to the top makes it financially and in every other way; the executive who misses still has few material complaints—except that, if his last two working decades coincide with a periodic spring cleaning or national recession, he could be (maybe gently, but still shatteringly) put out to grass.

Far better, for all concerned, is the carrot-and-carrot company—if you can make it work. The most ardent advocate of the green-belt company, which starts off with no organizational ideas save belief in having as little organization as possible, is Robert Townsend. The *Further Up the Organization* thesis is explicitly "down with the organization," utilizing the motive power of challenge, managerial independence, profit-sharing financial rewards, and plain fun to obtain the kind of growth that Wilbert Gore has won with Gore-Tex, the rainproof material that breathes, and which, typically, was turned down by Gore's former employer, du Pont.

According to Townsend, Gore's objective has been to make his company as little like du Pont as possible. Without question, this rejection of big-company norms, this turning to what Apple's John Sculley calls "no-manager management," is of itself a powerful motivational force. Having something to kick against always is—especially if the object deserves kicking —and managers in the mighty corporations have been through a mighty bad time. The wholesale firings of those whose services are no longer required are harsh examples of the disrespect in which middle managers are held. As Boston management consultant Emmanuel Kay once observed, "To them this is grim evidence that they are not in a uniquely favored and protected position just because they are the echelon immediately below the top executives."

Managers who survived with ease the threat of the computer are now anxious about whether the electronic office will undermine their positions. Some hope that the new tools will enhance the manager's individual freedom of action and decision, but in most organizations that is just a hope. As John Thackray wrote in 1981, "Instead of reflecting on job enrichment, self-supervising work, on T-Groups and Theory Y organizations, most large corporations today are bent on increasing their organizational scope and anonymity through further mergers, acquisitions and consolidations."

That accusation becomes more valid with every passing megamerger. The Apples and the Gores are bound to seem more and more attractive against this background. But it isn't their free and easy ways that will ultimately call the tune. Just as the test of IBM is its ability to survive its own errors and turn them into triumphs, so the issue is whether Apple can continue to combat that same IBM profitably, or Gore to repel his new rainproof rivals. The proof of these motivational puddings isn't how well they're cooked, but what they taste like— to the marketplace, not the managerial palate.

The issue always comes back to the motivation of the firm. How individuals respond to treatment depends above all on the behavior that is the organizational norm. Where the bland are leading the bland, all the behavioral scientists in the American universities will not improve performance. However, it's important to note that these scientists have obtained impressive-seeming results below the managerial line by allowing workers to plan their own operating schedules or salesmen to organize their own selling. Under the stimulus of Japanese competition and in the sporadic lust to imitate elements of Eastern competitors' methods, ideas like quality circles and quality-of-working-life programs have paraded the surely obvious truth that the more you involve men and women in their work, the better the results of that labor will probably be. The behavioral scientists and the Japanese management experts should try persuading a few more corporations to allow their executives actually to execute; then the behavioral geniuses will really earn their fabulous fees, though it shouldn't require a posse of expensive professors to teach chief executives how to suck that particular egg.

20

Centers
of No Profit

The idea of the *profit center,* of slicing a business into the maximum number of accountable components, has taken its time to work through. For instance, it didn't start to penetrate the nether regions of du Pont, the first bastion of American capitalism and of decentralization, until the start of the 1970s. Many large companies have still missed the message entirely. In a way, the benighted can't be blamed, because many (perhaps most) profit centers don't make any profits, and they aren't centers. But the device satisfies a great managerial yearning to imagine that every cell of the corporate body is a business like one's own.

Top executives in profit center companies brag that they want every junior to run his center as if that were truly so. It's an answer to corporate flatulence, a medicine to revive the flow of entrepreneurial blood in stiffening arteries, a means of ideal

238

progression for the executive—earning his spurs in his very first little profit center, moving on from center to center until he arrives at that big profit center in the sky, the chief executive's suite. This ideal hankers back to the golden past when the business was small enough for one man to run and the founder in his buggy could supervise his first clutch of salesmen from the end of the road. The profit center, with its one man and his show, is a spiritual snub to corporate bureaucracy.

But the profit center is no more a manager's own business than a self-drive car belongs to the customer. Like Hertz or Avis, the company leases out a piece of its property; but it retains full possession, and it exacts a heavy toll. The center can't be run like one's own business because the real owners (not the de jure ones, the stockholders, but the de facto ones, the managerial Mafia) don't want it run that way, whatever they say.

The small businessman must answer only to himself, his family, his conscience, his professional advisers, and his tax collector. Nobody makes him submit an annual budget, plus his plans for the next five years, for scrutiny and approval. Nobody tells him how much he can take out of the business or put in. Nobody vetoes his bright new ideas or his choice of staff or his business proposals. But the powers kept by top management include all this—and more.

In any event, the profit center can be so arbitrary a creation that it isn't a business at all. In chemical companies this little fact is at its nastiest. Much of the work in chemical companies is for a sole customer—the company itself. Profit Center A sells all its output to Profit Center B, which sells all its output to Profit Center C, which finally offloads the stuff on the public. At this stage, the company at last makes a profit.

The game is played to well-known rules such as: Never make anything inside that you can buy cheaper outside. Philips Lamp of Eindhoven plays the game more than most, since it has diversified into almost every component under its sun. But what happens if Philips satellite A, buying component X from satellite B, finds that Xs are a drug on the outside market and selling for peanuts? Will B give up its Philips business? Not on your life: it will cut its internal "transfer" price down to the outside level, and the stockholders will be left with yet another unprofitable chunk of turnover. Earnings per share at Philips fell by 22 percent in the 1960s, and much the same dismal tale of sales growth failing to generate tolerable profit expansion was retold in the 1970s—with only slightly better excuse.

Chairman Wisse Dekker, who took charge in 1981, wisely didn't blame Philips' futile shortfall on external recession. He accepted the fact that internal defects of management structure and marketing were equally to blame, and set about the tough task of correcting both. Never before had the tightly knit bunch of top Philips managers admitted that their bureaucratic organization had militated against their monetary returns (not to mention their marketing; the local managers in some of the sixty-two countries in which Philips operates, when unable to gain head-office approval for new products they badly needed, sometimes used to introduce them unofficially—what might be called black-market innovation). With world recovery giving a powerful assist, Dekker raised profits threefold in the first three years of his regime—meaning the final profits at the end of the corporate line.

Any striking of profits down the line is merely an imaginative hobby, at which corporation executives pass many an idle hour, day, and week. What's more, A, B, and C are all lumbered with charges for central overhead—basically the costs of the head office, over which they have not an atom of control. So even their accounts bear very little relation to those of an independent company, especially since A and B largely depend for their sales growth and investment projects on how those SOBs in C make out in the market.

The consumer markets see the most contorted attempt to slice up the corporate cornucopia—the concept of the *brand executive.* His "business like his own" is a brand, and the lucky man (normally young) is responsible, in theory, for everything from its packaging and pricing to its advertising and distribution. If the brand is a proud and treasured heirloom, however, the company will tie the brand executive to its apron strings so tightly that he can hardly breathe.

The only brand executives allowed real freedom are those with products on which the corporation has given up; and then, if the bright young man puts real management muscle behind his baby, he comes up against the sound barrier—the corporation won't provide any more spending money. It's all earmarked for Daz, or Maxwell House, or some other boring product without which the whole corporation would cease to be a center of profit.

The total profit center (the corporation) won't genuinely atomize itself, for mechanical and emotional reasons. This hard fact matters most to those who share the ideal of the small business. The theory is that the large business breeds inefficiencies out of its size (true), and that small businesses are therefore more efficient (false). Most small businesses are just as incompetent—that's why they stay small, and why so many go bankrupt, passing unnoticed and unwept over to the other side. Every now and again the true course of events in a small business gets known outside, and the picture can be quite fantastic.

There was one modest-size, fast-growing company whose boss demanded only one management accounting statistic—weekly turnover. As long as turnover was rising, this happy entrepreneur was tickled pink. After all, he knew his percentage profit, didn't he? He didn't. In any case, the turnover figure was inflated by double-counting whenever (as it largely did) the sales division sold to the hire side. The company duly descended into bankruptcy, turnover figures still bounding upward, as the result of infantile errors that any competent accountant, if allowed, could have eliminated in an afternoon.

Small firms are always publicized as the backbone of the economy, especially in the United States, where the image of the little entrepreneur is as strong as that of the pioneer frontiersman. But neither, in point of fact, made the United States economy what it is today. The small firms dominate only numerically. In qualitative and quantitative terms the clumsy mammoths lead. Without them, America and Britain would still be stuck at the Greek level of economic progress.

This runs counter to much modern economic philosophy, fervently espoused by right-wingers—like the Reaganites in America and the Thatcherite sisterhood and brotherhood in Britain. This school of thought (and action—small business has never had it so good in terms of government handouts and concessions) was greatly heartened by David Birch of MIT. He opined in 1981 that most of his great country's jobs were not created by the giant corporations, but by the modest employers: to wit, firms with under 100 employees had generated 82 percent of the entire mass of new jobs created from 1969 to 1976. This was most remarkable, not to say odd, at a time when total employment in small business seemed unable to budge from 40 percent of the jobs total.

In fact, the true figure for small business creation of jobs appears to be around half, a creditable performance, to be sure, but one for which, according to a White House report of 1983, "a fraction of small firms" is responsible. The most conspicuous contribution comes from small firms sponsored by the venture capitalists, who raised $3.4 billion in 1983 for 1,500 different businesses. But that's a drop in the numerical ocean of all new business formations (10,000 a week), and even smaller in the financial context of a $3 trillion economy.

True, the impact of that venture dribble gigantically exceeds its initial scale. Venture-capitalist Ben Rosen has calculated that $50 million launched Intel, Apple, Microsoft, Rolm, Genentech, and Tandem, for which sum, among other marvels, the U.S. economy gained the microprocessor, the personal computer, and memory chips (all developed, significantly, in under two years, against the thirty-year gestation period for radar). But those half-dozen companies are highly atypical. Far more typical are the 85 or 90 percent of small firms that, as John Thackray writes, "go through long fallow periods when they don't create a single job."

The record of one small British textile company is representative of the way that little firms merely cling to life like limpets on a rock. After fifty years it was earning less profit and making fewer sales, in real terms; its investment in new plant had been negligible; what there was had been wasted; and much of the energy of its management had evaporated in internecine disputes that made boardroom politics seem like cozy parlor games.

No big corporation would want any segment of the business managed as a small company really runs; and it is stupid to moon over a nonexistent ideal. The profit center cannot work as a way to make managers think like individual businessmen. It is only another good, vain try at resolving the conflict between the corporation as a decision-making entity (that is, head office) and the corporation as a business (that is, the sharp end, the places where the money is made).

As H. G. Lazell, the great marketing man who brought Beecham to the States, once said, "That's the struggle all the time, the battle between head office and division, the battle for power." The profit center is a fiction to give the divisions the idea that they are winning the struggle. But the divisions know the real score; and they resent the millions that (as they think) they shell out for central expertise, control, and direction, which in divisional eyes seem more like expense and interference.

This is why ICI executives make that jest about the Millbank headquarters in London as "Millstone House," or why an aggressive divisional boss in Unilever says about central charges, "You have to pay your club subscription . . . but there are few operating skills of our sort sitting in the middle." There does, in fact, seem to be an uncanny correlation between the size of the head office and the ineffectiveness of the company. It was a richly symbolic gesture when ICI, under the new chairmanship of the iconoclastic John Harvey-Jones, decided to sell Millstone House. The message was unmistakable. As Harvey-Jones told *Newsweek,* "The thing I'm really interested in is how you make large organizations work." That meant, in practice, not only cutting out still more superfluous employees and unwanted products, but also reducing the board by a third and decentralizing the authority to make decisions. Killing the centralization of Millstone House was essential if ICI itself was to live.

By the same token, Helmut Maucher of Nestlé, another new boss, knew exactly what he was doing, and what it symbolized, when he sold off a brand-new office building, designed by I. M. Pei, in Purchase, New York. As Maucher, another keen decentralizer of decisions, explained, the old building was "good for a long time yet." Maybe somebody had told him that a large company's stock often nose-dives when it moves to spanking new offices. The Vickers armaments group, which put up what was then London's most ambitious skyscraper, and then saw its stock promptly halve in half a dozen years, is one awful example. Union Carbide, tragically accident-prone, is another; one year its Park Avenue skyscraper had to stand in suspended animation until earnings picked up again. Both Shell and BP, too, ran into profit constipation and organizational purges after they moved houses; and there is clear managerial logic involved.

Overhead always shoots up, because the new building invariably costs much more, and it's temptingly easier to add more central staff, more central departments, and hence still more central cost. So it was a good omen for the Vickers stockholders (and divisional managers) as occupancy of the tower shrank from the original thirteen floors to a mere half dozen. It was a bad sign for the owners of the British steel industry (the Labor government) when their newly nationalized British Steel Corporation moved next door to Buckingham Palace. The same offices had housed one of the most notorious cost centers in Britain, headquarters of a defunct electrical dinosaur, whose 800 central employees compared with 160 in its purchaser, the three times larger GEC. The U.K. steel industry promptly lost some £140 million in four and a half years.

Even that was a mere bagatelle compared to the £1 million a day the corporation was losing later on, at the height (or depth) of its powers. The losses were stemmed only by staging a command performance of the Incredible Shrinking Steel Industry, to which the grandiose headquarters seemed increasingly inappropriate. None of these moves and expenses are undertaken at the request of the profit center. The head office, the cost center par excellence, imposes its levies whether the divisions like it or not. And the levy is never light. In modern times only a brilliant giant has pretax profit margins of 10 percent; so incurring $10 million of extra central costs, in effect, cancels out at least $100 million, very possibly $200 million of profitable turnover. Yet the onus is never on the head office to prove itself; the onus is always on the divisions and that onus is to pay on demand.

The profit center practice finally breaks down here. Executives shouldn't be held to account for expenditure that they can't control. They can never run their bit as if the business were their own, because it isn't. The recipe, however, is to let them run it as if the *money* were their own. The money isn't theirs either, and don't let them forget it, but it can be made to look that way. Start off by imposing no central charges except for specific services (such as market or product research), which can be charged for specifically. After all, the head office ultimately collects all the loot, anyway, and it can afford to pay its own expenses.

The counterargument is that excluding the central overhead gives a false view of divisional profitability; but so may the arbitrary allocation of that load around the joint. The most remarkable operation of this kind is at the du Pont Company in Wilmington. There the decentralized divisions share the same monumental offices as the headquarters. Elaborate apportionments of the central costs have to be made continuously, as if the divisions were headquartered in distant places like Nome, Alaska.

Du Pont, moreover, acts on the typical big-company principle. Because a division is making a bundle of money, it doesn't mean that it can spend a lot. It follows, of course, that even though a division is making no money at all, it may be authorized to invest like wildfire. In logic, a high earner should cash in on its luck; an unprofitable unit should suffer the pressures of its own misfortunes. The notion of running a business as if the money were your own demands no less.

Running it when it truly is your own teaches powerful lessons in reality. As a fascinating example, advertising agencies were once notorious for managerial incompetence, which some of the brightest and best displayed *in excelsis* when trying to diversify. But in Britain, where local circumstances encouraged spin-offs and new agencies eager to crack American dominance, the breakaways showed how quickly, under pressure, even advertising men could learn the ropes. Two of the newcomers, brothers Charles and Maurice Saatchi, in fourteen years magically multiplied $1.5 million of billings into $2 billion, which in 1984 ranked the group as the world's seventh-largest agency. It was managed, though, by keeping its separate agencies just that way—separate. In a world in which the difference between triumph and tragedy lies in ideas, and in how the brainwave is presented to the great consuming public, the idea merchants no longer occupy the lowly position that, in traditional industry, was reserved to the manservants of manufacture.

Neither do Saatchi and Saatchi and the other creations of this new world organize themselves as the manufacturers did; because, in the service industries, the business is typically of recent foundation and funded with the entrepreneur's own limited resources, the own-money philosophy tends to come on hot and strong. What hurts with your own money is not the earning of it but the spending. Profit centers are strictly speaking cost centers, and it's costs that executives should agonize over. But in real life the detailed head-office control is over one kind of spending only—investment. A divisional director must line up, cap in hand, to get permission for a $900,000 extension while, out in the sticks, a factory supervisor is incurring extra current costs of exactly the same amount, without the head office even knowing.

That problem is supposed to be dealt with by the budget. But nobody can accurately predict all costs for a year ahead. Targets, too, are seldom set in cost terms, and managers are not assessed on their cost-cutting ability; witness the sluggish acceptance of value engineering, which expresses the devastatingly true idea that no product is ever designed for manufacture in the most economic way possible.

Executives are natural spendthrifts with other people's money. One great company chairman excused his company's total lack of control over a trade investment—this "profit center" had to be saved from dire losses and bankruptcy—because the dollars involved were only a few million, compared with, say, $450 million for sales of a major division. This is a man who would be hurt by a personal expenditure of a few hundred.

If he had been taught to think of the company's money in the same way as his own, that few million might never have been lost. The relative amounts are irrelevant—it is all money, and other people's too.

When the big-corporation director starts to think of millions only as numbers, the termites are in. The head office's prime duty is to remind executives that money is real, which naturally means that the head office must take the same unpalatable view. In fact, directors do customarily treat the corporation's money as if it were their own—but not in the proper sense. They spend as if in recent receipt of a rich uncle's legacy.

Few firms reach the opulence of one British company that kept three kitchens for the directors, each offering a different national cuisine; owned a grouse moor; provided two houses for the chairman; and hired private trains for the board's annual pilgrimage to its Midlands factories. But few companies follow the austere standards of one chief executive who bars all fringe benefits and all padding of expense accounts, even with tiny sums. (He somewhat spoils the picture by refusing to work for a company that won't provide a decent car—meaning a Rolls-Royce—for every director.)

How the director in the profit, cost, or loss center down the line behaves is a function of how the executives at the top behave and of what they expect from others. They should start from a known truth: that the head office is an unnecessary evil unless proved otherwise. They should confine headquarters functions to those central areas that are central by definition (patents, law, finance, and the like). The executive directors, kept as small a band as possible, shouldn't attempt to duplicate in any way the operating functions in the divisions. They shouldn't spend their time second- or third-guessing the operating directors to no good effect, or waste money providing services that the divisions either don't need or can perfectly well, and much more cheaply, supply for themselves.

And the head office shouldn't become a luxurious men's club for the chosen few, nor should expense accounts be high-class pocket money. Nor should the inhabitants pretend that central expenses are low because only a few people work in the West Coast pad or Manhattan glass mansion. Many a company has a tight headquarters only because all the central staff are stacked up around the main factory site. But that is where staff should be wherever possible—not in the company's Taj Mahal, but close to where it's all happening, close to the factory, or to the market, or to both.

A head office can be every bit as bureaucratic at the plant, of course, as in White Plains, Wilmington, or New York City; and the bigger the plant, the better (or worse) the chances of bureaucracy building up. Wilbert Gore, the Gore-Tex inventor, is only one of many people who hold strongly, convinced in part by experience, that when it comes to plant size, small is very, very beautiful. As soon as Gore found he had 180 persons working at his first plant, he started another factory, and another, and another—and none of today's Gore plants has more than a couple of hundred people, all highly motivated and allegedly all having fun, just as Robert Townsend said they would.

But it's not only smallness that helps give a real sense of ownership—it's ownership. Townsend argues that any executive worth his salt should march into the owners of the business (pretty difficult if it's du Pont, but never mind) and demand that 15 percent of the profit be set aside, forever, for distribution to the employees. What if the owners say no? You politely shake hands, say good-bye—and move to some other company that has the sense to realize that 85 percent of a fortune is worth vastly more than 100 percent of nothing very much. Indeed, companies with a brilliant record of motivational management do tend to share the spoils—or to insist that they are shared: at People Express, which in half a dozen years has carried 15 million passengers, to its great profit, each employee must buy company stock as a condition of employment. But this insistence goes with an organization to match. "Everybody has manager status in a flat structure," according to *Management Today;* "employees work in small teams which set their own goals and are self-managing within the company's objectives." Actually, the ownership of stock (witness the multitudinous cases of failure despite employee stockholding) isn't the only form of possession that counts, not by a long shot.

Owning the job is at least as important. Interestingly, executives at IBM (deluded or not) use the first person a great deal. It's "I" did this or that, and "my" plant, and "my" plan. The sense of job ownership is concrete and a real force for managerial good. It's facilitated, too, by the breakdown of corporations into small, discrete units, capable of making both managerial and economic sense, which is happily the prevailing mode among managements that think about their managing. In this recipe, the head office functions as banker (you can't leave cash lying around all over the corporation) and almost as an independent investment trust whose business is owning operations, taking in dividends, and reinvesting the money. But this banker has the unique advantage of being able to demand performance from the executives running its investment. If the profit center concept really meant anything, this would be the only role reserved to the head office. By minding their own business, the management Mafia would in truth be able to run the company as if it were their own. But they want passionately and insistently to manage, and to manage the wrong things. Consequently, the executives under their authority feel that nothing is their own and they manage just as you would expect.

21

Merchandising the Future

An electronics tycoon, famed as an emperor of automation, hated to be told that he made and marketed hardware. He would retort with heat, "I'm selling the future." His firm later became more and more unprofitable until it was sold (at too high a price) to an even larger and equally troubled seller of futures, which duly disappeared in exactly the same way. Those who sell the future, like those who buy it, face a heavy risk of being sold a pup. No law, economic or moral, holds that all technological advance must provide rewards. In many industries, technology not only advances slowly but its significant moves exploit innovations that are scientific ancient history.

The larger the advance, the greater the chance that the executives will end in the most uncomfortable, exposed, and expensive posture of all: sitting well ahead of the market. The postwar history of the aircraft industry should disabuse executives who believe that if you look after the future, the future will look after you. The jet engine saw late action in the last world war. Boeing's 707, itself a development of a military tanker, made its first flight in 1954. Yet to win orders, Boeing felt it had to price the plane to the bone. When the wide-fuselage jumbo (embodying even less significant technological advances) flew along, this sad history was repeated, with much the same financial results. You could argue that Boeing's biggest stroke of luck came when Washington denied funds for the next great leap forward in technology, the Supersonic Transport. That left the world market wide open for Britain and France, who proceeded to scoop the pool—all of sixteen aircraft, built and subsequently flown at losses horrendous even by aerospace standards.

The aerospace industry's troubles stem partly from the conviction of its executives that, like Everest, the next technical peak must be scaled, because it is there. The aerospace managements love their technology even more than their money. That being so, nobody (including their financial backers) should be surprised when technological effort ends in financial failure. What's more, disaster strikes even though the companies are largely spared the bugbear expense of research and development. Fantastic largess has been invested in this group of businesses by governments, especially in the United States, all because of their importance to national defense and technical prestige.

Europeans commonly cite the American figures with anxious awe as the most unfair disadvantage under which European competitors labor. But the so-called spin-off from military work is small both in absolute terms and in relation to the total U.S. federal spending on research. The military is a highly specialized customer; and, in any case, executives are incompetent at transferring technology from one market to another, even within the same company.

The men making missiles and space shuttles are not interested in machine tools or refrigerators, even if the advanced technology is cheap enough to be of any use (which it isn't). Rockwell, big maker of automotive components, had the hilarious notion when it bought North American that the latter's aerospace know-how would help Rockwell itself. Al Rockwell later sadly admitted, "We did overanticipate that there were some products at North American that we could tool up and take off the shelf and manufacture."

The most advanced technology is often worse than expensive—it may not even work. The record of electronics in weapons systems supplied to the Pentagon, with six out of eleven major systems begun during one ten-year spell achieving 25 percent or less of specification and only two coming up to snuff, does not inspire faith in applying defense goodies to mass-produced goods. The spin-off from civilian industry into military technology is probably much greater than the reverse spin: for instance, all the du Pont products in the Apollo program had originally been developed for down-to-earth sale. Those industries (data processing and electronic components, for main examples) that have been utterly transformed by advanced technological developments are exceptions. Those apart, there is no evidence, so far, that the rich economic prizes go hand-in-hand with technological preeminence alone.

On the contrary (but perfectly logically), the greater the leap forward, technologically speaking, the greater the risk. This isn't only a fact of microelectronics—although Trilogy didn't even get off the ground with its state-of-the-art superchip, while at least more humdrum failures, like Osborne, had enjoyed a brief spell of glorious sales and profits. Look at any industry, and you will find at least one example of ambition overreaching itself. Thus Dow Chemical constructed an ethylene plant in the Gulf of Mexico, based on the brilliant idea of using crude oil direct, without the intervention and cost of an oil refinery. For all anybody knows, the process might have been a brilliant success, but the plant has never operated (resulting in a loss to the company of half a billion dollars), not because of technological defect but because Dow couldn't get a big enough supply of the requisite crude at the requisite price. Aim for the moon, in other words, and you may hit the ground.

West Germany's record in high technology is about as inspiring as its performance in management education: nil. Yet until the oil price shocks it had the world's second most successful economy, the most brilliant being a Japanese economy led, originally, not by space-age whiz products but by supertankers (which are nothing but floating boxes), motorbikes, cameras, portable radios, hi-fis, and autos. And how about hovercraft, carbon fibers, metal oxide semiconductors, fluidics, and glass transistors? All of these are technological marvels of the 1960s on which, well into the 1970s, any investor would have lost most of his shirt; indeed, only three of the five had come into their own by the 1980s.

None of this will stop a manager from bragging about his research and development spending, as if the money itself promoted something beyond the continued employment and well-being of scientists. Big-company executives are sure that research and development is intrinsically good and absolutely essential; yet its results in big companies are generally disappointing. Rather than conclude that there is something wrong with the management of the whole company, directors decide that the fault lies with the specific management of research and development. Consequently, quantities of intellect and trouble have gone into attempts to make research and development live up to its billing as a fountain of profit.

The most discredited of these pastimes is "brainstorming," in which all the participants are encouraged to throw onto the table every idea in their heads, however asinine; and that's what you get—asinine ideas. The most intellectual game is known as *technological forecasting.* The object is to show companies where, given the likely developments, they should concentrate their efforts. The names of the technological forecasting techniques (Delphi, morphological research, relevance trees, and the like) are a poem in themselves; their weakness is that, by the time the forecasts are proved right or wrong, it's too late. If you back a wrong horse (for instance, if you happened to choose the steam engine in preference to internal combustion), excellent research and development will inevitably go to waste. Technological forecasting won't solve the problem that makes research and development genuinely baffling to its directors: that its results are so hard to predict and to measure that the directors cannot quantify what they want.

This vagueness has its charms—the executive can (and usually does) merely avoid making any sensible calculations at all. Investors have the same entranced rapture in face of the future. The case of Viatron can stand as their monument. The hot technology idea was to apply MOS (metal oxide semiconductors) to LSIC (large-scale integrated circuits). Investors who couldn't tell an MOS from an MTB, or an LSIC from LSD, rushed to buy the stock on issue—even though the prospectus said candidly (as U.S. law insists) that the management had no reason whatsoever to suppose that it could make anything but a shambles of the business, which it duly did.

Under the banner Never before have mass production methods been applied to the computer industry, Viatron offered to lease its System 21 wonder terminals for $39 a month. This low, low price, in a typical hot technology gambit, was not justified by economics, but by the necessity to get high orders, without which the price of the MOS magic could not be lowered from sky-high levels. The inevitable end was a collapse all along the management line, a switch to selling the terminals at much higher prices and a bankruptcy that stranded all the stockholders high and dry—and nobody could say they didn't deserve it.

The moral of Viatron is that greed is no substitute for intelligence. The company's own statements made it clear that Viatron was a monstrous gamble, which in any context save that of high technology and buying the future would have been shunned like Central Park at night. The Viatron backers got mugged. Any attempt at purchasing the future can be reduced to figures, and all that Viatron's known statistics showed was loss, loss, and more loss. Against this known chasm, its executives and supporters set the prospect of entirely unquantified Xerox or Polaroid-style gains—if the technology, marketing, general management, and following wind were all set fair. That's like jumping out of an aircraft without a parachute.

But sums fly out of the window when the future comes in the door. At a more prosaic level of technology, and of market appeal, the Nimslo camera succeeded in uncovering all the same naïve eagerness as Viatron in very recent times. What *The Financial Times* labeled as among the ten greatest technological flops ever ran through enormous sums of money: $43 million of losses in 1982 and 1983, on top of $38 million of capital supplied by investors who might have been able to read balance sheets but couldn't apparently understand simple facts—like Nimslo's need to capture a share of the market that was ridiculously high by Polaroid standards with a product that plainly had less appeal.

The market sums just didn't add up. But to those intent on the hope of emulating Polaroid without a Polaroid, sums are unimportant. Even in the death throes of the Nimslo apparatus as a consumer product, the latest management was cutting the price while lowering production to fit a financially crippling shortfall in demand. To innocents in these matters, the more reasonable course of action might have seemed to be (a) a price cut accompanied by higher or unchanged output or (b) a price increase linked with lower production. But when you look at life through three-dimensional spectacles, the results are different. The logical alternatives didn't apply, because the product itself was illogical: that is, 3-D photography has no advantage sufficient to attract more than an inadequate minority of the public. The backers made the fatal mistake of being seduced, not by the market potential but by the technological promise.

Similar lessons should be engraved on the hearts of all futurologists, high and low. In estimating costs, work out an honest number and then double it. Nor is the future priceless: there is always a point where the price becomes too high. Whether the cost lies in research and development or in operating losses in a new business, the question is always the same. How much can current earnings be sacrificed for future benefit? In this context the only sensible (and often only too accurate) way is to treat research and development as pure loss. The minute a company starts to kid itself that scientists' wages are an asset, it is writing its doom on the wall.

How much a company shells out depends on personal taste and the quality of its research and development staff (a quality that nontechnical managers, being ill equipped to judge, are prone to exaggerate). Given that research and development is always to some extent a game of chance, it is dangerous to spend less than the other players; you may as well have the same number of throws. The research and development write-off can also be regarded simply as a firm's subscription to the industry club, as the license fee that entitles it to stay in business. Whatever the firm spends, however, executives must do the kind of back-of-an-envelope sums that far too many managements either fail to scribble down or else ignore. It's no use putting big money into a transistorized combination electric toaster, tea-maker, and radio clock; the likely demand for such a toy will never generate the needed earnings. (One firm actually did produce a combination portable radio and camera, which is just as weird.)

If a company is going to lose $10 million this year—or spend it on research and development—the financial pain is only worth incurring for a sure *extra* $2.5 million profit after a five-year wait. "Anyone who enters the Continental computer market must be prepared to stand a loss operation for five years," said a Honeywell man sagely. He didn't add (because he didn't know) that the five lean years would not be followed by the five fat ones that would have made the losses worthwhile. Obviously the longer the wait, the larger the return has to be. Any executive who lets money drain away today without knowing which tomorrow will bring the payoff, or even what size that bonanza will be, is leaping into the dark with somebody else's cash.

Expensive research work can be sorted out by a simple question: If it succeeds, what is the maximum potential financial benefit? Once the spending has passed the point at which the return is worth having, the answer is equally simple—halt. A new and potent danger sign pops up at this point: the just-around-the-corner complex. Just as prosperity was always around that next bend during the Depression, executives persist in believing that the loss-making business, the failed new venture, the great research and development program, is going to pay off—any moment now.

The complex has a subsyndrome: "We've spent so much already that it would be silly not to go on." If $100 million has vanished without trace into a project, and "only" $10 million more will bring the breakthrough to a $5 million return, the investment seems marvelous: only $10 million for a $5 million annual payoff! Gee! But the return on the total outlay is still hopelessly inadequate. Even supposing that the latest forecast turns out to be right (and it won't), simple payback will take twenty-two years. The result is a permanent drag on the business, or when the same argument gets applied to some prestige aerospace venture such as the Concorde, a heavy permanent tax on the national economy.

The Beecham group learned how not to research, and how to, in the most telling way, which is the hard one. Its former chairman, H. G. Lazell, believed in the goodness of research. For years he defended and sustained Beecham's research effort single-handedly, with no valuable results at all. Then Lazell saw his error. Nobody had decided what Beecham wanted from research; therefore, the company could neither concentrate its efforts nor define them. A chastened Lazell chose to concentrate on one of the lush pharmaceutical markets; taking his expert adviser's expert advice (another rare virtue), he put all Beecham's research money on fermentation chemistry, and came up with a well-bred, wealthy family of synthetic penicillins.

Beecham could still have failed. Its research was still undiluted risk; rumor says that a rival company's penicillin was only narrowly beaten to the tape. But Beecham knew that it could easily survive the loss if the project failed. Just as important, the reward, if success came, was certain to return the research and development investment many times over. That is much more intelligent than spending money you haven't got to achieve an objective that is either not worth reaching or impossible to attain.

The Ninth Truth of Management is: *if you are attempting the impossible, you are bound to fail.* Worse than that, you will fail abjectly, because the Eighth Truth—as shown in the still-unfinished saga of Digital Equipment and the small computer —also operates its malevolent magic: *because what you are doing is wrong, it will be done badly.* Hot competition, led by IBM, in the scientific and engineering markets, where its mini-computers had once reigned supreme, left DEC no option but to tackle other, broader sectors. Its attempted strategy in the new markets was the same as that which had succeeded so brilliantly in the old: aimed at the same customers, with the same low level of promotion and the same emphasis on established, reliable technology rather than innovation.

But the market consisted of new customers who could be reached only by massive advertising—and could be convinced only by technological novelty and prowess. Setting off in the wrong direction, DEC was too late and too lumbering. In consequence, it won no significant position in personal computers or work stations—and it began to stumble over minis as well; its Venus supermini, according to *Business Week,* was two years late in 1984. Small wonder that DEC's margins have halved since 1981.

The implausible, if not the impossible, can be achieved. But the process is essentially romantic, random, unplanned. No big corporation, being prosaic, routinized, and formal, could have contrived, say, the extraordinary encounter of two Hungarians and a German who created Syntex and the whole birth-control pill business by processing progesterone from the barbasco root, a yam grown wild in the Mexican jungle (into which the shy German later retreated as a recluse).

The pursuit of the impossible explains the long, lugubrious record of airline manufacturers outside the United States. The back of an envelope used to say that projects could coin money at a production rate of only eight a month, with the break-even point somewhere around three hundred copies. (This was the calculation that proved to the satisfaction of everybody, except Lockheed's executives, that their beloved Tristar was a financial flying flop.) Because no outside manufacturer, given the predilection of U.S. airlines for buying American, had any hope in this world of that kind of orders, all their projects were doomed to economic failure, either relative or (mostly) absolute. The equations held good right up to the end of the 1970s. Even then, the U.S. sales of the European Airbus didn't disprove the point. The mold-cracking Pan Am order came about, in part, only because the desperate, heavily subsidized Airbus consortium had built so many "white-tails"—planes for which there were no visible customers.

He who seeks the most advanced, sophisticated, versatile, and technically interesting product reaps enormous development costs and a heap of trouble. In many markets, he who wants the most foolproof, rugged, purpose-built, and technically boring product can make it more cheaply and sell it on those humdrum qualities alone. Customers who buy conventional power plants have a reasonable expectation that they will come on stream on time and on cost. Customers who buy U.S. nuclear stations, judged by the experience of the past decade, have a reasonable (or unreasonable) expectation that they will be horribly late and will cost anything up to ten times the original estimates. Even with conventional stations, it was always the newfangled high-technology mammoths—such as New York State's Big Allis—that were the ones that worked half the time, with luck.

The real edge in U.S. technology always lay more in improving established commercial technology and production techniques than in genius in the labs. Europeans have been wise to whip across the Atlantic to see what new productive wizardry the Americans have wrought. Great fortunes were built in this elementary way in the days when the United States ruled the production roost. Now it's often the Americans who travel hopefully abroad in search of the technological advances made by others—for instance, almost every postwar innovation in steel production. The ultimate blessing of technology, though, is that you can buy what you cannot invent. So do it. The Japanese have developed this to so fine an art that they have long been licensing back to America products and processes originally brought from the United States.

One of the little ways in which Western competitors love

to deceive themselves, however, lies in arguing that the Japanese are not creative technologically. Any camera buff knows that this is nonsense; so does anybody who has operated a personal copier, or donned the earphones of a Walkman, or switched on a video recorder. Japanese manufacturers have an incurable itch for invention—they generally insist on building their own production machinery; and it's their makers of robots and other advanced automation equipment, not the Americans or the West Germans, who have the numerical lead in world markets. The prime characteristic of Japanese innovation, though, is that it is genuinely market-led. Like IBM, the company that they so much admire, the Japanese are less interested in the technology than in whether they can sell it.

Steel's basic oxygen furnace is a wondrous illustration of today's real technology race—invented in Austria, applied widely in Germany, taken up late by the Americans, perfected by the Japanese, and adopted last by the British. There can be virtue in coming first. Like everything in management, however, it depends on the price, and sometimes it is better, richer, and safer to come a very good second.

Your technologists will oppose bitterly your refusal to allow them to waste your money by trying for first. They will also oppose any new idea that didn't spring from their own brains. Don't let them get away with either idiocy. Technical experts are always wrong until they prove themselves to be right; and it's the layman, not the scientist, who is most likely to spot a market opportunity or sweep aside some technological roadblock put up by well-educated blockheads—as did one executive who made his name by refusing to believe that drop forging couldn't be made continuous. You're not after a Nobel Prize, but an innovation that is useful and thus commercial. Remember that the zip fastener has made far more money than the vast majority of high-flying products of high-spending labs all over the world. Bear in mind that, leaving out oil, inheritance, real estate, merchants, and other accidents of nature, the greatest fortunes in America have lately been made in hand-held calculators (two guys called Hewlett and Packard), computer facilities (Perot), and word processors (Wang); all technology-based, to be sure, but about as far removed from nuclear power stations and the higher technological risks as you can imagine. Which, of course, is how and why the fortunes were made.

22

The Conglomerate
Capers

The shocks and shake-ups of the 1970s have had several salutary effects on management—not least the death or diminution of the myth that a manager could be an expert in nothing but management itself. Today the wise executive goes no further than calling himself "professional," meaning that he is paid to apply professional aptitudes and attitudes to performing a management task. His professional background may encourage him to transfer from cola drinks to personal computers, as John Sculley did in moving from Pepsi to Apple. But there's a world of difference between such transfers, the bread-and-butter of the executive headhunters, and the old conglomerate claim that it doesn't matter at all whether the product is pop or PCs. Part of your true professional's equipment is the knowledge that different businesses require different types, styles, and techniques of management, that only the rare (and maybe yet unborn) genius can manage whatever you give him with equal success by applying his expertise in his real business, which is management per se.

That was the selling pitch of the conglomerates. Since management does not exist, however, neither did the conglomerates, not in the sense in which they sold themselves to a fond public. Even the conglomerate-makers seem to have suspected their image; at least, some affronted aces in this hole did their best to escape the name.

As John Brooks pointed out in *The Go-Go Years,* they coined futile phrases such as "multimarket company," though conglomeration described their activities rather well. All conglomerates, the respectable and disreputable alike, use financial techniques to pile together unconnected businesses. They manage the results in the way of all holding companies since their time began (which was long ago). The purchases are shoved into common accounting and reporting systems and generally left to paddle their own canoes, leaky or buoyant, subject to varying degrees and forms of helpful and unhelpful head-office intervention.

The basic financial technique of conglomerate accounting was no more a business innovation than the management method. Financiers have been able to work out simple sums for a long time, and few sums are simpler than the one by which $10 million Company A, earning $10 million a year and valued in the market at $200 million, buys $10 million Company B, earning $10 million, but valued only at $100 million, and so neatly boosts its own earnings per share from $1 to $1.33.

This performance should not have fooled the management professors. But very few foresaw, as Peter Drucker did, that the red-hot conglomerates of the 1960s would become the corporate hulks less than a decade later. There are transferable management skills, and there are transferable executives. But it doesn't follow that all management skills transfer, or that one central team can possess all necessary skills, or even that all conglomerates had management skills of any kind, or that all executives can shift easily between all businesses.

This fallacy has been cruelly exposed, yet again, in the latest phase of conglomeration, the recent lust for financial services. It's understandable—almost inevitable—that industrial companies like Xerox, Armco, and Control Data should burn fingers, even whole arms, by meandering into investment banking, business centers, reinsurance, and so forth, businesses about which they knew nothing and for which they paid plenty. What these optimists were after was stability. What they got, to take Xerox as an example, was a $116 million collapse in earnings from Crum & Foster, its billion-dollar insurance buy, in just nine months of 1984.

But what about Connecticut Life and, still more, American Express? A life insurance company surely isn't too far removed from property insurance; at least, that was the thesis behind the Connecticut merger that formed CIGNA, topped up by the investment banking buy of Blyth Eastman Dillon. That deal didn't work out because (as CIGNA's chairman confessed) "we had a difficult time integrating Blyth. . . . There may be some companies that will be successful, though we certainly weren't." Undeterred by that experience, or by CIGNA's lackluster return to its investors (a crawling 5.2 percent compounded over the past decade), others have tried over and over to prove the CIGNA man right. Amex doubled its bet with no less than two investment banks, mutual funds, and international banking. The cost of this prize package was $3 billion and a great deal of pain. That results partly from having no less than eight outfits jostling each other for the money-management businesses of the institutions. As an Amex man said, mildly enough considering the circumstances, "The risks are that we don't pull it together. The risks are that somewhere the process breaks down, and that we don't benefit from having all these parts."

That's the same cry that marked the death throes of the old conglomerates that were in unrelated businesses. "Two and two makes five" synergy and transferable management have proved just as hard to obtain when executives are dealing in the ostensibly homogenous commodity known as money. Not only has Amex lost the wizard who built its recently purchased Geneva bank, it lost so much money on casualty insurance that, for the first time in thirty-five golden years, the Amex parent suffered a decline in earnings. At Sears and Prudential, similar woes have been won instead of the glittering prizes, and yet all the managements concerned were deeply experienced in what is loosely (too loosely, as it turned out) known as "financial services."

Given the billions lavished on these buys, this episode of conglomeration has been a hideously expensive proof that companies are effective at managing only in a certain line of business and some of their skills are nontransferable, intrinsic, and essential to that business. Because this is so, large corporations are bound to find diversifying less diverting than it seems. But at least diversifying is extraneous to their main activity. For the conglomerates, diversifying was their only business, and in the long run, that's generally a bad business to be in—or so the majority of U.S. experience would suggest.

A couple of *Harvard Business Review* writers, Salter and Weinbold, took a look at the capital productivity of thirty-six widely diversified companies—like Norton Simon, ITT, FMC, and Bendix. The diversification strategies that were supposed to raise performance actually brought their average return on equity *down* between 1967 and 1977. Compared to the *Fortune* 500, the demon diversifiers had made 20 percent more on equity at the start of the decade (thus obtaining the wherewithal for their diversifying). At the finish, though, their return was 18 percent less than the 500 average. Over the whole ten years, the dirty three dozen produced returns a fifth or more below those of the 500.

To descend from the general to the particular, diversification has proved to be so bad a business for ITT that, according to one analyst, nearly all the profits reported by the giant in the first three quarters of 1984 existed only on paper: its assets, estimated *Business Week,* were selling at maybe half their breakup value; the dividend had been cut; and in the wake of that last trauma, a financier was preparing a raid on the wreck. ITT's latest CEO, Rand V. Araskog, had cut the dividend to finance the investment badly needed, and shamefully overdue, to restore ITT's strength in its base market, U.S. telecommunications. But, of course, the entire rationale of conglomeration was to enhance the financial strength of the whole by combining its parts. In ITT's case, the original Geneen strategy had plainly had the reverse effect.

Yet ITT is a senior conglomerate citizen, which, like its fellows Litton and Textron (also the subject of a late 1984 raid), hated being tarred with the same brush as the sharper conglomerate-makers. So did the industrial establishment, which was offended by the sharp practices of the latter, and said so. But just as conglomerate web weavers lied in claiming to be a new form of business, so did the established companies who swore they were anything but conglomerates. All but nineteen of the two hundred largest U.S. companies were in at least ten different manufacturing categories as long ago as 1968. At the height of the conglomerate passion, no avowedly multimarket company had such multiple markets as General Electric. And even staid old citizens such as du Pont (now up to its neck in oil) see no reason why they should stick to chemicals; like the conglomerates, and with no more reason, they think their skills and resources are universal. After all, didn't they build the atomic bomb?

Large companies mostly decide to diversify at the moment when their profits from the businesses they really do understand are wilting. New sources of profit are the standard prescription at this juncture. But relative failure in fields you know is no great qualification for success in strange pastures. General Mills was the world's largest flour miller when it decided, under the stirring leadership of an Air Force general, that milling was a no-good, low-margin business, and that it would shift to emphasis on growth in earnings per share by risk-taking diversification. After costly purchases of food companies and European businesses as far afield as fashion and toys, General Mills is no longer the mightiest miller. Its earnings per share in the 1960s rose by precisely 69 percent. Fuddy-duddy old Pillsbury, the other Minneapolis flour giant, more than doubled in the decade.

Move on to 1973–83, and it is still investors in Pillsbury, the later and cannier diversifier, not those in General Mills, who have most reason to thank management, for an annual return of 17.9 percent against 10.35 percent. The best business is the simplest: a firm that markets one product in one market in one way and lives happily ever after. That phrase comes from fairy stories. Real life is different. At the start of the 1970s any executive in full possession of his senses would have traded an Avon for a GE any day. Avon's elementally simple idea of door-to-door selling by agents yielded almost one third of GE's profits on one eleventh of GE's sales, with a tiny proportion of GE's anxieties. Yet Avon's day was soon to be done. As its market worsened and its method became obsolescent, Avon slipped—until on a ninth of GE's sales it was earning only a twelfth of the giant's net.

Plenty of one-market examples exist to rub in the old Avon point, though. Dr. An Wang's single-minded concentration on processing words by computer, even in 1983, a year of greatly toughened competition, produced for the Wang company a quarter of ITT's net on a ninth of the sales. But Wang was one of the nineteen companies singled out by *Business Week* for strategic failure: the idea ("become the leader in the office-of-the-future market by introducing new products to combine data- and word-processing") had been "largely unsuccessful because of the rise in personal computers." Even a champion one-marketer is bound to get nervous eventually about the golden eggs sitting in that one beautiful basket. It begins to diversify, to stretch its market span, to spread (that is, to increase) its risks.

The more bets you have on a race, the more bets you are likely to lose. True, because the industries are widely spread, if some components are down, others will be up. But executives seldom spot the opposite truth—if some parts of the company are up, it follows inexorably that others will be down. The company is condemning itself to mediocrity, and to more conglomeration; for one diversification (like the first step on the primrose path) leads to another.

Before top management knows where it is, its preoccupation has ceased to be thermostats, or tires, or computers, but becomes the management of diversity. A brilliant Harvard Business School team, primed to the ears with accurate information about U.K. companies, came to the conclusion that British management's prime failure lay in mismanaging diversity—as if the Americans have proved any better. The confessed conglomerates and the diversified nonconglomerates have discovered alike that management doesn't work in the abstract. In practice, the many-eggs-in-many-baskets corporation either has to fall back into today's typical rut of unhappy compromises or abdicate a management role on classic lines and settle for a banker-investigator-stimulator function.

Effective diversified businesses do exist. Even though most businesses make odd bedfellows, strangeness doesn't rule out a happy sex life. Clothing companies shouldn't even dream of going into food. But after the war, Britain's Marks and Spencer, second only to Sears as a textile retailer, did so, and with more success than in its basic business. The company had abilities, premises, and policies that fitted both lines, and it capitalized on those genuine strengths, not on its mythical abilities.

Tobacco companies, in Britain and in America, had reason (à la Levitt) to think that their strength lay in marketing packaged and branded consumer goods. They were truly adept at selling cigarettes, a very different commodity, being neither necessary nor always competitively priced, from food. At R. J. Reynolds Industries, the transformation from tobacco could ultimately be achieved only by the wholesale import of executives from the consumer businesses that had tickled the tobacco men's taste buds; the latter's marketing abilities, it appeared from some damning with faint praise by the imported chieftain, lay mostly and merely in market segmentation.

You can crash in from scratch, as IBM did with electric typewriters and personal computers, and get away with it, but that depends on having a decisively better product and a transferable asset such as IBM's immovable indoctrination of office bosses (and secretaries) with its name. The further out a new line is (Rolls-Royce once even tried making saucepans), the less chance there is of making it succeed (Rolls couldn't even get the things to stand up).

As at Reynolds, food has attracted more diversifiers than any other dreamland, on the unsubtle argument that people will always eat. But even in inexhaustible markets a rule of thumb usually applies to all companies in all fields: only the two largest competitors and one specialist make big money. The price of becoming number two from scratch, let alone number one, is so ruinous that executives often run their behinds off to budge not one financial inch. If it's a virgin or *demi-vierge* market for the diversifier, he must buy his management experience. The lack of this asset, which can only be acquired over time, ensures a costly initiation.

This might seem to endorse that famous work by the

Boston Consulting Group which suggests that the greater the market share, the richer the accumulated experience, and the more profound the ability to extract the highest profitability from a market. So buying a small unit to get your feet wet— or developing one—may not be such a masterstroke after all. Don't rely on something your company doesn't have, transferable management skills, to develop something else it lacks, a worthwhile share of the market. But the purchase of companies with a lovely plump market share comes no cheaper. One American diversifier has kept its nose reasonably clean by refusing to pay more than fifteen times earnings for any purchase. On that none too demanding criterion (it means a payback over seven years, assuming, as you must, no increase in profits because of your own brilliant management), many diversifications by acquisition would never have been made, to the eternal benefit of the stockholders—and even of the executives.

Company executives seldom reflect that nobody forces them to diversify. They can afford to be greedy, to wait for opportunities where the criteria are all satisfied—rate of return, degree of risk, use of real existing strengths. That last criterion almost certainly restricts you to vertical acquisition—buying firms that fit onto existing interests. In a study of mergers by John Kitching, no vertical amalgamation failed, but 42 percent of the conglomerate mergers went phut. And while executives wait for the right buy, they can concentrate on their central assignment—making the most of existing major markets.

These foundation businesses—the data processing of IBM (still a highly specialized company, but evolving fast, in 1984), the base chemicals of du Pont or ICI, the instruments of Honeywell—in the end make the accidental conglomerate a better bet than the deliberate multimarket, whiz-kid creations were. The basic, solid sectors, however, bore executives. They want to pioneer new commercial frontiers. They love to quote the progress of new businesses, to boast how acquisitions have blossomed under their gardening—though a one-point drop in margins on the bread-and-butter business would wipe out the profits of every new jam tart in the group.

This gross disproportion encourages executives to hang on to their errors, in the forlorn hope that some miracle will avert the admission that they have bombed with stockholders' funds. Something about losing money warms an executive's entrails. It proves that he is doing what executives are supposed to do —building for the future. Capitalist mythology holds that all great businesses start by losing money, until the tide turns, the risks pay off, and the risk-taking company or entrepreneur finally gets his just glory.

Since most great businesses started small, this must be untrue. Small businesses can't survive years of loss—or couldn't until the mid-twentieth century. The bull market of the 1960s saw the American invention of the perpetually loss-making potential growth star: one hot Wall Street tip was an electronic tape firm that had lost money for fourteen successive years. The truly great and good product pays off early and piles up wealth incessantly. Where the payoff takes years, only a handful, like RCA's color TV, are genuine gambles against time. Mostly simple management mistakes spoil a perfect setup. Just as Boeing underpriced the 707, so did du Pont originally sell and manufacture Orlon for the wrong uses.

Neat little financial tricks are used to ease the pain of diversification losses. If managers buy companies, they don't calculate the return on the actual capital expended. If managers start new ventures, they work out returns only on the capital spent—the current losses made before that elusive corner is turned are forgotten as if they had never been. The exception comes when the firm's current profits aren't big enough to bear the strain; then the losses are "capitalized" as development spending.

But these pigeons always come home to roost when the management is finally forced up against the reality that its precious venture is kaput—stone-cold dead in the market. Then the only financial recourse available is the write-off or write-down: slicing a chunk off the corporation's assets and throwing in the accumulated operating losses, which, if you're really unlucky, may mean a sum like Texas Instruments' $660 million. That was lost in a home computer business founded, not on an accurate perception of a market gap that TI could exploit, but on a desire—irrelevant, in market terms—to offload some more of the company's own gigantic output of microprocessors.

Another American giant, whose bold geographical diversification had at long last broken into profit, kept its prodigious pride unmarred by memory of the losses incurred over the past years. Asked when accumulated profits would exceed accumulated losses, that is, when the European push would finally yield a clear cent, the corporate treasurer said, "I wouldn't know what to do with that number if I had it."

The secret of being a conglomerate (after first confessing that you are) is to be far more exacting and sharp financially than that—and to insist that money is paramount. If an operation justifies itself in money terms, you have an executive there who clearly knows his business. Don't bother him too much so long as he goes on proving it. Save top-management time for operations on which the group prosperity really swings, and for those that are going wrong. The easiest way of dealing with sour apples is to throw them out, but that means taking the easy route, when executives much prefer to have dramas and excitement instead.

The above principles aren't theoretical. They have been proved in practice. Two British groups have come from somewhere out in left field to achieve substantial scale, not least in the U.S. market. Hanson Trust, which late in 1984 tucked U.S.

Industries under its belt, has used exactly this approach to grow over a decade by 1,989 percent in sales, 1,730 percent in capital employed, and 2,520 percent in return to stockholders. The BTR performance outdid even that: 1,673 percent growth in profits (against Hanson's 772 percent), leading to a 5,891 percent enrichment of the stockholders. These groups are diversified with no logic at all, but they are organized on strictly logical lines to extract the most from the acquisitions that have been the key to their supergrowth: their business is buying and managing diversity—and their looming problem is how to sustain the growth when the buying has to stop.

The same point must be made of successful diversifiers who don't rely on acquisition skills. Procter & Gamble is the most frequently quoted case of ace diversifying, building up its paper-products business with rare success on the base of a relatively tiny acquisition. But these examples are good only as long as they last; General Mills was also praised for its rapid development from small to large of the Red Lobster food chain, which, by 1984, had become one of the corporate drags. Philip Morris was praised for years as the most successful of the tobacco diversifiers because of its work on Miller beer. By the time the beer binge had gone flat, the Seven-Up purchase, as noted earlier, had also proved a humbling failure.

The fatal error is to diversify merely because deep strategic thinking, or highbrowed strategic thinkers, convince the board that diversification is essential. That approach converted a respectable and respected engineering contractor like Fluor Corporation into a conglomerate with a sky-high stake in metals (it paid $2.3 billion for St. Joe Minerals in 1981, just in time for the slump in metal prices) and gave it enormous difficulty in showing a decent profit. It came about simply because the Fluor management wanted a cushion against the ups and downs of the capital investment cycle. Ten of the nineteen failed strategies reported by *Business Week* involved major

275

diversification. In contrast, of the fourteen plans classed as successes, nine involved increases in concentration, often with disposals of past diversifications thrown in (or out).

Any fool can end up with a corporation that has nothing for anybody—its backers, its stockholders, or its employees—except the ability to grow bigger and broader like the fat lady in the circus. Wide industrial spread is a misfortune that piles burdens on managers as they struggle to achieve genuine expansion in earnings. The irony is that, for a spell, some conglomerates set about the management of agglomerated multi-market companies in a realistic, demanding, and financially alert style. Their tragedy was that they came to share all the follies of the established and conglomerated nonconglomerates, including that of believing their own myths.

23

The Computer
Comes Clean

Of the changes that have conspicuously altered the world of management in the last decade, none is more obvious, more pervasive, and probably more important than the unpredicted revolution in computery. From a point when the pocket calculator didn't even exist, management has moved en masse into the age of the user-friendly, ultraversatile personal computer— sitting on his desk, even lying in his briefcase, capable of responding to an infinite number of demands. Plainly the powers of this device, its ability to communicate, compute, inform, and remind, will change the life of managers and the nature of management—maybe.

The qualification is necessary in light of previous failures in computer futurology and sociology. The computer used to scare more managers than any other invention—even the allied myth of automation, which is also now being made flesh. Yet business throughout the West ran into its worse postwar troubles with human labor at the end of the 1960s, which was about the time when, according to the more eager prophets, advanced mechanization would be making the two-legged factory staff redundant or servile, or both. The computer industry likewise ran into its first recession around the same date, when managements, according to the less realistic pundits, were already supposed to be recasting their entire corporations around the machine.

The computer robots were to allow chief executives to recentralize their corporations, to reduce middle executives to mindless functional roles, and to concentrate the information flows of the company into one glorious "on-line, real-time" system, in which to know was to obey—with the computer issuing the orders. The threat, though, never materialized. IBM and its competitors (once called the Seven Dwarfs before they shrank to five) did try to sell customers on so-called management information systems—huge, ambitious complexes designed to take the guesswork out of management and, incidentally, to sell rich quantities of computer hardware.

Never mind that the first commercial examples of these wonder complexes were unconvincing—taking many years to break even and providing absolutely no information for management. Never mind that the first efforts of software houses to dream up monster projects collapsed because time and cost were underestimated. The ventures were on the right track, as the later development of successful, almost routine projects showed, but at the time the venturers lacked the right hardware and the right software—even the right thinking.

Univac even sent some hardy pioneers to Europe to publicize its achievement at a plant in Marietta, Georgia. The Georgia customer, too, added some of its men for the ride in its pride over this ultimate in management control systems. The wonder was designed to reap extra profit from tight control by, among other things, giving a running account of actual expenses and updated estimates of production costs, keeping the program on schedule and even building in automatically the financial results of any change in specification (the plant's major product was a gigantic complex job whose costs history was critical).

The Georgia company was Lockheed Aircraft, and the project, the C5A monster transport, overran its budget by $2 billion, worked none too well at the end of the process, and would have sunk the company without trace in 1970 but for a Washington rescue act. It was a spectacular demonstration of the truism that any computer is only as good as the assumptions and information fed into it. A human being determines what results his marvelous machine can produce; more than that, he determines what use to make of the results.

The common old complaint of executives that they were "disillusioned" with computers was bathetic; the executive was really disillusioned with himself. Appropriately, what gave executives back their virility wasn't just technology; their own independent high spirits greatly helped. When the Apple II computer was first born, its creators had no notion of cracking the business market where IBM and (in those days) its mainframes reigned supreme. The personal business computer was invented by its users, executives who dodged the computer overlords by buying Apples and other microcomputers for their very own use. Not only did IBM miss the beginning and significance of this revolution, it was still grossly underestimating the scale and importance of the PC when its own model, after a remarkable two-year crash program, hit the market.

Notoriously, IBM's first-year sales vastly exceeded its projections for the entire U.S. market. The revolution has been spreading like a forest fire, all over the world. Take Europe as an example. According to International Data Corporation, there were 11,800 personal computers being used for business and professional purposes in Europe in 1978. Five years later, the numbers had swollen to nearly three quarters of a million —a sixtyfold surge. As sales in their billions of dollars rolled in, IBM was forced into sweeping change—not just in its marketing organization (for the small devices had to be sold through the retailers IBM had almost never used before); not just in its manufacturing (for all the components, even whole assemblies, had to be purchased from outside); the corporation's entire strategy had to be reconstructed around the micro.

The battle is now to dominate (or, for IBM rivals, to stay in) the market for the intelligent terminal: the desktop unit that will double as personal computer and access to the formidable powers of the mainframe. In the excitement over micros, the mainframe market has been ignored, although, to quote *Management Today,* "developments in the area of mainframe general purpose computing have been at least as great as those in other areas. . . . Over 70 percent of expenditure on data processing is represented by large general purpose computer systems."

One good reason this mainframe dominance has passed largely unnoticed is that purchasing powerful and even superpowerful computers, while still expensive, is no longer traumatic. The technology and the technologists have advanced to the point that the things actually perform as planned. Managers not only know how computers work (thanks to their own experience with personal and even home computers), they have learned hard lessons from the mismanagement of the past, and can even afford to laugh at the memory of its fiascoes.

The computer horror stories are legion. The builders of the liner *Queen Elizabeth II,* for instance, blamed their installation for an almost overnight collapse into illiquidity, with $37 million of liabilities against only $4.3 million of assets. The accounts, said the boss, had all been put on the computer, and it took six weeks to get them out. At Lockheed the delay was measured in months, not weeks. It took from December to

September for the cost projections to catch up with unexpectedly rapid wage-price inflation on the Galaxy; "fully integrated management by real-time computer" thus proved unable to signal a $2 billion crisis for nine months.

Managers very often took it for granted, without even doing their sums, that investment in computers would save money in the present while storing up even greater benefits for the future. No wonder that something between 40 percent and 70 percent of computer users—depending on whose figures you liked—were disappointed; or that, according to other calculations, 80 percent of installations didn't show an economic return on investment. In 40 percent of the cases the experience was far worse: these users reported a significant degree of deterioration of performance in computerized areas.

Computers were bought that didn't match each other, or match the purpose for which the management wanted them, and stood around forevermore, idle, costly, unloved, and unmated. One group had four main subsidiaries that opted for four separate, incompatible sets of hardware. As a result, one executive found his overhead up by the equivalent of three research chemists or four salesmen because his payroll had been computerized—to fill up computer time. Companies that badly needed the improved systems that a computer could provide poured huge sums into computer setups but not into the systems. Rolls-Royce, Lockheed's partner in crime with the Electra flop, had $5.5 million of IBM computers (with its usual eccentricity, it had forty-six of the things, all bought instead of leased) and spent over $2 million a year on running them: yet its cost control was painfully weak.

Any management that, in this age, is not in control of its computers, as well as its costs, is not only naked, but should be deeply ashamed. Yet the new dawn has brought new problems, some of them looming as large as the old. One is the sheer pace of technological advance. There are plenty of monuments

to past errors in this unavoidable form of technological forecasting: like the airline that built a whole new multistory building to accommodate its future computer needs and, in the
mid-1970s, found itself with a wholly adequate installation (obsolescent at that) occupying just part of one floor. What computing power, in what size package, will be available in the
mid-1990s? As one expert wrote, "Data processing has always
had a strong body of futurologists, keen to explain what will
eventually happen in a computerized world, but their predictions have a way of remaining predictions." In other words,
nobody knows.

Fortunately, it may not matter in most circumstances. It's
a long time since managements agonized over typewriters and
telephones, and computers are passing into that same realm of
purchases cheap enough to be expendable. Indeed, typewriters
and phones already come with computer power attached, and
managers ain't seen nothing yet. The argument over the office
of the future concerns how fast and how far to move, but no
corporation will be risking its own future, or any manager
laying his on the line, in deciding which supplier to use or what
systems to computerize. Electronic data processing is already
becoming part of the furniture—literally so.

Similar developments are racing ahead in the plants,
where actuality is surpassing Lockheed's failed Galaxy dreams.
The control of inventory and production is already routine;
robots are on the march; and computer-aided design (CAD),
tied in with manufacturing, is a fundamental of modern output
—even of corporate economics. The Iacocca renaissance at
Chrysler, for instance, was powerfully aided by the CAD system; without it the crucial line of K cars couldn't have been
produced at the same vitally low costs. For the equally crucial
H cars, starting in 1985, Chrysler has used CAD for two thirds
of all components; twenty-eight mainframes, eighty minicom-
puters, and 1,000 terminals will comprise the hardware for a

gigantic system that, according to a consultant quoted by *Business Week,* has given Chrysler "a 10-year jump on the rest of the industry."

Since the rest of the auto manufacturers, like their counterparts in most other forms of manufacture, are doing likewise, the future looks as golden for suppliers as it does for customers, although manufacturing systems are the area where companies can still very easily make the same brilliant bobbles that office users perpetrated in the past. The Raleigh bike company poleaxed itself, in the midst of a desperate drive to emerge from years of losses of markets and money, by installing a system that, by delivering the wrong parts to the wrong places, brought the entire plant to a grinding halt, at ruinous cost.

Ironically, but predictably, some of the major snafus have occurred at the very microelectronics plants that are at the heart of the factory and office revolution. Two companies making lap computers (portable units, no bigger than a paperback book, which are one certain wave of the future) ran into almost identical roadblocks. At both Gavilan and Convergent, reported *Business Week,* "Soon after designing a production prototype, each group was plagued by manufacturing problems." Gavilan was four months late in beginning manufacture, which promptly ran into "new production glitches." At Convergent, the manufacturing troubles led to abandoning its Workslate altogether. Over at Apple, there was a nasty moment when failures seemed briefly to threaten the totally automated output of Macintosh computers, on which the company depended for its very survival.

Such grisly experiences only repeat what has always happened to firms (even IBM, with the notorious 360 glitches) vying in a data-processing or information-technology market of inexhaustible promise but easily exhausted cash. The history of Control Data is only one example. It seemed to have the business of fighting IBM taped. "We had and have the best strategy in the industry," it boasted. "We didn't hit IBM in the hardest part of their big belly." But choosing the softest part, the large-computer market, didn't save CDC from coming seriously unstuck in 1970, only five years after an earlier setback. By 1984 a different set of problems was bedeviling the business. Its project for making large disk drives plug-compatible with IBM had to be expensively abandoned; money-losing business centers had to be closed; earnings were still declining after two years of falls; the stock had halved to a point where the company was valued at only 60 percent of book value—and this was in a highly rated, high-performance company in high technology.

Control Data had basically got that famous strategy wrong: making bad decisions on which computer areas to enter and which to shun. Consequently its 1983 sales were only 11.4 percent of IBM's, its profits a feeble 3 percent. The company that took up the torch of racing IBM in supercomputers is Amdahl. Even after an amazing rise to 350th in *Fortune*'s sales rankings, thanks to the design genius of Gene Amdahl, the company ended up on an earnings roller coaster. Every essential new model, because of start-up costs and delayed customer orders, crunched profits—down to an almost invisible $7 million in 1982, then up to $46 million next year as the new number-crunchers came in. As one analyst told *Fortune,* though, "The company is at the beck and call of IBM. It can make no rational product or pricing decisions on its own. It must react to IBM."

Dancing to IBM's tune has become the fate of many companies that once never thought to compete with the company that, more likely than not, supplied their own computers. Just as managements that knew nothing of the office-of-the-past market (RCA, Univac, GE, Honeywell, and umpteen others) were seduced, sometimes fatefully, into data processing by the promise of an unlimited future, so the office of that future has brought more companies tumbling in—far, far more. When *Newsweek* produced a supplement on office automation (OA), predicting $262 billion of world sales in 1983–87, it was sponsored by companies whose core products were, respectively, copiers, cameras, computers, telephone exchanges, radios, typewriters, electrical goods, and printers. That list only scratches the surface of a competitive lineup never seen before in business history. How did all these would-be office automators expect to make a living, let alone wax rich? If this market is truly inexhaustible, if it really can accommodate all comers, it will be the first such cornucopia in history—and it won't be.

The first batch of the inevitable dropouts includes the biggest entrant of them all—Exxon. After a total investment of $600 million or so in office systems, the company may have lost as much as it sold in 1984—$70 million. Not surprisingly, at the end of the year, the oil company bowed out of a market in which it literally never had any business. Yet still they come. Eastman Kodak astounded one and all by announcing at almost the same time as Exxon quit that it was going to compete in the business telecommunications market. Kodak is to telecommunications as Ronald Reagan is to flower power. Its past record in its own core business of films, where the Japanese have come up so fast on the outside, hardly encouraged faith in its future in office systems, despite its existing market position in copiers. And what goes for Kodak applies to most other runners in the new computer race started off by the microchip.

The inside track had to be held by those with the strongest positions in personal computers, or PABX, or facsimile, or copiers, or word processors. But the insiders, too, have a problem: they must build on these bases with other compatible products—that being, of course, the grand strategy to which IBM has committed itself. It's impossible to avoid a strong sense of déjà vu. Just like their predecessors in mainframe competition with IBM, companies that should know better, all

285

equipped with even more computing power supposedly to help them reach the right decisions, are sailing off into certain loss. The mind is mightier than the machine—even when the mind is dead wrong.

The new availability of communicating, computing, and information power can't and won't of itself prevent managers from making as massive a mess of their corporate affairs as ever. The stones that managers were so fond of hurling at computer experts are no sharper than those the experts could hurl back. Being logical, computers can handle only systems that are logical. The typical corporate system, given half a chance, sprawls all over the place, working only because those in charge have gotten familiar with its mysteries, like travelers on the New York subways. Even though it functions after a fashion, the established system (no matter for what purpose) is certain not to be the simplest and clearest way of organizing the flow. Therefore, the first step in computerizing is to simplify and clarify the system, and very often the main economic benefit of the computer has lain in doing just that.

The computer will never eliminate the executive's need to think for his living; in some respects, it has made his task harder by introducing a new area of anxiety. For today the computer really has begun to revolutionize management. Terms such as *real time* and *on-line* are no longer sales talk, but commonplace reality; managements can get usable information about what is happening as and when it happens—as a matter of course. Computers have at last graduated from bookkeeping to running the basic routines of the business and pitching in at the rarefied level of planning and decisions.

The parallel is with management consultants. The latter graduated from walking around with stopwatches timing production workers to (much more profitably) advising giant corporations on their future. The difference, however, is that the consultants did the advising. The computer (until the promised advent of artificial intelligence, that is) will act only in the capacity of millions of calculators, filing cabinets, and message centers. The information capability any big company already has will be multiplied enormously, but the primary function, even when (or if) the "expert systems" start taking more far-reaching decisions out of managers' hands altogether, will be unaltered—to be used or misused by the human executive.

The sheer explosion of information is already causing human difficulties. It isn't just a question of deciding what in a huge data base is actually useful, or even wanted, but of marrying different sets of data. Putting a bank's savings accounts in touch with the same customers' checking accounts, for instance, sounds like child's play, but the two sets of information will be on two different computers, and the task is actually of inordinate complexity. Worse still, the systems are also live—the business of a bank, an airline, a store, a manufacturing plant increasingly depends on the computer staying in operation; in fact, that's why Tandem built a remarkable success story, growing by at least 90 percent annually between 1976 and 1981, largely on the provision of nonstop or *fault-tolerant* computing: that is, the things wouldn't (unlike everybody else's computers) let you down with a nasty, expensive electrical short.

It's a measure of both the volatility of management's new computerized world, and of the weight of technological advance, that Tandem's share price slumped by two thirds in eighteen months, not only because its growth rate fell sharply but because standard computers have become too reliable for fault tolerance to be a sufficiently strong selling point. Managers on both sides of the revolution, the customers and the suppliers, have a tiger by the tail. The saving grace is that it is now, by and large, a friendly tiger. Those who get bitten, or eaten alive, will have walked into it—not so much by mistakes in the technology itself, more by management errors. Tandem's stumble, for example, is honestly enough blamed by its own people on poor planning of product launches and too great a move away from the original business—plus the pressures of such rapid growth in itself.

That, too, is no change from the past. Monumental mistakes in computerization were made, not because computers were unmanageable, but because they were badly managed. In a way, managers could be excused. The computer had added considerably to the complexity and perplexity of management at a time when it was becoming more complex and perplexing for other reasons—as it still is. There's now a good chance that the friendly computer will actually reduce complexity and perplexity by making them easier to handle. It's the suppliers, in all shapes and sizes, who will most likely, many of them, suffer the greatest agony. For managers and customers in other industries, this will make a pleasant change.

BOOK V

Shell Games

24

B Grades
for B Schools

Executives, the most intensively educated group of adults in society, are very possibly educated to the least effect. Any executive could spend three hundred working days a year—and several thousand dollars of company money—at individual seminars, without coming near to exhausting the rich table that consultants, academics, training firms, associations, publishers, and other do-gooders spread before the business world. Their altruism is spiced with lucre. The teaching of executives has been the best-paying branch of education, and by a very long way. It has also been a soft market; only a few heretical voices have ever questioned whether you can really teach executives, that is, make them better at their jobs by any general course of instruction, short or long.

The Harvard Business School is the ark of the tabernacle in management education. Many schools more or less ape it, especially its "case study" method of instruction—though munching over out-of-date business anecdotes is about as helpful in actual management as waging war by tramping over old battlefields. When the dean of the HBS publicly queried the relevance of the method, the effect was roughly similar to a pope's casting doubts on the validity of his Church's attitude on birth control. The expression of doubt, though, merely reflected a widespread questioning of the value of B-school education in general and that of Harvard in particular—a mood reflected in a highly critical *Time* magazine study, just one of several broadsides fired against the business academics in recent years.

Any particular discomfiture suffered by Harvard can't be confined. Even those business schools that self-consciously follow a different route do so by reference to the Harvard standard. These others mostly concentrate on "quantitative" studies; in other words, as a maverick educator, Reg Revans, pointed out, they teach much the same subjects that students of economics or statistics have always fed on. The specific management element in these mind-bending studies is hard to isolate. Although executives should be numerate (and many are not), they don't require skills in higher algebra, and many great businesses have been created by men who all but count on their fingers.

A story tells of two schoolboy friends, one brilliant at math, one innumerate to the point of idiocy, who meet much later when the first is a professor and the second a multimillionaire. Unable to control his curiosity, the professor asks the figure-blind dunderhead how he managed to amass his fortune. "It's simple," replies Midas. "I buy things at a dollar and sell them for two dollars, and from that one percent difference I make a living." The business world is full of successful one-percenters who live, not by their calculators, still less their personal computers, but by knowing the difference between a buying price and a selling price. It is also full of clever fools who work out elaborate discounted cash-flow sums to justify projects and products that a one-percenter would laugh out of sight.

The clever-fool syndrome would explain why one controversial study of Harvard Business School students found that, after a flying start, the alumni (presumably among the ablest young men of their day) gradually slipped back to the general level inside their chosen management hierarchies. A Harvard graduate has no reason at all to suppose that he will manage more effectively than a less-instructed contemporary. The Harvard man can only claim that he is more highly educated; and high education and high achievement in practical affairs don't necessarily go together. John F. Kennedy found that assembling America's brightest brains in Washington neither got bills through Congress nor avoided the Bay of Pigs; and many companies have discovered that business-school diplomas are a thin defense against incompetence.

An overwhelmingly large proportion of the highest and best American executives did study business. All this proves is that an overwhelmingly large proportion of business-minded undergraduates got the real message, which is that a diploma will be good for their careers, starting with starting salaries. It does not follow that the education was of any other direct benefit either to the executive or to his firm. Nor does it follow, of course, that the schooling was wasted. As a general rule, the wise man recruits the finest intelligence he can find; and good minds are far better for good training. The question is only whether academic training in subjects that seem to have some connection with management is the best education for managing, and that is something that nobody can prove either way.

The business school is really good at teaching future business-school teachers. But teaching the raw young is only the starting point of management education and its big money.

You can detach an experienced manager for hours or years and you can attempt any form of education, from familiarizing him with computers to changing his entire personality. *Attempt* is the critical word; for some of the objectives are very curious. They start from an odd proposition: that management is a body of abstract skills, like those of mechanical engineering, which can be applied equally successfully to any number of practical situations.

Once you've built one suspension bridge, very possibly you've built the lot—although the modern history of bridge accidents questions even that. But the abstract principles of launching a new toothpaste are too loose and vague for analogies to apply. And once you've launched one new toothpaste, it doesn't mean that you can launch the next in the same way, much less that you can use the same methods for a cake mix. The absurdity of the educational proposition is stunning when applied to personal relationships. The most successful single products in the business-school business are prepackaged courses for managers designed (like midwestern evangelism) to change the behavior patterns of the human beings involved.

In the supreme (so far) development of this art form, the evangelists seek to change the behavior pattern of the entire company. Organization development (OD) is a religion whose creed is so extreme that, as with the harder-nosed heresies of the Middle Ages, true believers are few, far between, and fervent. The OD consultant may never actually talk about people, preferring "human factor management" or "human resource development," as he practices "a process for implementing the improvement of the organization, particularly the effectiveness of relations among its members."

Writing in *Management Today*, Paul Rowlandson listed some of the ways in which OD "human factors" set about this daunting task. There's the "Intimacy Program Questionnaire," whose fifty-five questions include "Have you ever been tempted to kill yourself?" and "What do you think about nudity?" These very naked managers are submitted to exercises like "knee-balling" (you sit directly opposite somebody with knees touching and stare into his or her eyes); "yelling" (you yell); or "elimination" (you nominate another group member to be eliminated from the group, and so does everybody else). Psychologist Carl Rogers defends such processes as a necessary way of "stripping the self," so that "in time, the group finds it unbearable that any member should live behind a mask or a front."

This is the end result of postwar developments admirable in aim and relatively innocent in content—like the Blake and Moulton Managerial Grid, which sounds like an electric toaster but is billed as a mechanism "for achieving corporate excellence." The griddled managers are supposed to plot their characteristics on numbered squares that range from 1.1 ("minimum concern for people and minimum concern for production") at the bottom left-hand corner to a 9.9 paragon at top right ("work accomplishment is from committed people: interdependence through a 'common stake' in organization purpose leads to relationships of trust and respect"). In fact, the grid really leads to a rigid, expensive, intense, and sleepless attempt to indoctrinate the executive in the philosophy and psychology of the magic 9.9.

The umbrella name of "sensitivity training" is inapt for a process that is often insensitive to the point of butchery. By confessing his shortcomings in front of others in grid sessions, T-Groups, or similar gatherings, the executive becomes psychologically purified. The North Korean brainwashers and the hippies at the Esalen Institute shared this same belief in inducing spiritual change by humiliation. This is achieved for executives by giving them an "unstructured" problem to discuss.

They have no points of reference, no idea what they are supposed to be doing, and no protection against attack. The more unbalanced executives have sometimes been tipped right over the brink of breakdown. Others have come away feeling better and wiser and more effective men. But all uplift wears off, and it wears off long before the uplifted one has any real chance to transform his performance through his transmogrified personality.

If the existing executives are not performing very effectively (which is probably true), it is more painful to change them than to try and change their behavior. But the only result of attempting to modify their personalities is to strengthen the conformist pressures that are already too strong inside the corporation. That is also the main, if undeclared, purpose of much so-called in-house training—when groups of executives from the same company are herded together at some away-from-it-all location such as the stately homes often maintained by British companies, or Starved Rock, Illinois, of which a Caterpillar Tractor man once remarked, "Executives don't leave Starved Rock and become better executives without working at it. How do you get to it? Feedback, results, tests, self-appraisal, counseling—you're the salami in the sandwich."

These sausage factories feature the requisite appearances of the requisite academics. But their high point is the sacramental unveiling of the boss or bosses, and it is his speech or their speeches on which the acolytes hang. The whole enterprise is surrounded by an atmosphere of forced intimacy, of flattering selection, of general devotion to the greater good of the corporation, of total immersion (like Baptist converts) in its ethos. The evangelical note is again strong—and again effective, until it wears off. These high-level in-house courses, too, smack more of indoctrination than of any carefully metered attempt to improve management performance in measurable, practicable ways. But they do at least let middle executives get a close-up of their supreme bosses.

In this respect, in-house courses serve the same purpose

as conferences of the Soviet Communist Party. The faithful are rewarded with the opportunity to applaud the leader, who can at the same time applaud them for their faith and seek to reinforce it. Yet in-house education actually has far greater, mostly unexploited potential. Outside courses can get at an executive only by taking him away from his job; inside courses can teach him in the best place of all—which is on that job.

That is actually one of the selling points of the OD special-ist—that the organization is developed in situ, increasing effec-tiveness all along the line. That isn't what happened at Tonka Corporation, according to author James A. Lee. After OD intervention, profits fell by a third, the chairman was fired, two vice-presidents went the same way, the president resigned, and the new chairman promptly blamed the OD interventions as the principal cause of Tonka's troubles. All the same, there's no question but that managers, just like workers on the line, learn best at work, "sitting next to Nellie."

That simple principle has been translated into a significant new emphasis on *coaching*, the manager's responsibility for developing his subordinates by using their work as an educa-tional tool. While the idea is extremely sound, and while some form of coaching is inseparable from any relationship between the boss and the bossed, neither the pressures of his own job nor the predilections of most managers are truly conducive to enough or good enough coaching to develop a manager's ability and equipment fully. What is certain is that the company, like it or not, is an educational establishment, good or bad. You don't have to go as far as Apple's John Sculley, who says of his company, "We're trying to create a unique learning institu-tion"—but a teaching and learning role is inescapable.

Lecturers to business audiences know that the attention quotient rises sharply if the executives' superiors are in the room—the underling wants to show how alert and brisk he is, even if he has to laugh at the lecturer's jokes. That apart, any training given where the executive works and which is directly related to his work is more effective than education outside. At one-day external seminars nobody notices if the executive dozes off into languorous half-sleep, opening glazed eyes just in time to sprint for the early train. Well-attested studies show that people absorb only 10 percent of spoken information; they do twice as well with visual information and six times as well with sight and sound combined. So at most seminars, naturally, the customer gets little or no sight and sound; about 10 percent visual display, if that; and 90 percent of unadulterated, mostly unabsorbed spoken words.

Even if the seminar's subject is relevant to the man's job, even if he has absorbed a significant part of the information (both unlikely conditions), the executive still faces what is known as the reentry problem. He may have found a better way up there on the managerial moon, but will his unenlightened colleagues back on earth let him disturb the even, set tenor of their ways? Will they, hell. The more an executive is exposed to external ideas of how a modern business should be managed, the longer he spends away from the shop at this university or that seminar, the more alien and obtuse the actual real-life conditions in his company can seem.

The company, unlike the business schools, is enmeshed in real life. The academic inevitably teaches of an ideal world in which the personalities of all chief executives (to take one illusion) are equable, open to persuasion, and eager for change, and in which (to take another dream) markets respond logically to logical plans logically arrived at. There is no other basis on which the academic can operate, but it is not the basis on which a company works.

The main criticism of business schools and their graduates is precisely that, and has been for years: that their education and their attitudes are not fitted to real-world business. Many of the graduates, anyway, don't head in that direction. In 1983 nearly a quarter of the Harvard graduating class went into consulting. As John Thackray reported in *Management Today,* one MBA, back for his fifth reunion, was "shocked that very few of my classmates were making a product, running a plant, or drilling a hole in the ground. Almost everyone was on the financial side." Almost everyone, too, was earning about two thirds more than if he had started his career straight from a liberal arts education. Though there have been times when a few but very important companies (Xerox, the Bank of America, Ford, and General Motors among them) have cut back on hiring MBAs, the commodity has remained in generally high demand.

This can't have much to do with what they're actually taught. As Thackray says, "One of the more frequent carpings of business today is that MBAs show an over-reliance on mathematical techniques and quantitative methods (usually computer-based) which business doesn't want (or doesn't know how) to utilize effectively." Or, in the delicate phraseology of one banker, quoted by *Time* magazine, "If we shut down the business schools for ten years, we would not suffer a very great loss. A lot of what is preached at business school today is absolute rot." Another business executive alleges that there has been a profound switch from his B-school days, when "the analytic process was disciplined logic and common sense, supported by a few analytical tools," to a situation "where the tool is so sophisticated that it is mistaken for accuracy it doesn't have when faced with a commonsense problem."

This manager argues that consequently "it's very difficult to train an MBA to become a decision maker today." At American Can, the complaint is different, though equally heartfelt: "It is difficult to entice MBAs into jobs as first-line supervisors or territory sales representatives that give you a first-hand feel for the business." So why would Exxon, in 1983, have informed the University of Chicago that it wanted the entire graduating class? Because, very simply, the best brains in America with an active interest in business enter the B schools. It isn't what they're taught that counts so much as gaining entry in the first place. The more highly educated they are, true, the harder it will be to assimilate them into or back into the corporation. But this is a very unconvincing argument for putting up with second or third best.

The reentry problem is less likely to lead to burnout if external training is treated like good in-house education; that is, equip a man to do his job better, and as he moves to another mystery, equip him for that in turn. An executive in his first marketing post needs specific knowledge about certain techniques (for instance, how to arrive at a price or run a promotion). Most executives need better education in management accounting, which means managing by the real financial implications, not by the abstractions in the balance sheet. But no academically acquired knowledge is any use until it is applied at the crunch point, where mistakes will be made and hard real-life lessons learned. And the shorter the gap between learning and application, by far the better.

Every executive once knew enough of Latin, chemistry, history, or some similar recondite study to pass an exam of fair difficulty. Within a few years of disuse, his knowledge has decayed to the status of childhood memory. Exactly the same rusting away happens to management knowledge. So, the more general the course, the more will be wasted—simply because the executive will be limited in what he can use. On the job, anyway, he learns lessons that no course can ever teach: nobody can work out for every executive in every situation, or any executive in any situation, what will come to be the most significant, testing, and painful parts of his craft.

This presupposes that the executive has been taught how to learn—possibly the most valuable gift that education has to offer. Men who lack this general lesson are prone to take experience as a substitute for thought. All knowledge is the result of inquisitiveness—of asking why. Experience is another name for ceasing to ask because the answer has been prejudged. "We've always done it this way" is the worst reason of all, unless, that is, there genuinely is no better way, and that can only be established by inquiry. As businesses have grown more complex, this task of getting appropriate answers has also become more complicated, more difficult. And here the academic can offer analytical tools that do produce far better answers; but none of these gadgets is more than a small attachment to the great tool of skepticism.

The skeptical executive takes nothing for granted, including his own competence. He doesn't dismiss the whole effort to apply theory to business management, or to teach it. He recognizes that nobody knows, in the scientific sense of the verb *to know,* how to achieve the maximum results from managing a company—let alone how to measure whether those results have been achieved. He does know that executives must be encouraged (or taught) to recognize their own ignorance. They dare not copy one chairman, since stripped of his rank, who liked to show off a chart showing how his company would coin profits once output passed break-even and then moved on toward capacity. The weakness in this inspiring analysis was that the true capacity line lay where he had drawn the break-even point.

This error falls into the category of what every manager needs to know, and it's true that the amount of necessary information has greatly increased over recent years. That's why the best companies make an intensive educational effort, using internal and external courses, as well as job rotation, to inculcate what professional management means and to provide the professional equipment. Few companies in the West, though, take the process as far as Japanese groups like Hitachi or NEC. In fact, an NEC executive unconsciously echoed Apple's boss when he told Gene Gregory, a Tokyo professor, that "work in the age of information technology is permanent lifelong education. The enterprise has become essentially as much an educational institution as it is a place of work."

The education provided at the Hitachi Institute of Technology or NEC's Institute for Technology Education is exactly what the titles of these top-ranked institutions suggest: to a Japanese, education for managers is highly specific, highly technical. A company president won't just know about statistical quality control in general; even a man with a finance background will know the technicalities in depth, and will be expected to. In many Western corporations that spend heavily on management education, neither the expectation of knowledge nor the knowledge are present. Particularly now, with the arrival of distant-learning techniques, which bring education to the terminal on the desk, there's no excuse for a manager not knowing what he's talking about—and many don't.

Ignorance is a rotten foundation for thought. Making executives think isn't the need that business courses publicly try to fill. But it *is* the central issue, more so than the defect the schools themselves now confess—which is that they can't teach executives how to make decisions under stress. Nor can they. But before making a decision, under stress or at ease, it helps to have been guilty of constructive thought and constructive self-criticism. Apart from any other factors, thought helps the decision to make itself—which is always the most desirable way. Saying that executives can't be taught the power of decision at school, in any case, is only another way of saying that you can't teach executives to manage, for initiating action under uncertainty and pressure is one of the activities for which executives are paid.

The interesting question is whether business education has boomed in response to the increased complexity and bureaucracy of industry or is itself part of the long march to complication. The only organizations that match business life in devotion to schooling are the military ones, which can be said historically to have started management education. Just like executives, officers can spend all their lives on courses, if they are lucky. But even officers are better employed on courses that have some bearing on their needs and the army's. In peacetime, when soldiers mostly play at being soldiers, purely playful education matters less. In war the playing has to stop, and in war the amateur soldier, the civilian trained in utterly different skills and ways of thought, comes into his own. Just as the individualistic business entrepreneur outperforms the career executive, so the amateur soldier often beats out the professional, because on the battlefield, as in the marketplace, you seldom win by the book.

Great generals, like great executives, also rarely distinguish themselves academically. (Nor, for that matter, do military leaders show up well in business; they can prove as destructive as napalm.) The qualities that win wars, like those that create fortunes for companies or individuals, are expressions of personality rather than intellect. True, Field Marshal Montgomery did make a supreme contribution to the art of business, and war. But his old El Alamein one-two is more remarkable for its simple effectiveness than its intellectuality: first, assemble overwhelmingly superior force, and second, attack where the opposition is weakest.

The games that executives play at school don't elucidate such simple truths. They are more an expression of anxiety. I am not/the company is not/my underlings are not managing as well as I/it/they should. A child who is going to fail an exam, or a golfer whose swing is slipping, is given extra coaching—and surely coaching will help the executive. So it may. Even if the business coach himself is both unqualified in real business and inept at instruction, good can always rub off. But education is no substitute for giving an executive a job he likes, letting him do it the way he wants, helping him when he needs help, and demanding that he do the job to the best of his ability.

In the end, that's the best definition by far of coaching—and, for that matter, of organization development. If a company can't employ highly intelligent, highly educated people to its profit, that's a criticism, not of the graduates, but the company. It's easy to turn a B-school graduate into a clever fool, just as it is to get foolish management from an incompetent. But both misfortunes say more about the organization than about the individuals involved. The individuals can *always* be taught to manage more effectively; the issue is rather whether they will be allowed to do so.

In the typical situation, where the man is underemployed, overmanaged, and constantly let off the hook, a half-failed man in a half-failed organization, education of any variety won't help. And total failure must follow from the unpleasant delusion that classes can transform the adult mind and personality like some fairy wand. The less companies and educators expect to turn an incompetent into a polymath, or a bully into a Boy Scout, the more they are likely to achieve. As it is, too much of what now passes as management education isn't education: it is indoctrination, entertainment, or occupation of vacant hours. And it has very little to do with the management of business, which is the real business of management.

25

Conundrums of Consultancy

There was once a snappy answer to consultants, management professors, and other tradesmen who tell others how to mind their own businesses. "Ah yes" executives could say, "if you know so much, how come you're not rich?" There are variations to this arresting theme: "Those who can, do; those who can't, consult," or "He's never met a payroll in his life." The last gibe skirts around the fact that most executives have never met a payroll either, not in the sense of having until Friday to find the cash.

The gibes also seem beside the point at a time when consultancy itself is a big and booming business. True, even $3 billion a year (the sum that the 774 leading American management consultancies now carve up between them) is small potatoes by the standards of big corporate clients. But within that sum groups of clever men and women have been able to accomplish little masterpieces of niche building, market segmentation, and repositioning—the very arts and crafts they enjoin on their clients. Examples like Boston Consulting Group's invention of portfolio planning built around market share or Bain's branding of corporate strategy are a joy to behold—and have proved financially joyful to the partners involved.

But the most conspicuous joy must be that of McKinsey & Co. as well as that of the two consultants, Thomas J. Peters and Robert H. Waterman, who created a mountain of money with a single book, *In Search of Excellence.* Its million-plus hardcover sales make it the greatest business publishing phenomenon of modern times—certainly no straight-out business book has even approached such numbers, *Iacocca* notwithstanding. Not only did Peters (now ex-McKinsey, with five personal companies grossing over $4 million a year) and Waterman (lecture fees up to $12,000 a throw) become personal successes, McKinsey also cashed in; having funded the research into corporate excellence, it reaped enormous and continuing benefit from the publicity, while raking in half of Peters's royalties—and all of Waterman's. Even the most grasping of client businessmen must envy so shrewd a bunch. Plainly, the entrepreneurial juices run high in the bosoms of many consultants—higher maybe than in those who pay their bills.

Executives rest in the safe arms of the corporation, which always (or nearly always) makes sure that the payroll gets met and the creditors paid. These days executives are more like consultants—shifting from assignment to assignment, never soiling their hands with selling or manufacture, spending their time largely on reports, meetings, and investigations. But like those mentioned above, many consultants are more like businessmen than any executive in General Motors or General Mills.

The lucrative boom in "management," as opposed to "managing," has made many other consultants and professors far richer than any division general manager. Very few are festooned with Rolls-Royces, Cadillacs, or Lamborghinis. But consulting is paid well enough, and distributes enough of the swag in partnership devices, to retain men who could amble into $350,000 jobs managing some client company. Consultants like to say that it's not the money that retains them, but the intellectual challenge. They seldom mention an equally significant factor—consulting is much less risky than management, which for a former consultant can be very dangerous indeed.

The risk may only be that of losing a posthumous reputation, if, like a former boss of Westinghouse, you die in office before the mess you made of the company lands at your door. Profits halved in half a dozen years, partly because of exactly the kind of snafu that consultants are supposed to clean up in their sleep. "The major problem of the company," said the successor CEO, "in its management structure, was the fact that they had too many people reporting to the top operating man. . . . A bottleneck at the top is the worst place to have one." Westinghouse, however, is not the only company (RCA was another) to discover that while most consultants are good at business, they are mainly good at their own business, which is a very specialized and lucrative form of service industry.

In that industry, the marvels of marketing performed since World War II have elevated their status and profitability by strategic strokes that any entrepreneur would envy. The market has advanced to meet them, the usual phenomenon with hit products. Executives perplexed by the problems of operating their own clumsy corporate creations have cried for help, and they have really needed it in areas such as computers where technical advances left companies floundering in strange waters.

The consultants have been around in these quasitechnical

jobs for decades, but the rewards of such humdrummery are limited by an obvious ceiling—the amount for which a company can acquire its very own full-time specialist. Some executives are not acute enough to spot this fact. But consultancy rewards in general stayed unexciting until the sharper minds in the game raised their sights to a more sublime level, the holy of holies, the boardroom itself.

Advising on marketing strategy or corporate organization has one shining virtue. The consultant breaks away from the constraint of fees related to the time of his own employees and climbs up to far more gratifying levels of remuneration based on the expected future worth of his services. Nobody does know, can know, or ever will know how to measure that worth. There may be some difference between this approach and charging what the traffic will bear, but not much.

Client boards may fight about the fee for computerizing the accounting system; they don't even try to assess the value of a new organization structure or "marketing orientation." If the company is big enough and the high-level consultant good enough, it might add $10 million a year to profits, in which case a fee of $250,000 is too ridiculous to worry about.

The same argument, though, hardly applies to companies lower down the corporate scale, especially since, to quote one consultant, "there's been a tremendous escalation in the fees for quality consulting by the big firms. Just to diagnose a medium-sized company, with no implementation offered, can cost $100,000 for three months' study. So the lone chief executive of a company that size can't get good quality advice without paying through the nose." That word *implementation* is crucial these days—or said to be. Consultants used to be severely criticized for completing their fat reports, charging their even fatter fees—and walking away from the client to the bank. Now they stay with their recommendations, theoretically to make them work. That lone chief executive, in other words, might be buying nothing. But does experience prove that there's anything to buy?

After McKinsey consultants visited Shell, in fact, the latter's profits swelled gigantically—never mind the sheer impossibility of proving that a chain of cause and effect links the consultants with the profits. The story of Shell and McKinsey started in Venezuela, where two brilliant young consultants, Hugh Parker and Lee Walton, worked so impressively for a subsidiary that they were invited to look at Shell's head-office problems in London and The Hague. McKinsey at this time was still U.S.-based. But its adoption by Shell, widely supposed (and with some good reason) to lead Europe's management elite, was a gilt-edged visiting card into Europe.

If Shell, bristling with internal consultants, needed that extra something from McKinsey, then McKinsey obviously had something extra to give. Old-line British boardrooms, jammed solid with anxiety over modern problems of scale and complexity, for which they were ill equipped, rapidly took the point; so did thrusters unsure which way to thrust. One after another the blue-chip names—ICI and the Bank of England, the Post Office and Unilever, Dunlop and the BBC, and so on, and so on—found the McKinsey medicaments irresistible.

British consultants were consumed with jealousy by this American success in winning fat assignments and, adding insult to injury, publicizing it. One or two hinted darkly that the follow-up to McKinsey's work was less inspiring than its orders. Sour grapes, no doubt, but later developments, seen in this light, are still interesting. Spillers, the flour giant, went on a McKinsey course of reorganization and marketing orientation; its profits fell by one third in three years. That was merely preparatory work for the vast fall in earnings during the 1970s that led to Spillers' own disappearance—swallowed up by an agriculturally based conglomerate.

Dunlop was another good customer. In 1970, just before

its marriage with Italy's Pirelli was consummated, Dunlop's pretax profits had been stuck for three years running. That merger was probably the most disastrous corporate liaison in history—for the British groom, that is. By the time it divorced the Italians, Dunlop had lost huge sums of money on the deal and, far more serious, had lost its way in the technology and marketing of its base business, tires. Even total capitulation in 1984, selling the bulk of the tire business to Japan's Sumitomo, couldn't restore Dunlop to health. Later that year, the rump, racked by ruinous debts, was being kept alive only by the bankers—and an unseemly squabble took place before someone (BTR) finally bought and salvaged the wreck for peanuts.

The Post Office, set up as a new public corporation, combined big marketing fiascoes with huge deficits; at least, the Bank of England didn't follow this precedent, because central banks, by definition, can't lose money. But its record in the 1970s was one of unmitigated mistakes, in the course of which mass financial disaster was only narrowly averted. Even Shell, after a few years, found the McKinsey scheme of boardroom organization unworkable. There are other examples, but their lesson is not that McKinsey's work was bad. On the contrary, its consultancy was probably as good as money can buy. The defects were intrinsic to consulting itself—not to consultants. The client company gets for its fee, and for a time the services and advice of men who (if its choice has been good) have broader experience, superior intelligence, more impressive backgrounds, and sharper all-round competence than most of its executives. But the company doesn't get new management.

Most consultants tell of the assignment where the only essential, but impossible, recommendation was to heave out the boss. One man had a tough job even getting the family chairman to resign the title of chief executive, on which a vitally needed new president insisted. The embattled chairman, after many weeks, finally blurted out that he didn't see why he should surrender, not when Henry Ford II, at that time still in the auto company's driving seat, kept his chief executive title. "Ah ha!" said the consultant, seizing his moment, "but Henry Ford runs Ford." They settled the argument by ringing Ford in Dearborn and asking if he ran the company. "Sure as hell I do," said Henry, and with that the chairman surrendered.

But consultants don't find it easy to bite the hand that hires them; they are more likely, after cozy months with the board, to unearth unsuspected virtues in the directors. The information on which the consultants work, anyway, has to come from the company itself, and consultants naturally look at the business through the directors' eyes. There is no practical point in submitting a report that incenses the customer. First, it won't be accepted, and all the consultant's labor will have gone for nothing. Second, the failed assignment will be bad for the consultant's reputation, and it is on reputation, especially in boardroom work, that a consultant's business depends. (The golden rule of consulting is once in, never out—or lose anything except the client.)

The new emphasis on implementation, curiously enough, is a great help in obeying that golden rule. It guarantees that the consultants will stay around for a long lucrative stretch of time—and never mind the fact that the fashion for implementation springs from consultancy failure, not success. The implementing phase follows hard on the heels of the strategic planning era, and is really Son of Strategy. As Booz Allen & Hamilton president Jack Lescher explained to *Management Today*, "A lot of the strategies that were recommended ended up on the cutting-room floor—they weren't implementable." Quite why managements should believe that effective implementation will flow from the same people who gave them unworkable plans isn't clear. But the proposition has established a marvelous line in "technical support programs, manufacturing and marketing enhancement tactics, or a management information system that will support a company's strategic plans."

The words are those of Arthur D. Little's president, John F. Magee. He also observed that "one trend today is the recognition of the importance of the interrelationships between strategy and operations." Were there truly managements unaware of these connections in the 1970s? Were there (as presumably there must have been) consultants, too, who either didn't know or chose not to reveal their awareness? John Thackray puts his finger on the answer when he describes consultants as "like golf professionals who have never won any tournament but who are trusted to improve the top players' swing." Thirty years ago "the concept would have been laughed at . . . yet in today's climate of general insecurity the idea is evidently plausible."

Probably, this same sense of insecurity had much to do with the best-selling triumph of *In Search of Excellence.* American management, having suffered from a sometimes pitiful loss of confidence before the onslaught of recession and the Japanese, drew comfort and sustenance from a book whose excellent companies were all 100 percent American, in origin and direction, and whose message reinforced the necessary belief of chief executives that they can shape the destiny of their own companies. Reinforcement is one of the prime commodities that the CEO and his cohorts can purchase for their consultancy fees, and consultants are generally only too happy to provide it.

The facts play into the hands of directors who hire consultants for the most respectable bad reason—to endorse a decision that, in principle, has already been taken. Very likely, Shell knew that it was fat with surplus middle executives. But the necessary pruning was more comfortable, especially for a company that rejoiced in the avuncular nickname and traditions of "Joe Shell," when it was done, or seen to be done, on the disinterested advice of efficiency experts. This element in consultancy could be called the Pontius Pilate gambit; the hand washing comes expensive.

But suppose the Pilate gambit in no sense applies. Assume that the directors are genuinely in a quandary: they know not which way to turn, or how. At first sight, the most sensible action they can take, before going down for the third time, is to clutch at consultancy—even if it does prove to be a straw. But only at first sight. What the company needs is not consultants, but a whole new top management.

High and mighty executives draw high and handsome salaries to chart the destination of a company and decide how to get there. It may often be right, proper, and thoroughly sanitized to have competent outsiders double-check assumptions and plans. But any board that abdicates its role, and finances the abdication with stockholders' money, is worse than weak-kneed—it is incompetent to carry out the consultants' recommendations. The work will be doomed to failure, and the fees will run to waste.

That's precisely the point that Akio Morita, co-founder of Sony, and father of the Walkman, made in 1982: "I think Americans listen too much to the securities analysts and the consultants. American management no longer likes to make decisions. No one takes responsibility. That's why the consulting business is so good in the U.S." Or, to put it more crudely, in the words of a *Harper's Magazine* headline: "Why do experienced executives pay millions for the advice of young punks in pinstripes who've never run anything?" The rude question has a polite echo in what Bruce D. Henderson, the man who led Boston's spectacular growth, has to say on the salaries paid to those youngsters—that is, business graduates, more of whom go into consulting than anything else.

With $60,000 a year starting salaries, plus bonus, and even signing-on fees, this preference isn't surprising. But as Henderson says, "Some clients were not happy at financing, with their fees, these ridiculously high salaries." McKinsey's Jon Katzenbach noted that "if I had my way, I'd not pay them that much. A, they're probably not worth it. B, it creates the wrong image with my clients." C, he might well have added, it's very hard to argue that the seminarian in pinstripes can have anything useful to offer that any senior manager worth his stock options doesn't know already—or couldn't find out much more cheaply.

Random hiring of consultants isn't justified by any exclusive expert knowledge. The textbooks on organization and strategy are all freely available; and the favored approaches of individual consulting firms can be easily recognized, like hallmarks on old silver, by the cognoscenti. When a company was told to reorganize into product divisions, install long-range corporate planning, and establish a straight man-to-man pyramid of line executives, with a single chief executive at the top —that was the authentic hallmark of McKinsey; others have similar recognizable stamps.

Whatever their brand, few consulting firms are prepared to limit their juicy range of tempting services. One man who defines himself as a *marketing* consultant is happy to work on market strategy, new product development, organization of sales forces, diversification, corporate planning, and so on. The list stretches so far that very little remains for management itself to manage, and far too much remains to be provided from the consultant's own exhaustible resources; plainly, the more he specializes, the more expert, justifiable, and useful his work is likely to be.

But the dynamic of consultancy dies if this line of reasoning is chased too far. The true logic of consultancy is maximization of juicy fees. Only then can the firm provide its members with the glowing reward and warm satisfaction that, rather than the grandeur of the organization, are its objectives. This is a key difference between consulting firms and the industrial corporation, to which organizational grandeur matters greatly —which is partly why many former management consultants find adjusting to executive jobs in industry so tough.

Another part of the trauma hangs on the word *executive.* The consultant, whiz though he is, merely advises; he can only put his own delectable ideas into practice by quitting his field. In management, having ideas is wonderfully easy; turning them into reality leads to the pain of ulcers, losses, and angry stockholders. At that point, the top-level consultant is literally well out of it. His projects can only be judged, conveniently, over a period of years. If the outcome is disaster, the consultant can always argue either that the client failed to implement the advice properly, even with his help, or that the glue would have been still stickier without his advice, an argument that has the great virtue of being wholly irrefutable (and wholly unprovable, for that matter).

If a company wants to employ consultants effectively, it had better not use them where effectiveness can't be measured. So don't employ those clever brains where they love to be used —in substitution pro tem for the unsure intellects on the main board. The best reason for using a consultant is that he knows something you don't know. There really are consultants pumped full with all there is to know about "physical distribution management," that is, lugging goods about. There are consultants in how to sit, how to sell, how to plan, how to budget, how to interpret market research statistics; you name it, somebody knows it—and somebody needs it.

No management can be blamed for failure to have universal knowledge of the new business technology. But no management can be excused for failure to buy the missing knowledge —or for falling for the idea that general ignorance can be overcome by some single session, even one lasting six hours, at the feet of some guru or gurus. Whole-day seminars for the board are approximately as helpful to the company as a visit from Billy Graham. But the act of hiring and listening to an apostle of enlightened management is somehow thought to qualify the hirer as an enlightened executive. The intention substitutes nicely for the reality. Moreover, false enlightenment comes cheap. In a situation of hunger—in this case, for enlightenment—the man offering food to the starving has a great bargaining position, especially when even $5,000 a day is a drop in the ocean of corporate waste.

That waste is a subject on which one of the most valuable of all gurus, quality expert W. Edwards Deming, has forthright views. "American management on the whole has a negative value—it's like an old refrigerator you can't sell," he told *Fortune*. That being so, failing to get a return from Deming's seminar fees ($20,000) should be fairly difficult. Just mastering the eleventh of his famous fourteen points ("eliminate work standards that prescribe numerical quotas") should be worth many times the cost of attendance. That is one of the many Deming lessons that the Japanese have taken to heart. Observe, though, that this isn't general guidance, but highly specific, with results that can be swiftly and directly measured—just like the Japanese preference in corporate in-house education.

The Japanese not only use the specific, practical advice of consultants. They treat it exactly as they do manufacturing plant or purchased technology: they modify, improve, and develop. That's the correct way to use consultants—and they are usable; there truly is a real task in which the business academic, or the professional consultant, can always help. It arises from the same causes that often negate consulting work—the fact that the consultant is outside the business and will play no long-term role in managing it. In any company, no matter how good, internal blindness becomes a besetting sin. Blinkered by obstinacy, experience, and self-regard, executives can't see their own simple mistakes. The outsider can. But his use as devil's advocate depends on having executives who will listen.

Beyond this, the proper use of outside experts, in their fields of expertise, is as rifles aimed to pick off specific identified targets. To use them as shotguns, spraying in all directions, is a wasteful and uncertain method of getting bull's-eyes.

Calling in an expert to install a new management concept is like calling in the computer wizards. Unless the systems within which the new toy works are themselves effective, the toy will give no joy. In other words, it takes a high-class executive to know when he needs a consultant, to get full value, and to take the expert's advice critically and unemotionally. All consultants know that their best work is done with the best companies, a very obvious truth, even if it means that those who most need consultancy get least out of it.

The high-class executive is also less likely to run for help (or for cover) indiscriminately; it's the less-able executive who abdicates, who lets the consultants take over. Well-found consultants can stay in a company forever, moving from one divisional trouble spot to another like Arabs wandering from oasis to oasis. Many consultants would agree that for half of the time companies employing consultants really need new management. But they also feel that, for half the rest of the time, consultants are misused. Yet they can't complain too loudly, unless, that is, they want to lose their fees. As with all management, the possibilities are defined by the human factors.

Take the case of one supergrowth company that had plainly outstripped a rudimentary management system. One of the consultant's remedies was to kick the energetic, proconsultancy, but elderly chairman upstairs in favor of the highest-ranking relative. The chairman's attitude underwent radical change. While preparing to resume the reins, he was heard to mutter, "I don't think much of these consultants." That is the problem in a capsule. You can't make top-level consultancy work without breaking executives, and they purely hate to be broken.

26

The Innovational
Helter-Skelter

One obsession has recently united executives right around the world: the urge to innovate. Firms love to boast that such and such a percentage of sales is, or will be, of products unborn five or ten years back. The innovatory quest has spawned new consulting firms, new gimmicks such as "venture management," and new areas of aching loss. Consumers are showered with new wonders that they don't want, which don't work, which duplicate, which rapidly disappear—and still executives crave more of the same. Yet any intelligent executive granted one wish by the good god Mammon would beg not for a new product, but one that would become very, very old. The most desirable products, self-evidently, are those that last forever—and most of the world's great businesses earn their bread from just such blessings.

This truth runs counter to a cherished concept of the new

management—the product life cycle. Any academic can draw the smooth curve that shows the steep upward rise as the innovation takes off, the flattening out of profits as competition moves in—before peak sales arrive—then the slow decline through obsolescence to the morgue. From this, any student can mark the spot where new products must pick up the baton if the company isn't to drop out of the race. The picture is beautiful, beguiling, meaningless. First, theoretical life-cycle charts never have an actual time scale, and it makes a mint of difference whether the palmy days will last fifty years or five. Second, the words *new product* need careful analysis.

The Thunderbird is dazzlingly new compared to the Model T Ford. But the basic technology, as opposed to its refinements, variations, and additions, has changed surprisingly little in half a century, and this relative technical stagnation explains a commercial fantasy such as the Volkswagen Beetle, which ran unchanged forty years after its design and twenty-five years after its first sale. In food, today's top brands, such as Kraft, Maxwell House, and Bird's-Eye, have been bestsellers almost since introduction. That's true, even though in food the United States alone has been spawning five thousand to six thousand new products a year (of which only eighteen hundred reached the stores and only five hundred survived twelve months).

In magazine publishing, the *Reader's Digest* has outsold all competitors for decades. In soft drinks, Coca-Cola is still king, and even its great challenger, Pepsi-Cola, is no chicken. The common-or-household light bulb of today would be familiar to Edison. The aspirin has been the world's leading analgesic since 1898. In a hot British brand market such as soap powders, Persil kept a leading market share, even though technically less powerful than the new synthetics.

The Hershey bar, Vaseline, Kleenex, Quaker Oats—these are only a few of the legions of products that continue to dominate important markets (and to underpin the revenues of great companies) long years after the proprietorial genius showed them the light of day—or saw it himself for the last time. True, the top brand successes in any year will include products which Father (unless he is very young) knew not: like, to take 1982 as an example, names such as Activision, Burger King, Commodore, and Miller Lite. But Father equally surely did know other leaders in the fifteen big hits of that year: Chrysler, General Electric, Prudential, Jack Daniel's, Del Monte, 7-Up, Hilton, Maybelline, and Marlboro (though he might have known the last in its first red-tipped incarnation, as a cigarette for ladies, before the king-sized cowboy era). As for Tylenol, which became infamous as well as famous when some capsules were poisoned, that's nothing but good old-fashioned paracetamol, which has been the major pain-killing rival to aspirin for decades.

Nearly all these products have improved substantially since their dawn. But as technical concepts they are identical. The Thunderbird is more comfortable, more convenient, much faster than the Model T; but the driver behind the steering wheel and internal combustion engine, on top of the four wheels, won't get from point A to point B much faster. In Detroit's heyday, the products barely altered. Only the outer skin—the packaging—was changed annually at an alarming cost, which was built into the price of the vehicle.

This built-in obsolescence opened wide the doors of Detroit to competitors who did vary the concept: minnows from Europe and Japan beat the mightiest American management machines in their own precious market with their own technology. The built-in obsolescence turned out to be, not of the styling, but of the concept. The bungling of the auto bosses did not arise from lack of new products, but from missing the effect of changing tastes on old ones.

Brands lose market share or wither on the vine, not because they get overtaken by the march of history, but because executives stupidly neglect them. There is no automatic product life cycle; there is a mismanagement cycle. A confectionery executive once stumbled on this truth. He had an old line of cachous, a Victorian sweet that any whizzing young brand manager would have shot on sight. Apart from its creaking antiquity, its sales figures were convincingly bad. Over the years they had slid down the life-cycle slope to a quarter of their one-time peak.

The chief executive (who, since the family owned the business, was more possessive than marketing professionals) looked at the figures another way. Certainly, they showed that far fewer people wanted his candy. But the miracle, for unpromoted, old-fashioned gunk, was that so many still drooled for the stuff. It *must* have something. So he improved production to cut costs, spent the savings on promotion—and sales doubled. In Britain in 1984 you could still buy not only Victorian cachous, but also products such as Beechams Pills (b. 1847), Mackenzie's Smelling Salts (b. 1870), and Stone's Original Green Ginger Wine (b. 1744), whose packaging has barely changed since 1915. The mistake, once a company has built a market, is to throw it away.

Back in the 1950s, Howard Johnson was almost as symbolic of America as the Statue of Liberty—or rather, of Middle America. The ubiquitous orange-roofed restaurants were as popular with middle-class Americans as the famous ice cream was with their kids. But Middle America changed, and as it changed, HoJo didn't. On the contrary, for nearly twenty years the company spent not a cent on refurbishing its hotels and restaurants. By the time some foolish Britons, the Imperial Group, bought the chain for a fabulous (or fatuous) $630 million in 1980, matters had deteriorated so far that, even after $350 million of belated spending, ace hotelier Willard Marriott, Jr., could pronounce this thumbs-down verdict to *Business*

Week: "Howard Johnson has too much outdated product they can't do anything with."

Howard Johnson wasn't dying from natural causes, note. It had undergone slow strangulation at the hands of the old family management. As the magazine observed, whether the loss-battered Britons sold HoJo or soldiered on, "it appears that the orange roofs that dotted American highways for sixty years are going the way of wayside Burma Shave signs"—and for the same reasons.

Mind you, the temptation to give in to those seductive arguments, and to go on making an unchanged product until it simply stops selling, is very powerful, on a shortsighted financial view. Old-fashioned auto manufacturers, according to them, chose to run their wonders until they and their market dropped, to give the customer continuity. Actually, the firms couldn't afford the whopping investment in new or radically improved models. They also went on making obsolete cars on the specious financial argument that the production equipment had all been paid for with "depreciation" money. In reality, the old cars with their antique design engineering were even more expensive to produce than the new ones—and were stealing the latter's sales.

Behind successful cars that seem to change but little, like the Mercedes-Benz line, lies a massive investment in both manufacture and R & D, spending that in relation to sales is hardly less significant than the amounts committed by manufacturers in the mass market, where model lines must not only change, but be seen to change.

All businesses need an old product policy—how to make the best of what the company has. After World War II, Beecham built its considerable fortunes on three oldies: Brylcreem, Macleans, and Lucozade. Even at the end of the 1960s, this unglamorous trio—a gooey hair cream, a crisp white toothpaste, and a sickly sweet glucose drink—were providing, with the genuinely new Beecham penicillins, about two thirds of group profits. The old brand has the cumulative weight of years of heavy advertising, of use by (more or less) satisfied customers, of high acceptability and established image. So long as astute managers improve and upgrade the product in step with the market, and modify the image with the times, the dreaded turning point in the life cycle can be put off indefinitely. Because executives get bored or complacent with old products, however, they quite unnecessarily condemn them to fast death or slow neglect. Beecham's veterans, Brylcreem and Macleans, had so much life in them that a substantial U.S. business was promoted on their backs. (A newer Beecham condiment, Silvikrin Shampoo, failed expensively, however; its name made the unacceptable suggestion to Americans that they were going gray.)

One of Beecham's American markets, contrarily, seems to prove the life cycle: toothpaste, where the old U.S. brand leaders have all been ejected by upstarts (including Macleans and more recently, from the same stable, Aquafresh). The whole American industry was turned upside down by stannous fluoride. Here was a true technological advance, the first toothpaste whose advertising need tell no lies. It knocked the makers, Procter & Gamble, for a loop (P&G, of course, being a big company, didn't invent Crest—a university did). The hucksters could sing the therapeutic virtues of toothpastes that, hygienically speaking, were no better than any other. They couldn't cope with Crest, which truly was better. After painful false starts, the American Dental Association ended the agony by endorsing the product. A simple, unglamorized ad baldly stating the facts thereupon succeeded superbly where the traditional ballyhoo had failed.

A great new product has to differ so sharply from any joy already on sale that its qualities—as long as they are good— sell themselves. P&G's competitors made the gratuitous error when they launched stannous fluoride toothpastes, called Ace and Cue, of making them almost indistinguishable from Crest. New products fail, and in phenomenally high proportions, because they offer no advantage worth having or, more simply, because they are bad. Even an admirable original (such as xerography or the Polaroid camera) customarily starts life badly: it is clumsy, hard to use, expensive, unsatisfactory in its results. But their unique concept allowed Xerox and Polaroid to override initial error. When similar defects in use attack products that merely vary somebody else's theme, the customers will stand clear in droves.

The highest mortality—nine out of ten—is in cigarettes, where the novelty mainly lies in the marketing. Each cigarette is the same as some other cigarette, and those that fail are as good (or bad) as those that win. New product calamities, in fact, stem from confusion about newness. The pet venture may be a straight or crooked copy, or an attempt to break into somebody else's racket (IBM trying with scant success to muscle in on Xerox, or Xerox, with even scanter success, trying to muscle in on IBM), or the newness may lie in replacing a similar product of your own (adding enzymes to an existing detergent mix). There may be real technological novelty in replacements. But "innovations" such as the Boeing 707 don't produce whole new markets. People don't shave more because stainless blades are superior to carbon steel, and more airliners would have been sold in the 1960s if the jet engine had never been invented.

The genuine innovations, creating whole new markets, thrusting old companies into oblivion and new ones into preeminence, are so rare, and so rarely emanate from big corporations, that the giants are best off avoiding the chase. Their "new product" is usually a "me-too" (an imitation of somebody else's wow), or, far better, some variation on their own themes. The latter pays fine dividends. Stick an extra carburetor, a new paint job, and a few fancy extras on the same car, call it the GT or the GTO, and collect a bundle of extra cash from the customers without the financial and technical pain of producing a new supermodel. Far better to devise a new method of processing an existing fiber, and open up new uses, than to invent a new shoe material called Corfam and embark on the long, expensive effort to foist it on a wary world that prefers leather.

The second, even if it succeeds, produces only a long-haul yield. The former, with minimal fortune, pays off at once, and if it fails, costs little more than some executive's self-respect. Even that bruising will be mitigated by executives' reluctance to remember their failures. Marketing books are full of success stories, but failure has no friends and few case histories—even though collapse is far more common. On one survey's conclusions, there is an eight out of ten ratio of technical failure, while only one in every three technical successes (meaning that the product works) goes on to commercial triumph.

The lessons of failure are always the more valuable. When executives look back at the successes, like generals brooding over old campaigns, they always rationalize and mistake perfect luck for perfect performance. Triumph often catches its perpetrators completely by surprise, like the runaway hit in the United States of two novel light scotch whiskies, Cutty Sark and J & B. Both were owned by respectable London wine merchants who in those days knew far more about prephylloxera clarets than about marketing.

Look at Coleco Industries from one angle, for instance, and it's a marketing marvel. The angle is that of the Cabbage Patch Kid dolls, possibly the biggest single hit in the history of America's toyland, still selling phenomenally in a second season when they were expected to earn half a billion dollars in a single year. Yet the company was up to its neck in debt, and having trouble breaking even—all because the same management has made a mess in home computers every bit as big as its hit in dolls. Of course, the hard-to-buy Kids couldn't save the hard-to-sell Adam computer (sell just one of these, and the sales clerk got a doll, a $500 scholarship, and a bonus); the product was killed at the start of 1985. Much less can be learned from Coleco's success with the Kids, essentially a brilliant combination of luck, market perception, and timing, than from its failure to replace its fading ColecoVision electronic game with a properly produced, timely product—a botch-up that lost the company $7.4 million in 1983.

All too often managements under threat—from product obsolescence or competition—react either too slowly or too ambitiously. When Gerber and Campbell's came beefing their way into Heinz's U.K. gold mine, attacking Heinz's canned foods and ready-to-serve soups with bottled and concentrated goodies, Heinz didn't botch up its response. It put out its own bottled baby foods and concentrated soups, just in case the British housewives changed their tastes from cans to bottles and from ready-to-serve to concentrates, and it battered the opposition with massive promotion. Gerber and Campbell's were clobbered. But more often companies get locked into their technology as well as their management habits—and even more dangerously.

"Maybe Xerox will come first when the inevitable happens," I wrote long ago, "and its cumbersome, unreliable reprographic money spinner is replaced by a more efficient, less unwieldy process. But don't bet on it—and Xerox shouldn't bet on having the good fortune of IBM." The first Univac computer (produced by men who IBM had sent packing) appeared, and made IBM's entire product range obsolescent, four years before IBM got a computer on the market. Univac, however, so crunched up the greatest postwar commercial discovery that IBM, despite its errors and delay, roared past Univac into staggering riches. My misgivings about Xerox, though, proved well founded. The challenge came from Japan; the Japanese did not, like Univac with IBM, give Xerox space to recover from its errors. By the time Xerox had woken up, both its total dominance in the world market and its technological leadership had gone for good.

You can bank on the opposition being stupid some of the time, but not all the time. That is the trouble with me-too products. Assuming that the market is established, the me-too executive is gambling that his product will be better and better marketed. This ignores logic. Trying something different is always better than competing directly, for in the latter case, you may lose. The small companies that creep to riches under the skirts of large Auntie corporations do so by specializing, by doing something different. Nobody got near Kodak's mass market in conventional cameras and films until the American firm unwisely let the Japanese steal a lead on costs. Before that, though, Polaroid got in under Auntie Kodak by offering a clear difference—instant photos.

Self-deception is rampant. No executive confesses, even to himself, that the opposition does indeed have a better product (if the opposition has been making the goodies longer, it probably does). No executive readily concedes that his time and other people's money have produced a lemon. Only the most self-aware executive takes honest account of cannibalization, or robbing Peter to pay Paul; thus an auto company's new wonder hits the sales of its next model down, so that total sales don't rise by the numbers of the new winner. Thus Apple, in introducing Macintosh, ran the risk of the new product stealing sales from the established Apple IIe; while IBM, presumably in the effort to stop the PC jr eating into the PC market, produced in self-defeating fashion a cheaper model that not only was inferior but looked it. The logic is inescapable. Freeze-dried coffee had to clobber ordinary instant (in the case of General Foods and Maxim, it did so at tremendous cost, including forty-three months in test market). Without the new product, life might have been much ghastlier—but, with it, existence may not be any richer.

As that example shows, while high-technology launches are notorious for high costs and high risks, so are new products that are lower in technology but high in marketing requirements. The marketing cost of a new grocery launch in the United States is now put by *Business Week* at anything from $10 million to $15 million—and only one eighth of the launches proceed from test market to success. In the face of such harsh facts, the option of shunning new products looks increasingly attractive, but hardly anybody dares to take it—and rightly.

The hectic chase after innovation, which keeps executives busy and advertising agencies in funds, may be expensive, but it isn't a luxury—not anymore. Present prosperity for all companies, and prosperity for a good time to come in the fortunate cases, will rest on old products, from which great fortunes and fabulous returns on capital will be made. But the future, more than ever before, must rest on genuine and continuing innovation. The overwhelming reason is that, in a context of sharpened and worldwide competition and generally accessible technology, product leads last too short a time for any leader to rest on its laurels. The process of generating new products and processes has to be endless if companies want to stay in the game.

This being so, it makes no sense to stay in the majority, that is, to find three quarters of your new products failing absolutely, with many of the rest obviously failing in relative terms. Some companies reckon that only 6 percent of their development money ends up in commercial successes, which is not only perverse but perverted. The condition won't be cured unless the organization of new product development is made a key activity of the corporation, welded into its structure, springing out of maximum informality and creativity, but then tightly and efficiently controlled to maximize the chances of success.

But what actually happens? In company after company, innovation is entrusted to R & D or some other department, instead of being made a line management function; access to the decision makers is the only thing that's tightly controlled, much too tightly; actual execution programs are sloppily managed and allowed to run so wildly over budget on both cost and time as severely to jeopardize whatever slim chances they had. That's one way to guarantee that three quarters of all new products go on failing. But if they do, so will the corporations that perpetrate the failures.

27

The Technology of Techniques

Ask executives what they want by way of improving literature and most will call for a richer menu of management techniques. They can't have enough of barely comprehensible inventions such as Monte Carlo simulation, management by exception, statistical sampling, linear programming, Markovitz Portfolio Selection, and the other contents of the technical basket. Their approach almost suggests that management techniques are like handbooks on car maintenance: master the latter and you save garage bills by doing it yourself; master the former and the business will respond to the magic technical touch. The analogy breaks down at several points—including the fact that many techniques (among them the most valuable) can't be left to enthusiastic amateurs.

Neither can technology. But this raises an obvious and increasingly urgent problem. The advent of the Silicon Age has brought into managers' lives new and complex technology of a type they seldom encountered before. The problems are, of course, especially acute in the companies actually supplying the new technology. So intense have the pressures become in the highest high-tech areas that its prodigies are beginning to talk of a new technology of management itself. Thus Andrew Grove, the president of Intel, is fond of talking about VLI^2—meaning Very Large Integrated Investments—and the wholly new concepts that managements in this game must grasp.

The Silicon Valley syndrome is that every decade the microchip markets in which Intel leads become ten times larger; the devices ten times more complex; the density of the circuits ten times greater. The only thing that gets smaller is the price—again, by ten times. The techniques used by businesses where the key factors don't follow this exponential course simply don't apply, argues Grove, to a situation in which a state-of-the-art wafer factory, which will cost $200 million by the end of the 1980s, cost half that in 1984 and a tenth of that in 1973. The plant could generate revenues ranging from $300 million (guaranteeing a thumping loss) to $900 million (a smashing profit), depending on whether its operator gets the yield and pricing right or wrong—and that in turn depends on correctly judging the ten times development in applications. So what's the answer?

According to Grove, it's *process-oriented management,* the human equivalent of the artificial intelligence advances that, in the shape of so-called expert systems, are now able to give better diagnoses of the meaning, say, of medical or geological information than the human mind can ever achieve. The evolution of a business like Intel's would be a continuous development, constantly modified (maybe eventually by computer) as new information appears, achieving a life of its own, independent in a sense from the managers who are ostensibly in charge. If Grove is right, the apotheosis of management techniques is at hand. Without them, management will become impossible, especially in the world of VLI[2].

If so, it truly will be a new world. In the old world, a central difficulty is that of translating technical lore from the page to the battlefield. Imagine the higher executive leafing through a spunky article on the mathematical approach to the product mix, the number and variety of products a company puts out. If the company is typical, several products could be ejected without any effect on profits. In fact, by making room for other lines (not one of which is ever made in the optimum numbers), a bout of slashing must boost earnings. But the elevating cases in the product mix article won't exactly fit any other company. And the boss's first reaction will be to call some subordinate's attention to the offending pages. If this beleaguered man is using the technique, he fires off a brisk retaliatory memo; if he isn't, his defensive mechanisms come into play—and the most valuable of these is sheer delay.

This technique, found in no textbook, works wonders. The two main defensive gambits are diametrically opposed. Method One is Don't respond at all until forced. This way (the most common) amplifies the chances that other and weightier matters, like an overpriced bid for another company, will supervene, and the boss will forget all about it. Method Two is Respond at speed in overwhelming and enthusiastic detail. This embarrasses the boss in turn. Now he must make a decision, which he too dislikes, and his defensive mechanisms take over. With luck, he will never make the decision at all. A Method Two twist was applied within one great engineering group. Its new management ordered a full survey of production facilities to find out which could be rationalized (a euphemism of the same order and meaning as "liquidated" in Soviet Russia). The gigantic tome ended with one short arresting sentence: "Nothing can be done until future product plans have been decided."

This illustrates the difference between techniques of management and management techniques. Techniques of management are used to procure the result a manager really wants—in the above case, inaction. Management techniques are the tools that an executive may or may not use in the pursuit of those real objectives. The true aim of an executive who wants to bone up on techniques is to feel more efficient, more modern, better equipped. He isn't, like the genuine techniques expert, obsessively interested in applying a mathematical method—such as exponential smoothing or network analysis—to obtain better operational results.

But that—obtaining better operational results—is the name of both their games, and the test of all management activity, high technology or low. Grove of Intel is by no means the only gee-whiz manager, though, to insist that the higher the technology, the higher the technique. Over at Apple, president John Sculley's "in" phrase is *management degree zero*— "We're going to purge the word 'managers' from the Apple vocabulary." For managers, read culture; a *"new* culture. We're discovering that we have to make our own models as we go along. Out of this will come new management concepts. . . . After the end of the decade managing will never be the same again."

Maybe it will, maybe it won't. Without doubt, there's a sense in which management in the new industries is different; managing new industries always has been. Maybe in Silicon Valley, as Grove says, "no project will be brought to completion by the same people who started it" as VLI[2] enforces its stern laws—and as changes in management style and techniques are enforced in step. Yet the new jargon does have the ring of old, dead attempts to reinvent the managerial wheel. Remember Harry Figgie and his "nuclear theory of management" in Chapter 1?

Like Figgie and the other conglomerators, the Silicon Valleys have had a plentiful crop of flops. From Osborne to Trilogy they were brought down to earth not by their inability to cope with VLI² or failure to create (as Sculley dreams of Apple) "a unique learning institution," but by straightforward low-technology management mistakes. When Honeywell lucked out at Synertek, for example, one of the main problems was that the Minneapolis company, having bought the chip-maker, wouldn't let it use Prime computers. Why not? Because Prime is a spin-off from Honeywell. Less than a year from takeover, Honeywell had only one of the Synertek founders and officers left on the premises; the affiliate was hopelessly overdependent (80 percent) on Atari for its sales; and a $50 million new facility at Santa Cruz came in too late to forestall the competition. Much the same story of mangled management can be told of the other electronic catastrophes. The Synerteks of the new world don't drop 38 percent of their sales in three years by modern management failures; good old-fashioned bungling is all that they need.

As that sorry story shows, though, the new technology has provided plenty of brand-new opportunities for mismanagement, and in a field where the risks are unusually high. Sculley's own Cola-to-Apple example proves that nontechnical managers can bridge the gap between technologist and management, and in no time at all. But the divide exists all the same. It's a reflection in its way of the conflict, often deadly, between executives and technique experts inside the corporation. Not only do executives get the big money and make the big (and small) decisions, they are also free to use, abuse, or not use the expert's expertise. To the experts, there is something deeply wounding in being forced to support their surefire cost-saving ideas with voluminous reports, while any nut in the upper echelons merely has a brainstorm in the bath, and the experts promptly have to study its inane implications—in depth too.

The inanity is often immediately apparent. Professor P. M. S. Blackett, the Briton who invented Operations Research to improve bombing efficiency and convoy deployment in World War II, wanted to restrict "systems analysis" (which is the Everest of management technology) to "calculations that can be done on the back of an envelope." Rather than use the same small tool for his simpler sums, however, the executive loads his own failure to clarify his thoughts onto the shoulders of the misnamed management scientist—misnamed because none of the sciences is in any way specific to management, and because the work is seldom scientific either. The science rests only in applying measurement and logical deduction to known fact, something that executives are supposed to do for themselves.

Take a typical case—the executive who opposes a price rise, or wants to invoke a discount, or open a second sales office in a region, or revamp the corporate image. Rude questions have to be asked: If we raise prices by half, how much will sales fall—10 percent, 20 percent, or 30 percent? At what level of sales and prices will profits drop? How much more business will we get through this discount, or new office, or company face-lift alone, and what will it cost? The cost is always precisely measurable, and you can always work out simply how much in *extra* sales is needed to cover the *overall* loss of profit.

Executives fail to make this easy, speedy test, not because they don't know the techniques of simple arithmetic but because they are dead set on a course that they have chosen for other reasons entirely. The man wants to cut prices because he thinks vaguely that it will help the sales effort; he wants to open the new office to widen his empire; he longs to beautify the corporate image—to enhance his own. These are emotional drives. Sitting down with the back of an envelope is a cold-blooded affair that rarely satisfies anybody except the technical

335

expert. And he is too insignificant in the hierarchy for his pleasure to matter.

The greatest operations research calculation of all time was supervised (on a blackboard, not the back of an envelope) by Henry Ford I, whose enthusiasm for management technology was only slightly warmer than his love for unions. The sum showed the economic consequences of raising Ford wages to $5 a day. The calculations proved that elevating Ford workers into potential Ford buyers would leave Henry with enormous profits. Note the sequence of events. Ford had an inspiration, which men of less peculiar genius would have missed or misunderstood. Then, like a good engineer, Ford checked his brainwave by the simplest relevant calculation. Then he put his idea into practice—again like a good engineer.

Engineering is the right analogy. Much management technology is like most production or design technology—the general manager has no necessity to know the details, but must know that the technology exists. Mathematical and computational techniques are the machine tools of management—and some are as abstruse as the Cabbala. As one authority wrote, "Some of these techniques require highly specialized knowledge or equipment for their correct use. Probably only a few dozen people in the country fully understand them . . . [others] are as yet barely understood by more than a few experts." So relax. You wouldn't be able to use them if you tried.

In fitting out a factory, a good general manager decides what to make, but buys an expert to tell him how. The manager's judgment then tests the expert's words to confirm (say) that he isn't proposing to use a multispindle automatic when a hand drill will do nicely, or isn't hiring expensive computer time to try some assumption on which no profit hinges. An American chemical plant contractor was disconcerted to find that a British customer insisted on his using the sophisticated, costly technique of "network analysis." Back home, it wouldn't have been thought necessary—it wasn't either.

A second category of techniques is essential to almost any manager; it mostly boils down to applied common sense. Much of this indispensable technology is financial, meaning that the executive (although he will resist it) has to reduce the implications of his actions to money terms. There is always a simple, back-of-the-envelope truth involved, such as the basic discounted cash-flow thought, which is that a pound in the hand today is worth more than a pound in the bag tomorrow. Old-line executives in their ignorance used to rely on payback— how long their money took to come home, which assumed, falsely, that money received in three years' time had the same value as today's. The supposedly sophisticated Americans still have a deep sentimental attachment to this ancient concept, and to a degree they are right.

Old-line executives were not as silly as they seemed. Payback enshrines a truth. Until you do repocket your capital, the enterprise is pointless. Say a firm invests $10 million in a plant that produces a discounted cash flow of $1 million a year for a decade, and then has to be replaced by another plant of equivalent cost; its effort has gone for nothing. The quicker the payback, too, the less an executive needs to worry about discounted cash flow or anything else.

Forrest Mars, in creating his confectionery empire, used a crude, but highly effective, measure, judging executives by their return made in real money (with no allowance for so-called depreciation) on the real money that, historically, he, Forrest Mars, had put into the business. In other words, Mars looked at his wealth as an individual proprietor naturally would, and there is more logic (and money) here than in the big bureaucracy's more complex, convoluted measures.

The tycoon grabs hold of a simple, single idea that makes sense to him and applies it consistently and ruthlessly. But Patterson of NCR, Watson of IBM, Lord Leverhulme of Lever Brothers, Henry Ford, the founding Agnelli of Fiat, and the other emperors had something else: they knew their businesses.

337

Management techniques are only adjuncts to management. They don't cope with one basic fact—that the nature of the business partly determines how it is run. You don't have to be a lifelong butter and egg man to sell butter and eggs. But the lifetime knowledge of those who do know one end of a cow or hen from the other is critical to the success of the business— as turnaround men, or company doctors, often find out, late and to everybody's cost.

The turnaround artist, the expert called to revive failing firms, is frequently loaded with technical lore. Often he is a renegade management consultant. To judge by several experiences, there is at best a four-year rise-and-fall cycle: the technical touch first produces radical improvement, then yields diminishing returns, and is finally blunted by business troubles. The technically adept executive manager is asked to create an effective, fast-growing, efficient, and professional company out of one that is ineffective, sluggish, sloppy, and amateurish— which is why the wunderkind was called in. But for all his professional equipment he lacks the one technique that the dozy oldsters all possess—feel and affection for their special market. Lasting success depends (more than professionals can see, for it reduces their personal marketability) on how fast the newcomers can absorb the facts of a strange market and on how responsive that market really is.

Uncovering and eliminating the oldsters' mistakes is the easy bit. One taken-over motorcycle veteran vehemently opposed dropping a brand name because of its popularity in the Middle East. Inquiry showed that the company's Arab sales could be counted on one maimed hand. Uncovering and eliminating your own errors is no more difficult, judging by the experience of a group of American industrialists who visited Japan. According to Harvard professor Robert Kaplan, they found that the percentage of Japanese products that didn't need reworking went as high as 92 percent. How much higher was that than the results back home? They didn't know—that was the awful answer. Once they had taken the trouble to find out, they discovered an equally awful truth: the proportion *needing* rework was the same figure—92 percent. After being awakened, the industrialists turned their attention to seeking some kind of improvement. After six months, the no-rework statistic was up from 8 to 66 percent—and productivity was higher by a quarter.

Another example is market share. Whether or not you believe the Boston Consulting Group and PIMS (Profit Impact of Market Strategy) and proceed on the assumption that your profitability will rise with market share, the latter is plainly of considerable significance. But one *Management Today* writer found an executive who took a somewhat different view. He announced "with great pride that every time the firm put the price up 10 percent, it lost only 5 percent of its traffic—so it still made money." As the writer observed, "It needs no mathematical genius to work out that company's doomsday." This kind of nonsense tumbles out of the woodwork at the first application of common sense or management technique, call it what you will, as in the case of a battery company that only struck its profit at the year's end after counting the stock in the warehouse, though its deliveries to dealers were all on sale or return. The professional will settle such follies fast. The harder problem is to discover what the old boys did right, and, still more, to avoid new disasters (which the veterans would never even have imagined) in desperate attempts to overcome inborn defects in the market.

Mattel, having narrowly survived one disastrous period in its traditional low-tech toy markets (Hot Wheels cars, and so on), achieved brief respite in electronic games. Thus encouraged, the management went into home computers as well. Egregious errors in both markets cost shareholders dearly: the value of their holdings plummeted by 69 percent in 1983. Over at Hughes Tool, the core business that made Howard Hughes (and his fortune) a legend, the post-Hughes management tried well-production valves, pumps, and services in a bid to expand beyond the golden gusher of drilling bits. The result? The drilling business stagnated, the diversifications ran into the oil and gas recession, sales fell by 35 percent between 1981 and 1983 —and the company made its first-ever loss, no less than $90 million.

As the company retrenched to drilling bits, *Business Week* understandably remarked that "Howard Hughes' ghost seems to be saying: 'I told you so.'" The management technician's skills can stop the rot—thus part of Hughes's new recipe is cutting manufacturing costs by automation. But replacing the fungus with healthy growth requires different aptitudes. No mere technique can solve fundamental problems like Hughes's dependence on a one-product, one-market business, or Mattel's vulnerability to the cyclical, fashion-beset character of the toy trade.

Techniques are most valuable for correcting mismanagement. Thus the most important technique, positively guaranteed to wash any business whiter, is challenge. Since every business is managed badly, in the sense that every operation is capable of improvement, savings can always be made without any loss of effectiveness—and often at little cost. Simple technical analysis will always reveal bad cases of common defects, such as the overhead obsession. One company maintained a money-losing plant just for its contribution to overhead: it was tying up $4 million for a $65,000 contribution. Another firm kept a large loser going on the same specious grounds—the loss-maker, far from making a contribution, practically was the overhead.

Companies often suffer under the delusion that by juggling costs around the organization, even with no new money coming in, they can enrich its finances. The best use of technicians is not to chart corporate forays into the remote and uncertain future, but to uncover the errors of its present management. This is unlikely to be popular; it falls foul of a basic lie of management—any mistakes were made by the previous incumbents. The Tenth Truth, however, is that *the easiest way of making money is to stop losing it.* Dealing with customer complaints used to cost Heinz $6 a complaint, until some unsung genius thought of issuing a 30-cent voucher every time a can of beans or tomato soup came to grief. That's real management, and it doesn't need a computer.

The task isn't to understand what is meant by, say, "a system using doubly exponentially smoothed average demand forecasts coupled with safety stocks being set with a Trigg Tracker and the modules of the Trigg Tracker used to control the parameters of the exponential smoothing." It is to know rules of thumb such as this: operational research techniques will enable most companies to cut inventory by 30 percent, saving delicious sums, but eight tenths of that saving will come from better recordkeeping; "just in-time" systems will provide still greater savings, but most of them, too, come from better organization—this time of production. Or (and expert help will show you where) five distribution points will always provide second-day delivery to 80 percent of the entire United States. Never disparage a good rule of thumb; that digit is as valuable as any computer. But to discover and exploit such verities, you need the ability to challenge, check, and check again.

Beyond that, the vital technique of management is the use of analytical methods to picture reality. Managements are always being misled, like the U.S. paper company that thought it had developed a great trade in disposable surgical dressings. It applied a much abused technique (market research) and found that doctors actually used the products as de luxe hand towels. Luck, that most valuable of all management techniques, had played its usual, indispensable part.

If you attribute your success to pure luck, you will not only be right, some of the time, but you will be better prepared for the repugnant job of criticizing your mistakes, which are plenty. An executive in one of the more efficient retail giants once remarked, "Anybody listening in on our meetings would think it was the worst-run business in the world." That is the only safe assumption. Discontent is commercially divine—the manager's best friend. But like the techniques it employs, self-criticism won't create a wonderful business. The tycoon doesn't need techniques, and can afford self-adulation, because he can think and act along the straight line between a marvelous idea and its realization. Executives who are hired hands and tend to think in circles need all the technical aid they can get— especially from themselves.

28

The Organizational Obsession

The most prevalent organizational blight is organic—the growth of the corporate organism into an end in itself. Executives may swear that they exist to make money, sell safety matches, build power stations, market lingerie, or whatever, but insensibly they slide into serving none of these ends. Instead, they serve only the corporation. The business exists to sustain the company. The company no longer exists to do business; it exists to exist.

Consequently, a mind-bending preoccupation of senior executives is with the form of the beloved organism. Like some collector of stamps or rare coins, they fiddle constantly with the object of their love, and they call in other avid enthusiasts (in this case, management consultants) to help in rearranging, pruning, and swapping. Corporate reshuffles are nonevents—for everybody outside the corporation. Inside they are of lasting fascination, like a restatement of religious dogma. Their initiation alone accomplishes nothing measurable. A bad business can never be swung around to supergrowth by redrawing the organization chart.

Boards huff and puff about strains on the previous structure, about growth imposing new pressures for which the old machinery was inadequate, about it being time for a new look. (For the real reasons, read bad business results, uncomfortable awareness of falling behind the fashion, a takeover bid miraculously averted.) But the ultimate cause is simply that introspection, which all bureaucracies enjoy, has to come to a great orgastic climax at periodic intervals. After their game of musical chairs, the managerial bureaucrats, purged and satisfied, settle into their new seats—and carry on much as before.

The obvious analogy is the way in which Japanese companies rise above the hierarchical obsessions and social rigidities that would stultify any Western company. The form is one thing; the spirit is another. But organizational forms can powerfully affect performance in two ways. First, they can actively obstruct effective operation. Second, a change in organization can do more than anything else to symbolize and thus effect a change in corporate ethos and direction. The difficulties in obtaining these changes can be frightful—as William T. Ylvisaker found in his heroic bid to turn Gould from a mainly low-technology engineering conglomerate into a high-powered, high-tech electronics combine.

The interventionist, high-profile leadership that turned Gould into a $2 billion company didn't fit the transmogrified corporation—and neither did the first organizational attempt to make it work. In 1981, Ylvisaker told *Business Week* that "we are eliminating corporate structure, pushing down responsibility, and increasing incentives—division by division, group by group." A year later, a different song was being sung. Now four distinct product groups took over in a marketing-oriented structure, each group with its own seven-man operating board —headed by neither Ylvisaker nor his president. Even this, obviously, isn't enough. Gould managers wear a gold-plated numeral I on their jackets to match the new company slogan, "We are One"—and not, as some might uncharitably think, a hodgepodge of expensive high-tech buys.

Whatever form a company adopts, and for whatever reason, there is one eternal basic principle: that he who is supposed to manage should manage. It has nothing to do with the letter of the chart, but everything to do with that spirit of the company. The useful purpose of reorganization is to stop that guiding spirit, whatever it is, from being bogged down in organizational routine. A brisk game of musical chairs sharpens everybody up, the catch being that, if the executives are too slow when the music starts, they will still not be speedy enough at the end (a point where eleven out of Gould's original twenty-one top managers weren't even there—they had quit or been fired).

The sacred scrolls of the organization's tabernacle are the manuals and, above all, the organization chart. Like the sacred documents of many religions, these charts often mean very little, even to the initiated. Some iconoclastic managements have tried to stamp them out, with as much success as Nero had against the Christians. In one American multinational where charts were officially forbidden, the executives drew up unofficial ones. Nothing can destroy the self-preserving desire of the inhabitants of a bureaucracy to know precisely where they stand—or where they don't stand. Many executives are more eager to narrow their responsibilities (which gives them less opportunity for failure) than to widen them.

Very possibly, the unofficial charts drawn up by deprived executives are closer to reality than those blessed by the boardroom. These are abstract art, as highly regarded as Jackson Pollocks. The top management of a big company such as

Honeywell was even a bit ashamed that once upon a recent time it was chartless. But only the names and job titles are real; the lines of command reflect an idealized truth. The telltale symptom is the dotted line: the more dotted the lines on a chart, the less it reflects the way the company actually runs.

A crisp unbroken line is understood by everybody. It means that in theory Executive B reports to Executive A, who in turn supervises, controls, or pushes about Executive B. It does not mean either that B takes any notice of A, or that B manages his segment of the chart at all—A may swamp the fellow entirely. But at least everybody knows what their relationship is supposed to be. Neither A nor B may see it the same way in practice, however. In 134 cases where managers in one U.S. multinational thought they had told subordinates what to do, the latter were conscious of receiving only seventy-eight orders.

The dotted line, in contrast, is a thing of confused beauty and a joy forever. It fans out from boards to "advisers" or "planning units"—staff appointments, often at the highest level, whose work veers across that of the line managers. The chart of one large group, in the days before its disappearance, was festooned with dots of this description. Or dots connect a functional department (engineering, say) with a product division; here dots mean that the two are supposed to work together, all too often a forlorn but pretty fantasy.

If engineers dominate the company (as they dearly love to do) the dotted line is more authoritarian than the solid one. One production manager, invited to reveal his sorrows to a new outside director, pointed out that small differences in fifty virtually identical components forced him to maintain fifty separate production lines. He thought that the technical specification could be met by no more than five varieties. The director led him by the hand over to the engineers; they readily agreed that the production manager was dead right. The corporate

346

ethos, or the reality behind the chart, didn't allow production considerations, or production men, to intrude on the organizational dominance of the engineers—even to save money.

Other dotted daydreams cover bureaucratic miasmas such as independent overseas companies that are controlled by so-called international divisions but make the same products in the same way as domestic product divisions. Multinational companies (still the popular euphemism for American companies with overseas interests, though parents of other nationalities are now sharing much the same odium) have gone to extraordinary chart contortions to sustain the fiction that their foreign satrapies are independent. They have good reason for telling stories. Host countries (another euphemism, meaning the occupied territory) are not fond of reminders that control of large chunks of national markets or assets lies somewhere in the Midwest.

This kind of problem doesn't bother the Europeans one iota. The Swiss of Nestlé and the Dutch of Philips control their overseas companies with a tight-lipped Napoleonic firmness. "I personally still hold the view," wrote one of Nestlé's chocolate generals with heavy jocularity, "that . . . we are rather decentralized. But I am often surprised when talking to our own people in the markets . . . to find that they think the contrary." As for Philips, an internal wag commented that the electrical giant is the only company in the world where, no matter what your position, there are always more people above you than below you.

When new men took over both Nestlé and Philips in the early 1980s, both set out consciously to change that heavy-handed tradition. What put courage behind German Helmut Maucher's convictions was the Swiss giant's worst-ever profits fall. Crisp decisions, including a total retreat out of Libby's canned foods in the United States, followed smartly by the $3 billion purchase of Carnation, typified the new style. But more important even than the simultaneous assault on corporate bureaucracy was Maucher's decision, in *Fortune*'s words, "to give more authority and power to the line managers." In consequence of all this radicalism, return on sales jumped 60 percent between 1980 and 1983. At Philips, Wisse Dekker has taken much the same approach—and for exactly the same reasons.

The British are almost certainly more lax, or relaxed, toward managements in other lands. This has something to do with the tradition of empire (unique to the British). By the time bad news got back from India in Queen Victoria's day, it was too late to take any action, and British executives (many of whose companies, such as British Petroleum, grew up as imperially as the British raj) became used to letting far-flung executives sink or swim. So to this day earnest efforts at home are periodically drowned by disasters in Australia or India, the compensation being that bad domestic results are periodically salvaged by some far-flung miracle.

The American imperialists, even though bad news travels faster these days, have come to share the same experience—the fiascoes of Chrysler in Britain, France, and Spain were, if anything, more grisly than the company's pre-Iacocca catastrophes in the U.S. market. As design consultant Wally Olins described it, when Chrysler took complete financial control of British Rootes, French Simca, and Spanish Barreiros, "all names were changed to Chrysler. . . . The entire range of geriatric English cars, mongrel French cars, and Spanish-built inferior American cars was marketed all over Europe. The result was a catastrophe."

Not that you have to be American to mismanage multinationally. The entire Chrysler European inheritance fell into the hands of Peugeot, which "started all over again and christened the unsavory mess Talbot . . . another tale, equally unedifying." Peugeot had been, as the last family-controlled auto firm in Europe, secure in a solid, lucrative middle-income niche. Its strength lay in clear identity and cherished quality; the Peugeot family even boasted that its workers had the industrious, virtuous habits of the little old Swiss watchmakers who lived nearby. What drove the company to distraction and vast deficits ($360 million in 1983) was that inept swallowing of Chrysler's European interests. Multinational takeovers simply weren't in its experience, which (apart from Citroën) wasn't long on takeovers at all.

The more either Chrysler or Peugeot tried to impose their central will on their new subsidiaries, the worse the latter seemed to perform. Controlling subsidiaries with rods (or dotted lines) of iron may stop some mistakes, but it won't solve the problem, which is fundamentally one of power. The actual management of companies is determined by their power relationships, and these, because they are human and changing, cannot be depicted by anything less than a full Freudian psychoanalysis. Like all human relationships, too, they follow no rules. There are only well-known dangers, which you can survive, just as you could conceivably survive driving up the New York Thruway on the wrong side of the road.

First, if the man in charge does not have the power to execute that charge, he probably won't. He needn't be the man who the chart says is in charge, as long as some other executive has the power instead. But if the authority falls into an uneasy vacuum, with overlords sitting on managerial shoulders like so many old men of the sea, the results will be ineffective. Some of the bigger American success stories abroad have come under a loose rein—or no rein at all.

Black and Decker, managed by a tough Englishman named Robert Appleby, expanded so fast in Europe that it outgrew a parent that did little more than sit benignly by. Hoover grew to dominate the British appliance market under the independent British management of Sir Charles Colston, who took Hoover into washing machines and into Europe while the home board in North Canton, Ohio, couldn't see further than the sucking end of its vacuum cleaners. After the eccentric Herbert Hoover, Jr., decided to crack his little whip, before being ousted in turn by affronted American directors, British Hoover flopped into a much more dismal era, falling so far from grace, as noted earlier, that the independent British stockholdings were finally bought out by the American parent for what they were worth—which wasn't much.

The moral of this tale, though, isn't that the best organization is no organization at all. Few companies are more organized than IBM. Its local bosses have never had anything like the autonomy of a Colston. But the record of Sir Edwin Nixon's nineteen years as chairman of the U.K. subsidiary—a 3,726 percent expansion in sales—couldn't have been achieved without effective, vigorous performance at local level—a long way geographically from Armonk, New York, but fairly near to Paris, where IBM has its European headquarters. The setup could have been a tool for emasculation. It didn't work that way, not because of the mechanism but because of how the machinery was used—the corporate ethos, if you will.

There's even method behind the madness, or apparent eccentricity, of leaving Nixon in the same job for so long, like his counterparts in other key European countries, in a company where other executives are rotated like helicopter blades. It's part of IBM's answer to a basic problem of organization—the prime position. Do you or don't you have one man at the apex of the pyramid? The pressures of complexity are leading toward multiple management, not the multiple, hydra-headed variety long favored by companies like du Pont or ICI, still less the troikas of the "president's office" tried by several American giants, but a genuinely collegiate effort in which primacy doesn't go hand in hand with dictatorship. Once again, it's a matter of balance. The organization must have clear, single-minded authority at the pinnacle—hence the long-serving local bosses—but the right to that authority depends heavily on the readiness to relinquish, share, and even subjugate it in the interests of effective management.

Where hydra-headed management has grown up over the years, and has become built into the life-style, changing it can be as difficult as altering the whole direction and philosophy of the corporation. Shell found this out after its own McKinsey-advised reshuffle. There one director ended up as something called director of coordination, oil. Catch 22 was that Shell happens to be an oil company, the bulk of whose business descended, with backbreaking force, on this one man. His position, like the reshuffle, became quite untenable. Oil companies such as Shell face in acute form the dilemma of all organizations, which is to resolve the pull between the center and the lone executive down the line manipulating the physical facts on a day-to-day basis. Because oil is the most homogenous of businesses, the spider in the middle of the web can pull everything in toward it. But what about the happiness and self-esteem of lesser insects around the rim?

The decentralize-centralize problem can never be finally resolved. The gibe goes that the management consultant called in to a decentralized company says "centralize." Show him a centralized company, and he promptly decentralizes it. The bigger the company, too, the more likely the consultant is to push the top management upstairs into an ethereal chart zone known as strategy. But where does strategy begin and tactics end? Did Electrolux rise from sales of $211 million when Hans Werthen took over in 1967 to $4.2 billion in 1983 because of his strategy of buying the biggest share of Europe's appliance market (28 percent) until it accounted for half of turnover? Or were the tactical moves—like exacting high profitability, partly through efficient engineering—the real explanation?

Or take another Swedish example: Volvo. At one point the auto company seemed doomed as its strategy misfired: stuck with cars that were the laughing stock of the auto press; lumbered with what looked like a lunatic purchase of Daf in Holland; and searching desperately for mergers—only to meet with humiliating rebuffs. Has Volvo's remarkable rebound to $13 billion of sales come from the eventual success of the merger strategy? Or was it the continued high-quality operation at the plants that made its autos *(mirabile dictu)* cult objects in the U.S. market and pushed its return on equity safely into double figures? Is maintaining high quality strategic or nonstrategic?

The larger a company is, the more often strategy gets locked in by supposedly tactical decisions taken far lower down. By the time most issues have worked their way up the chart to the board or executive committee, the titans at the top may no longer have either the freedom or the time to reverse what some remote underling has wrought. The object of a decentralizing reshuffle is to consolidate this unplanned fact into a shining system of delegated responsibility.

But anyone can see the futility of, say, constructing a three-ring circus—the board, a trading board one ring down, and a permanent executive committee of trading directors below that. The overlaps between the three tiers meant that the seven managing executives on the trading board were responsible for their triumphs and misdeeds to a main board that consisted mostly of themselves (making life a little easier all around). The astrological complexities of systems like this (taken from the life of an oil major), with the nine trading executives as satellites of the seven managing executives, and regional and functional orbits crisscrossing all over the planet Earth, practically guarantee that the delegated power, like hot air, will rise right back to where it has always resided.

But some secret force makes a company work, more or less effectively, despite the efforts of bureaucracy to turn its management totally inward. Somewhere in the organization lurk the 20 percent of executives who (according to Pareto's law) do 80 percent of the effective work. Finding the 20 percent and removing obstacles to their performance is the only proper pursuit of organization organizers. An idealist might try to uplift the 20 percent proportion, but this is unrealistic. Maybe the active executives, like worker bees in a hive (only with a king bee or king bees at their head), need a large community of drones. In which case, the chartists should concentrate on keeping the drones in happy, mildly useful, and clear relationship to each other, and out of the hair of the workers.

This worker-drone breakdown could be synthesized into a new psychological theory of companies, like the popular contrast between authoritarian Theory X companies and easygoing participative Theory Y firms. The idea of hierarchical managements trying to loosen up is like Russian apparatchiks trying to give more power to factory directors. It fails because it isn't what the apparatchiks or the top executives really want. Styles of management grow out of traditions of companies and styles of people, and there is still, alas, no convincing evidence that Theory Y companies, although much nicer to work for, outperform the Theory X bastards.

All the same, there's more than sheer iconoclasm in the sermon that Robert Townsend preaches (at $6,000 for forty-five minutes) to corporations that are interested in moving in the radical, Theory Y directions he favors. To take one of his stories about the Gore-Tex company, it makes no difference to the efficiency of an organization whether or not people have job titles; so, if somebody, as one woman did, says she always wanted to be a vice-president, let her call herself anything she likes, as grand as she likes (this Gore lady ended up with "Supreme Commander" on her visiting cards). Nike, the sporting-shoe company, is another firm that has no respect for titles at all—and just makes them up as it goes along.

The new informality is no more effective in itself than the traditional ways. But what it stands for is an easier, freer form of association inside the company, from which greater effectiveness should flow. That's why Townsend's favorite steel company, built on a green-belt site by refugees from Big Steel, and now the fifteenth largest in the United States, has absurdly large hallways—so that people can meet and argue in them. This freedom of association is actually basic to Japanese managers, whose very souls would generally revolt at the kind of togetherness practiced in Adidas, Gore, or scores of Silicon Valley companies.

But you won't find in Japanese firms the organizational barriers described earlier in this chapter, which stop production from talking to sales from talking to marketing from talking to personnel. The barriers come down because the people on different sides of them, in organization-chart terms, don't regard themselves as different. They see themselves all as devoted members of the same outfit, with the same basic activity —being businessmen. Thus production, sales, marketing, personnel, planning, and so on, are all in on all business decisions, which affect them all. That's the essence of ringi—not the laborious method by which decisions are reached, stamped, and sealed, but the involvement worthy of the best Theory Y culture.

Even where a recognizable Theory Y company is a wow, there is a chicken-and-egg difficulty. As a company succeeds, so its executives, working cheek by jowl over the years, develop respect for each other's muscles, wariness of each other's weaknesses, and instinct for a management method that suits them all equally. Call this participation, if you will. But Theory Y can no more be credited for its success than Theory X can be applauded for ITT's swimming against the conglomerate tide for a spell under Harold Geneen, a sixteen-hour-a-day dynamo who devised a corporate structure that revolved around him like a top. A man can make an organization, and an organization in turn makes its men. But if the company falls on evil days, it won't achieve salvation without a change in the men as well as the mechanism.

29

Battle of
the Best-Sellers

The wondrous boom in management of the post-1973 era quite inevitably meant a wonderful something else: a boom in management literature. Managers desperately needed more knowledge to cover their nakedness, and books are where knowledge resides. Robert Townsend's original *Up the Organization* and Lawrence Peter's *The Peter Principle* proved to be the iconoclastic forerunners of a stream of nonacademic tomes, which became a spate—and then turned off in a new and unexpected direction. Even *In Search of Excellence* (the book that, as noted in Chapter 25, brought new riches to consultancy) did so in the time-honored manner, writing about the great and the good.

Time (and honor) have changed, however. Now the great, the good, and the not-so-good write about themselves. True, Townsend used his turnaround triumph at Avis as a peg on which to hang his enthusiastic ideas about permissive Theory Y management. But it was still definitely a management book. In 1984, though, the runaway, unprecedented best-seller success of Lee Iacocca's life and good times changed the name of the game. Iacocca's book is a full-blooded autobiography, more in the vein of *On a Clear Day You Can See General Motors*—the self-justifying account written for John De Lorean, a man with a great deal to justify.

In one way or another, though, all the tycoon texts are as interested in justifying or glorifying the self as in offering precepts for management. Since this vainglorious element is so obvious, what explains the public's hunger for reading the works?

One answer is simply that the tycoons (or their publishers) mostly had the wit to employ professional writers, and even to name them. Once upon a time, businessmen confined their literary ambitions to interoffice memos and annual reports, and that's how most of them write. But beyond the literary professionalism, and far more important, lies the same quest for certainty in an uncertain world that explained the equally unprecedented million-plus copies of *In Search of Excellence,* or the high-rise sales of books promising to reveal the secrets of Japanese business success. The management readers want reassurance; they want to hear that, if they only imitate this marvelous man or adopt that magical recipe, they can rise above the toughest challenges, as Iacocca did so superbly at Chrysler.

Not that more than a portion of Iacocca's amazing sales were confined to managers. But any budding boardroom authors inspired by its success should beware. Few other executives have lived through such tumult. None have become preternaturally famous through appearing (in 97 percent of U.S. households, sixty-three times each) in their own commercials ("If you can find a better car—buy it"). Few can tell a story that has so many elements of a *Dallas*-type television blockbuster. The Ford years alone brim with blood and thunder: the aging "despot" (Iacocca's word for Henry II) maintaining his cramping grip on a lavish and indulgent court at the price of destroying the ambitious, brilliant, thrusting Crown Prince.

Similarly, Mark McCormack has enough fame as the entrepreneur/agent who made Arnold Palmer into a multinational, megabuck corporation to give any book a flying start. But celebrity isn't the sole explanation: the sales of his *What They Don't Teach You at Harvard Business School,* of *Iacocca,* and of *Managing,* the testament of ITT's Harold Geneen, are also symptoms of a general upsurge of interest in the business of business. The issue is whether the books do anything for management other than line the already richly coated pockets of their prime authors; whether the readers obtain anything for the expenditure of a few bucks, other than a warm feeling in the heart.

To be fair, that question can be asked of any management book, including this one. The *Iacocca* phenomenon is only a mite more remarkable than that of *In Search of Excellence—* or that of *The One-Minute Manager* and its sixty-second progeny. That first slim (or minute) volume basically consisted of a crisp lesson as old as management itself, if not older: Don't hire a dog and bark yourself. Apart from that incontrovertible advice on delegation, and a simplistic three-stage guide to retaining control and motivation while delegating, *The One-Minute Manager* has little to offer except brevity. That's no criticism of the book, though, for the limited range of its lore isn't at all exceptional.

The eight basic attributes, the highest common factors, that the two consultant authors found in their search for *Excellence* among America's leading corporations can also be summed up in one page and read aloud in one minute. That's a vital mark of the business-book bonanza: the essential message, even if the volume, like *What They Don't Teach,* runs to

249 pages, can be expressed in very short compass. Thus, McCormack's argument is that what Harvard doesn't "teach you is what they *can't* teach you, which is how to read people and how to use that knowledge to get what you want." His "seven-step plan" to supply this academic deficiency occupies just two and a half pages and twenty-four key words ("listen aggressively; observe aggressively; talk less; take a second look at first impressions; take time to use what you've learned; be discreet; be detached").

Good sound advice it is, too. There are other equally pithy summaries en route to the epilogue: like how to deal with employees: "(1) Pay them what they are worth, (2) Make them feel that they are important, yet (3) Make them think for themselves, and (4) Separate office life from social life." Again, the words are worth their weight in silver, if not in gold: but they are hardly enough to fill a book. So what does?

The answer in McCormack's case is a wealth of anecdote, much of it inconsequential, and a welter of advice, mostly disconnected. The anecdotes are about sports more than management, for McCormack appreciates better than anybody (he should) the value of dropping a good heroic name, viz: "I bring up Arnold Palmer's name in business conversations all the time." But McCormack isn't as original or nonacademic as he would have you believe. Some of the lessons he offers are, in fact, taught at Harvard, like the 80–20 rule (which lays down that 20 percent of your customers provide 80 percent of your sales, and so on) and the art of positioning (which tells you where to place and price your offerings in the marketplace).

What Lee Iacocca learned in the hard school of Detroit, too, wouldn't surprise any Harvard professor. In the 16 pages (out of 341) that he devotes to "The Key to Management," the Chrysler hero advises on quarterly review of subordinates' performance (his favorite nostrum), on decision making, on motivation, on delegation, on the importance of having a strong ego (but never a large one), and on the vital role of team spirit. The note the Chrysler savior strikes here is similar to Mark McCormack's, and for similar reasons: both men are great salesmen. Iacocca's management methods—including the review device —derive from managing the salesman and sharing his prejudices; thus Iacocca waxes quite lyrical about the inherent conflict between "the guys in sales and marketing" and "the bean-counters."

The latter are the accountants, a breed of whom Iacocca is wary, even though, as he stresses, the terrifying problems at Chrysler included the fact that nobody was counting the beans properly. Without getting crisp, clear financial information about just how and where Chrysler was losing so many hundreds of millions, Iacocca and his team couldn't begin to stem the loss of corporate blood. But Iacocca wasn't really concerned to discuss the finer, or even the coarser, points of management. He was far more concerned to demonstrate that the Ford Motor board were deeply culpable for agreeing to the demand of Henry Ford (that "evil man") for the head of so splendid a president.

You certainly can't argue with at least three of the great man's achievements—anyway, not as he tells them. As the head of the Ford Division ("the happiest period of my life"), he found "a market in search of a car" and launched the Mustang, which netted over $1 billion in its first two years. That was after killing the Cardinal, a potentially disastrous plan to build a European-designed compact in the United States.

Later triumphs recorded by their author included the billion-dollar project, another crucial decision, to launch the small Fiesta in Europe. Add the revamp of the Lincoln division with the Mark models (one Mark equaling ten Falcons in profit terms) and you have a terrific track record. Which raises two questions: One, obviously, is why Henry Ford fired the champ; two is why, with so much Iacocca goodness going for it, Ford failed to emerge as a great, deeply admired, powerhouse super-challenger to General Motors and the world—especially Japan.

Iacocca's thesis is that the two answers are linked. Bad decisions by Henry (such as his veto of a terrific deal to buy Honda power trains for a U.S.-made small car) offset the Iacocca brainwaves, while the latter's good management was vitiated by Henry's bad habits (firing his brightest and best executives—including Iacocca's top auto man, Hal Sperlich—the hero weakly complied with this execution—and above all Iacocca himself). Yet consider this passage:

"The day after I was fired, Henry sent off a letter to every Ford dealer in the country, trying to reassure them all that they wouldn't be neglected: 'The Company has a strong and experienced management team. Our North American Automotive Operations are headed by talented executives who are well-known to you and who are fully attuned to your needs and the needs of the retail market.' Of course [writes Iacocca], if that were really true, there would have been no need for the letter."

But if that were *not* really true, if Ford *didn't* have a strong and experienced management team, whose fault was that? Iacocca had been president for eight years, after all. Then, consider the Pinto disaster. After "a number of accidents where the car burst into flames after a rear-end collision," Ford was charged with "reckless homicide. Ford was acquitted, but the damage to the company was incalculable. . . . We resisted making any changes, and that hurt us badly."

Iacocca himself asks "Whose fault was it?" and concedes that "One obvious answer is that it was the fault of Ford's management—including me." But surely, again, it was more Iacocca's fault than anybody's, on the basic management principle that the buck stops here—at the desk of the million-a-year man in operational charge. Presumably it was mere coincidence that "we voluntarily recalled almost a million and a half

Pintos . . . in June 1978, the month before I was fired." But Iacocca conveys a strong impression of taking 90 percent of the credit for all Ford's feats and little or none for its flops.

What this proves is that supermanagers aren't superhuman. They feel such common-or-garden human urges as the need to present themselves in the best possible light, their enemies in the worst. Given the chance to write history, they rewrite it to suit (literally) their book. In that they are no different from former Presidents of the United States. Just like the White House heroes, too, the tycoons can now, thanks to the best-seller industry, reap further large financial rewards, even if, as in Iacocca's case, the need for still more personal millions isn't especially apparent.

It's a fair guess that the money motive, even if powerful, comes well behind the passionate drive to exalt the self. This essential element of self-justification is as strong, if not stronger, in a book that doesn't even call itself after its hero— *Managing.* To read this work, you would imagine that its author, Harold S. Geneen, was one of America's most successful managers. And so he was, up to a point: that point being when he stepped down from the chairmanship of the company, ITT, of which he was the second founder.

In management, the evil that powerful men do lives after them; and (like Iacocca with Ford) Geneen would have to shoulder some responsibility for ITT's unhappy recent history, its sell-offs, slump in earnings, and vulnerability to predators, even if he hadn't hung on, Godfather-like, as a powerful and interventionist presence on the board. None of that is recounted in his book, though. The innocent manager would suppose that ITT was still regarded with deepest respect, even awe, at the time of writing. The less innocent manager, though, will guess from Geneen's own account, which does not spare self-praise, how the seeds of defeat were sown in the master's victories, and why they were bound to yield a bitter harvest. He tells, for instance, of 350 buys, mergers, and absorptions, many hasty, most acquired at asking price. Just how do you manage a consequently enormous spread of 250 so-called profit centers? Many, moreover, were bound, on the law of averages alone, to be duds—and expensive ones, at that.

In answer, Geneen's overall principle is "You read a book from the beginning to the end. You run a business the opposite way. You start with the end, and then you do everything you have to do to reach that bottom line." The bottommost line was ITT's target growth in earnings per share: 10 percent per annum compound. To achieve the bottom line (as he did, remarkably enough), Geneen set up an elaborate, exacting system of budgets, monthly reports, and interventionist visits at will by his staff experts anywhere in the company. Geneen calls this invigilation "open communications"; no doubt, some of the invigilated gave it less pleasant names.

But the centerpiece of the system was the General Managers Meeting. All 250 managing directors met Geneen and his cohorts (a strike force of 40-odd executives) once a month, either in Brussels or in New York, for sessions lasting at least twelve hours daily over several days. In all, says Geneen, ITT management spent thirty-five weeks of every year on planning, budgeting, and the notoriously inquisitorial meetings. Allowing for vacations, "That left a scant 13 weeks of 'other time' to run the company." Some men cracked under the stress of the inquisitions. But setting that aside, their still worse defect, shared with the whole apparatus, was just what the quote implies: most of the time, Geneen was running the system, not the company.

It was a system, too, that could be worked by only one brilliant, driven, and driving man: Harold S. Geneen. Moreover, it was a system uniquely equipped to seize tight control of an uncontrolled empire and provide a framework into which acquisitions could be speedily slotted and where they could be duly disciplined in turn. But Geneen, with his concentration on short-term results and distrust of planning ("There will be no more long-range planning" is the entire text of one early memo), seems to miss a vital point—that every business has two bottom lines: the financial one, of which he was the supreme maestro, and the organic one, which determines its future.

The organic bottom line would have included such objectives as intensifying ITT's technological power in its base telecommunications markets, instead of allowing it to slip behind, perhaps fatefully. The ITT giant was in too many businesses to manage them centrally, but its central system was much too strong for them to be managed independently. So long as Geneen was there, his own dynamic performance partially hid this reality. With him removed, painful reality came bursting through—but not for Geneen.

He writes witheringly about the man who "becomes unwilling to accept information which is contrary to some preconceived notion or image of himself held in his mind . . . [who] believes that he is smarter than everyone else, that everyone else is there to serve him." Outsiders at the time of his personal domination of ITT were led to think this scathing description of the "supreme egotist in corporate life" to be an excellent one of Geneen himself; it's an image that his book does little to dispel.

Inability to see themselves as others see them, even such spectacular blindness as Geneen's, isn't confined to managers. As observed in Chapter 16, though, self-deception is a common managerial vice—and blindness to personal defects, even worse, easily goes with the avoidance or ignorance of unpleasant truths about the business. Maybe the supermanager memoirs should all be accompanied by an antidote, a commentary supplied by a candid friend, or even an honest enemy, so the reader at least learns that the great man's character and conduct have a side other than the one he chooses to display.

There are also, of course, alternative views of the events he describes. Robert Townsend's version of events at Avis has been questioned by his co-workers, for example. In a famous passage in *Up the Organization,* Townsend describes how White Plains was chosen as the head-office site by imagining where "a man from Mars" would land as his chosen center for a multinational car-rental business. The revisionists say that the decisive factor came, not from outer space but from the fact that most of the decision makers lived nearby. Similarly, one old Avis hand complained that, sure, Townsend (as he reports) had no secretary, but he used everybody else's, and they hated it.

Be that as it may, does it matter? The "man from Mars" technique—trying to shake free of all acquired attitudes and received ideas before making a decision—is no worse for being based (if it is) on a misleading anecdote. Actually, the idea is very sound—and all the sounder if you gather, from the revised version, how difficult it is to be honestly Martian, truly aloof from preconceptions and predispositions. The issue of secretaries, what they are used for, whether they are truly needed, is one that's rarely faced, but should be. The story helps focus the mind, like all parables. And if you find that it may be a fib, that might help you to examine your own conscience for fibs, possibly harmful ones, of your own.

Does it matter anymore if the account misleads about actual and important events? If Lee Iacocca wasn't, say, as he has always claimed, "the father of the Mustang"? In the authorized, or Iacocca, version, the project sprang from his brain and was carried to sensational fruition by his energy. According to Ford's designer, not so: Iacocca was presented with a completed model on taking over his beloved Ford Division, and then ran with the ball. The truth matters in one sense, because truth always matters. But in terms of the managerial value of *Iacocca,* as of *Up the Organization,* that worth lies in the inspirational example, and the description of the market analysis that targeted the Mustang's sector is unquestionably valuable, whoever first conjured up the car.

All the same, the battle of the best-sellers has taken the managerial book far away from the scholarly, deeply re-searched, thoughtful works of a pioneering writer such as Peter Drucker; far away, too, from a book like *My Years with General Motors,* in which the between-the-wars supermanager Alfred P. Sloan, Jr., wrote, not about himself, but about the history of the great corporation of which he was the architect. It took Sloan 467 pages to tell a story that is still an indispensable management text. No doubt, gilded lilies and misreported events occur in Sloan's narrative, but it's difficult to believe, when reading that careful, dispassionate, fact-filled prose, that the lapses from grace are many.

For that reason, Sloan's magnum opus will probably still be around when today's megasellers and their hectic, "as-told-to" journalistic prose are long forgotten. That, too, may not matter. As Sloan wrote of the corporation: "No company ever stops changing. Change will come for better or worse. . . . The task of management is not to apply a formula but to decide issues on a case-by-case basis."

What's true of the corporation is true of management in general. Behind the hype and the hoopla, the best-sellers gain their currency (in both senses of the word) from a direct rele-vance to real and deep concerns of changing times, even if the relevance isn't too obvious. There *is* a strong backlash against the B-school academicism enshrined at Harvard, for instance. There *is* a powerful reaction against the awful internal and external abuses of corporations like Henry Ford II's Ford or the pre-Iacocca Chrysler.

There is, too, a general wave of acute awareness that the American corporation has been long overdue for a renaissance, for just the kind of managerial renewal that the sage Sloan foresaw. Whatever the motives and misdeeds of the hero-authors, and however many millions their books coin, reading about the experience of other managers is the best (and cheapest) method around of giving naked managers a few more clothes. It helps greatly if they don't fall for the supermanager myths, to be sure. It helps even more if they learn from their reading not to create myths of their own.

Epilogue

30

The Well-Dressed
Executive

Next to being told how good they are individually, executives best love to hear how bad they are as a bunch. Any course of myth destruction serves this therapeutic purpose, but at a price: that of building another myth, which is that all executives, being foolish and foible-ridden, make a bad job worse. All that I know about management was learned from executives, some of whom are my friends, many of whom I admire, most of whom deserve respect—clever men who work hard according to their best lights in circumstances that are often against them. This epilogue is for them. As for the idle, selfish, stupid self-deceivers, this is how to beat them and enjoy it.

The myths keep on coming, and from all directions—from the consultants and the professors, the gurus and the goops, the vain autobiographers and the eager army of business journalists. One grand myth in particular became firmly entrenched in the 1980s, with the aid of all of the above interested parties —the idea, akin to the big-bang theory of the creation of the universe, that there is One Big Solution. Whether it's the One-Minute Manager or the eight attributes of corporate excellence, the fundamental fiction is the same: that Highest Common Factors exist, which you can derive from study of the Highest Uncommon Companies or their executives.

Because you can find out what happens in corporations only by observing their activities, past and present, and drawing conclusions from what you see, it's impossible for any writer about management, including this one, to avoid perpetuating the myth. But the evidence, as savants in other fields would see at once, is purely anecdotal. Parables are marvelous teaching tools. But don't forget that the only thing winning companies have in common is their success—which may well not last. Merely look at the loss-making agonies of Caterpillar Tractor, one of the top stars of *In Search of Excellence* and for decades among everybody's top marketing companies. To get anywhere in understanding management, you have to move from the particular to the general. But don't let yourself be led beyond the general to the universal.

The temptation to follow those misleading footsteps, though, is well-nigh irresistible. Just imagine finding the secret of successful innovation, the key to market survival, let alone triumph, in the 1980s—surely the key lies among the successful innovators? That's what *Fortune* magazine thought, anyway. It looked at "Eight Big Masters of Innovation," selected by an exhaustive process, and sought to discover what American Airlines, Apple, Campbell Soup, GE, Intel, Merck, 3M, and Philip Morris could teach the sluggards. So what's the Holy Grail of innovation?

Surprise, surprise: "the management of each of the eight is convinced of the *need* to innovate, regarding new ideas as the essence of long-term survival." That discovery is about as original, and as useful, as announcing that water is wet. Then, "no matter how dependent the companies are on purely technological advances, they are uniformly devoted to marketing"— again, so what else is new? Other glimpses of the obvious are duly sanctified: "Listening carefully to their customers . . . clearly defined cultures . . . such mom-and-flag values as product quality, market leadership and [naturally] the necessity of invention." It's more valuable (but not much) to know that the eight "ruthlessly limit the search for new ideas to areas they are competent to exploit."

This meager result is par for the course. What lends the executive his peculiar charm and weakness, though, is less his readiness to swallow other men's myths than his inability to recognize his own nakedness—his impotence, incompetence, and error. So do recognize it: the shock of recognition will improve your performance and give you a lasting start on unshocked competitors. Make things easier for yourself, too, by simplifying everything you can, wherever and whenever you can.

William Blackie, when chief executive of Caterpillar Tractor, never said wiser words than these: "I deride the idea that an executive's function is problem solving—it is the bad executive who is up to his neck in problems." Blackie wasn't thinking of the real, monster anxieties, like those of his own successors as they wrestle with recession in key markets, deadly competition from Komatsu, and excessive costs in their own plants. He referred to the fact that, in the standard big company bureaucracy, executives stalk new problems with the eagerness of the hunters of the snark. As if ordinary life threw up too few troubles, they invent and invite extra complexity. Any business situation can be reduced to simple terms. If it is, the solution usually appears from the reduction, and the "problem" evaporates.

The surest way to simplify is to concentrate. Don't, if you

are brilliant at making executive jets, reckon that you will be an expert hand at autos (especially steam ones). If the company can find one lucrative activity or market in which it functions well, sufficient unto the day be the profit thereof. Concentration also means that the single-minded company must be single-minded about its overriding objective, which is to be the best at everything from production costs (the lowest) and efficiency (the highest) in serving the consumer. If you can supply more effectively on a lower cost base than anybody else, you must win.

The more a business concentrates, the less time its executives need to waste. The single-minded company, alas, tends to become monomaniacal as well; its executives are expected to live only for power tools or whatever, and they don't like to buck the system. So every last detail of the business is regurgitated to fill long days of discussion. Even in average circumstances, discussions take up half an executive's time, and interruptions do the rest of the damage.

According to a Swedish study, fourteen minutes is the maximum for which an executive is left on his own; and nine minutes is his top time without interruption. No wonder he can't think straight. Resist this vice strenuously. The object, as in management generally, is to get the most with the least, the maximum effective management thought and follow-up with the minimum expenditure of hours. Ask of every activity, and especially of every meeting, whether it serves any purpose directly related to the company's profit. Organize the company so that a normal working day will cover normal tasks. And pack executives (including yourself) off home at decent times (that is, unless they don't want to go). Never disturb them after hours without grave cause, and with humble apologies.

A dangerously narrow line divides a company that wastes no time from a stagnant bunch of idle corporate loafers. The best way to avoid stagnation is to manage young. That is, give men high responsibility as soon as you know that they won't stuff your bank (Penn Square) with so many bad energy loans, and pass them on to so many big bank suckers, that not only does your own bank founder, but the once-great Continental Illinois is only saved from collapse (and with it the entire U.S. banking system) by a $4.5 billion bailout. Mozart was dead at thirty-five. So are many living executives. The one great idea that, if Freud was right, is all any man is given comes early rather than late. If you wait until men are over forty, let alone fifty, to give them their most important job, you will miss their prime—and so will they. Young executives are no more all brilliant balls of energy than old ones are all sputtered-out volcanoes. But the good oldsters were better when they were younger, or would have been, if somebody had given them a chance.

And don't kid yourself that you've rejuvenated the company by lowering the average age of the executives from fifty-seven to fifty-three. That is different in degree, but not in kind, from the octogenarian chairman who decided to retire to make way for a younger man. He meant his son, a stripling in his sixties. Somebody, preferably that son, should long before have told the old roadblock to clear himself away. But the circumstances of the people almost certainly made serious criticism impossible. Don't let it happen in your company, and don't stay where it has happened. If an executive can't be frank with his colleagues and seniors, he won't be frank to himself either; both sins are equally dangerous.

Never take frankness as far as boasting. The Canadian press tycoon Lord Thomson should have bitterly regretted the day when he described his Scottish television franchise as "a license to print money." So it was; but it didn't take long before the government, alerted and offended, altered the license drastically in its own favor. Remember, as a better example, the Swiss Hoffmann-La Roche, the world's most profitable drug

375

company. For years nobody outside, except possibly its bankers, knew how much money Roche coined. When the facts began to emerge, under the pressure of government investigations, the reasons for Roche's secrecy became even more apparent: it was charging $10 a gram for tranquilizers that cost 56 cents to produce. Such conduct is extreme and not to be imitated. But "speak only when spoken to and avoid vainglory" is a sounder course than hiring a public relations army and missing no opportunity to extol your own merits. You may not have any.

For salutary proof of your demerits, follow up a few complaints. No criticism that has reached me in my game, however rude or ignorant, has been without a valuable grain of truth, and your game is no different. In some cases, it isn't just a grain of truth, but a whole Sahara Desert. To be specific, if an auto company delivers to a customer (probably several weeks late) a model that comes to pieces in his hands, and then takes several months of acrimonious correspondence, and several returns of the machine, before its offense is put right, then that firm is rotten from top to bottom and needs total overhaul fast.

Don't skate around complaints on the grounds that detail is not your business. The argument that board-level executives, or any executives, should look at the wood and forget about the trees is an incitement to, and an excuse for, unforgivable slackness. The good executive at any level can distinguish between a vital detail and rubbish, and a detail a day keeps the liquidator away. Sometimes, spotting even a beam in your own eye, let alone a few motes, is psychologically difficult. Overcoming this repression is where outside critics come in—so don't be like General Motors and try to wish your own private Ralph Naders away. Like Nader's Raiders, they will, more often than not, be right.

That, true, was in another era, and, besides, the auto Nader complained of (the Corvair) is dead. But GM's harassing of Nader's private life fell into the same pattern as the blind eye for its own faults, which culminated in dreadful reverses at the hands of the Japanese. The great corporation today is greatly changed, and none too soon, but it deserved its great punishment for infringing a creakingly ancient moral rule. Do unto others as you would have done to you: in other words, behave yourself. Few sights in world business are more unattractive than that of large companies seeking credit and praise for progressive labor policies, or for their antipollution, antiracialism, and antipoverty programs—as if they had some right, which they were generously waiving, to foul the environment, or exacerbate social tensions, or grind the workers' faces in the dust.

After Walter Reuther forced the guaranteed annual wage on GM, the company took credit for the innovation. Executives whose firms have ignored their social responsibilities for decades applaud themselves for doing so no longer. But in fact, the environment is still being polluted; and you will still find only slightly more Jews on the boards of U.S. blue chips than blacks in any executive role in any European company, and you will still find disgracefully few women in senior executive positions anywhere in the Western world (and you can just forget about Japan). The tide of women emerging from the business schools will change this sorry situation—but too slowly for the tastes of many able women. Like the Jewish immigrants before them, or the Asians in Britain today, they are creating their own opportunities as entrepreneurs. But corporate America will be poorer without them—and it will serve it right. If prejudice restricts a company's hiring policy, it will miss able people. In many mediocre giants, careers are still not really open to all talents. Change that, and you will change the giants, and possibly their mediocrity.

The company's social obligations begin at home. "In many auto companies life is like a jungle," said one escapee.

"Among executives, it is dog eat dog." That is no less barbaric than it sounds, and an uncivilized company is no more worth living in than a cannibal country. Even decent companies such as General Foods were in danger of forgetting that people are not pawns. "That place is much like being in the army," an observer once said. "They rotate people terrifically."

Don't let your company be like either a jungle or the services. Executives are neither animals nor conscripts; they can be made to behave like both, but at dreadful loss in both effectiveness and ordinary humanity. Employees are not "Honeywellers" and "IBMers," as companies like to call them; and it's fortunate for companies, as well as individuals, that changing social norms, the high pressures of high technology, and the work of the Theory Y enthusiasts have dispelled much of the aura of the old Organization Man. Employees produce their best work if they are treated as what they are, individuals. Their loyalty to the corporation is worthwhile only if it is voluntary, nonconformist, and, like undercarriages, easily retractable.

The only excuse for being displeased when a good executive retracts himself is if the move is a genuine mistake. If the manager is moving to a better job, and you can't outbid the opposition, be happy. After all, the man is supposed to be your friend; and nobody is indispensable (especially you). Huge turnover of executives is a bad sign; someone is either managing or hiring badly. But nil turnover is possibly even worse. The company can't be hiring and developing the ambitious, able, and energetic men it desperately needs; otherwise some of them would inevitably energize themselves out of the place. Moreover, if holes don't open up, you can't fill some of them with new talent, and that is fatal.

Fresh talent need not be imported; it can very often be dredged up from the company's own depths. But only these regular transfusions can save a corporation from the major surgery to which most eventually come. Unfortunately, the surgery only rearranges the same parts. The most effective shake-ups are cataclysmic, not kaleidoscopic. The best thing that ever happened to I.G. Farben, the prewar German chemical giant, was the breakup by the Allied occupiers of a lumbering, cartel-ridden mammoth into three aggressive and distinct component parts. The worst thing that happened to Krupp after the Nazi defeat was its preservation intact by a wily owner: that signed the company's death warrant as a leading European industrial force. "The first billion-dollar giant that deliberately hives off a few hundred million dollars of superfluous, profitable sales will make history and a fortune for its stockholders."

That last sentence is in quotes because I wrote it a long time ago—years before company after company proved my point by unloading division after division, including some mistakes that had only recently been purchased. In some cases the grounds were grand strategy (like Gould selling off boring base businesses to concentrate on gee-whiz electronics); in others, management was repairing past error (like Coca-Cola abandoning its attempt to lord it over California wine); in others still, the pressures were financial (like the need to reduce vast debts after du Pont's purchase of Conoco, or the megabuy of Esmark by Beatrice Foods). Whatever the motive, the consequences are the same: a business worth more to the stockholders and in a position, like any tree, to grow more strongly for being pruned.

Size, apart from its other drawbacks, kills homeliness. One common factor of unusually successful firms is their hick quality. They don't have plush metropolitan offices, or, sometimes, plush offices at all. Their heart is in some undistinguished locale. Their bosses know New York and London, but can't wait to get home. Homespun companies such as the boys from Buchanan, Clark Equipment (fork-lift trucks, and so forth), have built world interests in their concentrated specialties without succumbing to the tempting passion for sophistication and complication.

Simple principles sound laughably naïve: one modern tycoon built his fortune on an old-fashioned platform of paying for everything in cash, neither giving nor receiving credit, and never borrowing—but note that he made a fortune. Non-tycoons, lacking the intuitive quality of business genius, can't afford the same luxury of sticking to principles at all costs. The common-or-garden-variety executive needs flexibility, readiness to change course, even in midstream, willingness to look acidly even at success.

The Apollo program, hailed as a triumph of "good" professional management, is a caution in itself. Because you have landed a man on the moon by 1969 for a mere $50 billion, don't assume you've managed brilliantly—maybe it should have been done for $30 billion. Worry more about the worms inside the apple. The real lesson of Apollo is that, if the objective is attainable and there is no limit to the resources available, executives can achieve almost any task. That is not news. But don't manage (and many companies do) as if you are NASA. There are always limits to the resources of a corporation—first, that it isn't the executives' money; second, that behind the stockholders, the money belongs to the community.

Executives are highly privileged individuals. They receive sweeping power over society's economic resources—far more than that of politicians, but entirely in a private capacity—to do with what they will, under conditions of low accountability and virtual permanence. Few executives feel this burden of national responsibility. But they won't do their duty by the country's wealth until they see their work stripped of its mythological trappings and in its true, unflattering light—and thus do it better.

One persistent myth, which the Europeans used to believe

about America, is that some other national economy holds the antidote to whatever ails your own country. Americans have now fallen for this comforting idea themselves—the comfort lying in the fact that, if there truly were some magic ingredient that could be imported, a sort of managerial ginseng, economic ailments would be easily curable. The Japanese management model has proved unsurprisingly attractive to U.S. businessmen wondering and worrying about how these ace competitors from the East have captured so many home and overseas markets. It's true that, just as any sensible company constantly studies its competitors, and even counterparts in other businesses, to find ways of improving its performance, much can always be learned from other countries. But there are no panaceas available, from Japan or anywhere else.

The reality of Japan is that its magic consists of little more (though that's a lot) than dedicated application to clearly defined tasks, founded on the belief that constant improvement (in products, processes, efficiency) is always possible: built around the conviction that a corporation worth working for is worth fighting for; sustained by a tradition of mutual respect; and animated by a nonstop competitive drive. Nothing in Japanese management success should be strange to any American manager who has read the realities of lasting American success —as the Japanese certainly have.

The ten truths of management given in these pages form a simple antimyth kit. A wise reader of the manuscript objected that hardly any of the truths apply to executives only, but are common to almost all humanity. He had holed in one. Management is precisely that, a general human activity, to which the best guides are not the management textbooks, but history, sociology, and psychology. The first myth of management— that it exists—seeks to take management away from where it belongs and to put it on a pedestal of pseudoscience. Executives placed on pedestals fall from a great height. If the ten truths keep you off the pedestal, at least the drop will be much shorter.

1. Think before you act: it's not your money.
2. All good management is the expression of one great idea.
3. No executive devotes effort to proving himself wrong.
4. Cash In must exceed Cash Out.
5. Management capability is always less than the organization actually needs.
6. Either an executive can do his job or he can't.
7. If sophisticated calculations are needed to justify an action, don't do it.
8. If you are doing something wrong, you will do it badly.
9. If you are attempting the impossible, you will fail.
10. The easiest way of making money is to stop losing it.

Another truth lies behind all ten. One of the least attractive myths of management holds that nobody can get rich without at some point being a crook, a con man, or a mobster. Many crooks, con men, and mobsters have made great wealth. It does not follow that crookedness is the path to business success, or that executives can throw private morality overboard as they plunge into corporate vice. Ponder, rather, how it is that the Quakers and similar deeply religious gentry made so much worldly lucre. It was because they treated their people honestly and decently, worked hard and honestly themselves, spent honestly and saved pennies, honestly put more back into the company than they took out, made honestly good products, gave honest value for money, and, being honest, told no lies. Neither the naked manager nor the effective executive can ever find better clothes.

Acknowledgments

This book could not have been started without the help, direct and inadvertent, of the many, many managers I have met and talked with over the years. Neither could it have been written without the education received from Sir Gordon Newton, my first editor. I am permanently in his debt, not least for sending me as a correspondent to the United States, where I learned plenty. His chairman at *The Financial Times,* Lord Drogheda, among many kindnesses, encouraged me to start *Management Today.* At that magazine I have been taught as much about business as journalism—thanks largely to colleagues such as the late Jim Hunter, Michael Heseltine, Lindsay Masters, and Geoffrey Foster. The genesis of the book lay in the fortnightly column "Management in Action," published in *The Observer,* for which I am everlastingly grateful to David Astor, then *The Observer*'s editor, and to Anthony Bambridge, then business editor. Leopold Ullstein, the managing director of Barrie & Jenkins, thought of the book almost before I did; and so did my agent, Hilary Rubinstein, who buoyed me up at moments when buoys were badly needed. I owe many other debts I can never fully repay. Among others: to Sheila Black; to John Davis of *The Observer;* to Hugh Parker of McKinsey & Company; to Wally Olins of Wolff Olins; to Lord Weinstock of the General Electric Company; to the late Tommy Wilson of the London Business School; to John Diebold; to Peter Drucker, who has set the standard of perfection in writing about management; and to John Thackray, whose articles on U.S. business in *Management Today* are as invaluable as they are brilliant. I owe a debt of deep gratitude to many American business journalists, most of them working for *Business Week, Fortune, Forbes,* and *Time,* without whose work nobody could be fully informed on the unfolding U.S. corporate scene. Finally, like everything I write, this book should really be dedicated to the late David Roberts, senior history master at Christ's Hospital.

Index

INDEX

INDEX

INDEX

INDEX

INDEX

INDEX